Hugh Johnson's Pocket Encyclopedia of Wine

Simon and Schuster/New York

KEY TO SYMBOLS

r.	red	
p.	rosé	(in brackets) means relatively unimportant
w.	white	
br.	brown	
sw.	sweet	
dr.	dry	
sp.	sparkling	

★	plain, everyday quality
★★	above average
★★★	well known, highly reputed
★★★★	grand, prestigious, expensive
☐	usually particularly good value in its class

70 71 etc.
  recommended years which may be currently available

70 etc. years in **bold** should be ready for drinking (the others
  should be kept). Where both reds and whites are
  indicated the red is intended unless otherwise stated.
  N.B. German vintages are codified by a different system.
  See note on p. 60.

D.Y.A. drink the youngest available

NV vintage not normally shown on label

Cross-references are in SMALL CAPS

See p. 5 for extra explanation

A quick reference vintage chart for France and Germany
appears on p. 144.

Hugh Johnson's Pocket Encyclopedia of Wine
© 1977 by Mitchell Beazley Publishers Limited
Text © 1977 by Hugh Johnson
All rights reserved
including the right of reproduction
in whole or in part in any form
A Fireside Book
Published by Simon and Schuster
A Division of Gulf & Western Corporation
Simon & Schuster Building
Rockefeller Center
1230 Avenue of the Americas
New York, New York 10020

ISBN 0-671-23018-2
Library of Congress Catalog Card Number 77-79242
Printed in Great Britain
Designed by Florianne Henfield
Assistant Editor Kathie Chapman

Contents

Introduction

This book is an exercise in crowding angels on a pinhead, or students into a telephone box. It is deliberately the shortest book in which I could possibly squeeze a book's-worth of information. Conversely it holds as much information as I could possibly squeeze into a little diary-format book. Hence no prose: the whole work is played staccato.

Its arrangement is intended to be as helpful as possible when you are buying a bottle, whether you are on the nursery slopes or an old hand with a bad memory. You are faced with a list of wines or an array of bottles in a restaurant, wine merchant or bottle store. Your mind goes blank. You fumble for your little book. All you need to establish is what country a wine comes from. Look up the principal words on the label in the appropriate country's section. You will find enough potted information to let you judge whether this is the wine you want.

Specifically, you will find information on the colour and type of wine, its status or prestige, whether it is usually particularly good value, which vintages are good and which are ready to drink—and often considerably more . . . about the quantity made, the grapes used, ownership and the rest. Hundreds of cross-references help you go further into the matter if you want to.

The introduction to each national section will help you to establish which label-terms are the ones that count. In many cases you will find you can look up almost all the words on the label: estate, grape, shipper, quality-rating, bottling-information. . . .

For your browsing moments the introduction contains important background information about grape types; the first of all determining factors for the quality and essential flavour of any wine.

For planning meals and worrying about what to serve pages 10 to 17 contain over one hundred ideas for wines with dishes.

How to read an entry

The top line of most entries consists of the following information in an abbreviated form.

1. Which part of the country in question the wine comes from. (References to the maps in this book.)
2. Whether it is red, rosé or white (or brown/amber), dry, sweet or sparkling, or several of these.
3. Its general standing as to quality: a necessarily rough and ready guide based principally on the following ascending scale:

    * plain, everyday quality
    ** above average
    *** well known, highly reputed
    **** grand, prestigious, expensive

So much is more or less objective. Additionally there is a subjective rating: a box round the stars of any wine which in my experience is usually particularly good (which means good value) within its price range. There are good everyday wines as well as good luxury wine. The box system helps you find them.

4. Vintage information: which were the more successful of the recent vintages which *may* still be available. And of these which are ready to drink this year, and which will probably improve with keeping. Your first choice for current drinking should be one of the vintage years printed in **bold** type. Buy light-type years for further maturing.

The German vintage information works on a different principle: see the Introduction to Germany, page 58.

Acknowledgements

This store of detailed recommendations (which has never, as far as I know, been collected and published before) comes partly from my own notes and partly from those of a great number of kind friends. Without the generous help and co-operation of every single member of the wine trade I have approached, I could not have attempted it. I particularly want to thank the following for giving me material help with research in the areas of their special knowledge.

Martin Bamford
Anthony Barton
Michael Broadbent M.W.
Georges Foucquier
Francis Fouquet
Robert Hart M.W.
Tony Laithwaite
Michael Longhurst
Tim Marshall
Patrick Matthews

Christian Moueix
David Peppercorn M.W.
Jan Read
Dr. Bruno Roncarati
Steven Spurrier
Keith Stevens
Serena Sutcliffe M.W.
Bob Thompson
Peter Vinding-Diers

Grape varieties

The most basic of all differences between wines stems from the grapes they are made of. Centuries of selection have resulted in each of the long-established wine-areas having its favourite single variety, or a group of varieties whose juice or wine is blended together. Red burgundy is made of one grape, the Pinot Noir; red Bordeaux of three or four: two kinds of Cabernet, Merlot, Malbec and sometimes others. The laws say which grapes must be used, so the labels assume it.

So in newer vineyards the choice of a grape is the planter's single most crucial decision. Where he is proud of it, and intends his wine to have the character of a particular grape, the variety is the first thing he puts on the label—hence the useful, originally Californian, term "varietal wine".

A knowledge of grape varieties, therefore, is the single most helpful piece of knowledge in finding wines you will like wherever they are grown. Learn to recognize the characters of the most important. At least seven—Cabernet, Pinot Noir, Riesling, Sauvignon Blanc, Chardonnay, Gewürztraminer and Muscat—have memorable tastes and smells distinct enough to form international categories of wine.

Further notes on grapes will be found on page 120 (for California) and in the sections on central and south-east Europe, South Africa, etc.

The following are the best and commonest wine grapes.

Grapes for white wine

Aligoté
> Burgundy's second-rank white grape. Crisp (often sharp) wine, needs drinking young. Perfect for mixing with Cassis (blackcurrant liqueur) to make a "Kir". Also grown in the USSR.

Blanc Fumé
> Another name for SAUVIGNON BLANC, referring to the "smoky" smell of the wine, particularly on the upper Loire. Makes some of California's best whites.

Bual
> Makes sweet Madeira wines.

Chardonnay
> *The* white burgundy grape, one of the grapes of Champagne, and the best white grape of California. Gives dry wine of rich complexity. Trials in Australia and eastern Europe are also successful.

Chasselas
> A prolific and widely grown early-ripening grape with little flavour, also grown for eating. Best known as Fendant in Switzerland, Gutedel in Germany. Perhaps the same as Hungary's Leanyka and Romania's Fetească.

Chenin Blanc

The leading white grape of the middle Loire (Vouvray, Layon, etc.). Wine can be dry or sweet (or very sweet), but always retains plenty of acidity—hence its popularity in California, where it rarely distinguishes itself.

Clairette

A dull neutral grape widely used in the s. of France.

Fendant

See Chasselas

Folle Blanche

The third most widely grown white grape of France, though nowhere making fine wine. High acid and little flavour makes it ideal for brandy. Known as Gros Plant in Brittany, Picpoul in the Midi. At its best in California.

Furmint

A grape of great character: the trade mark of Hungary both in Tokay and as vivid vigorous table wine with an appley flavour. Called Sipon in Jugoslavia.

Gewürztraminer (or Traminer)

The most pungent wine grape, distinctively spicy to smell and taste. Wines are often rich and soft, even when fully dry. Best in Alsace; also good in Germany, eastern Europe, Australia, California.

Gros Plant

See Folle Blanche

Grüner Veltliner

An Austrian speciality. Round Vienna and in the Wachau and Weinviertel can be delicious: light but lively. For drinking young.

Italian Riesling

Grown in n. Italy and all over central eastern Europe. Inferior to German or Rhine Riesling with lower acidity, but a good all-round grape. Alias Wälschriesling, Olaszriesling (or often just "Riesling").

Malvasia

Known as Malmsey in Madeira, Malvasia in Italy: also grown in Greece, Spain, eastern Europe. Makes rich brown wines or soft whites of no great character.

Müller-Thurgau

Dominant variety in Germany's Rheinhessen and Rheinpfalz; said to be a cross between Riesling and Sylvaner. Ripens early to make soft flowery wines to drink young. Makes good sweet wines. Also grows well in Austria and England.

Muscadet

Makes light, very dry but not sharp wines round Nantes in Brittany.

Muscat (many varieties)

Universally grown easily recognized pungent grape, mostly made into perfumed sweet wines, often fortified (as in France's VIN DOUX NATURELS). Muscat d'Alsace is alone in being dry.

Palomino

Alias Listan. Makes all the best sherry.

Pedro Ximénez

Said to have come to s. Spain from Germany. Makes very strong wine in Montilla and Malaga. Used in blending sherry. Also grown in Australia, California, South Africa.

Pinot Blanc

A close relation of CHARDONNAY without its ultimate nobility. Grown in Champagne, Alsace, n. Italy (good sparkling wine), s. Germany, eastern Europe, California.

Pinot Gris

Makes rather heavy full-bodied whites with a certain spicy style. Known as Tokay in Alsace, Tocai in n.e. Italy and Jugoslavia, Ruländer in Germany.

Pinot Noir

Superlative black grape (see under Grapes for red wine) used in Champagne and occasionally elsewhere for making white wine.

Riesling

Germany's finest grape, now planted round the world. Wine of brilliant sweet/acid balance, flowery in youth but maturing to subtle oily scents and flavours. Successful in Alsace (for dry wine), Austria, parts of eastern Europe, Australia, California, South Africa. Often called White, Johannisberg or Rhine Riesling.

Sauvignon Blanc

Very distinctive aromatic, herby and sometimes smoky scented wine, can be austere (on the upper Loire) or buxom (in Bordeaux, where it is combined with SEMILLON, and parts of California). Also called Fumé Blanc.

Semillon

The grape contributing the lusciousness to great Sauternes; subject to "noble rot" in the right conditions. Makes soft dry wine. Called "Riesling" in Australia.

Sercial

Makes the driest wine of Madeira—where they claim it is really Riesling.

Seyval Blanc

French-made hybrid between French and American vines. Very hardy and attractively fruity. Popular and successful in the eastern States and England.

Steen

South Africa's best white grape: lively fruity wine. Said to be the Chenin Blanc of the Loire.

Sylvaner

Germany's workhorse grape; wine rarely better than pleasant except in Franconia. Good in the Italian Tyrol and useful in Alsace. Wrongly called Riesling in California.

Tokay

See Pinot Gris. Also a table grape in California and a supposedly Hungarian grape in Australia.

Traminer

See Gewürztraminer

Trebbiano

Important grape of central Italy, used in Orvieto, Chianti, Soave, etc. Also grown in s. France as Ugni Blanc, and Cognac as "St-Emilion".

Ugni Blanc

See Trebbiano

Verdelho

Madeira grape making excellent medium-sweet wine.

Verdicchio

Gives its name to good dry wine in central Italy.

Vernaccia

Grape grown in central and s. Italy and Sardinia for strong wine inclining towards sherry.

Viognier

Rare but remarkable grape of the Rhône valley, grown at Condrieu to make very fine soft and fragrant wine.

Welschriesling (or Wälschriesling)

See Italian Riesling

Grapes for red wine

Barbera
> One of several good standard grapes of Piemonte, giving dark, robust, fruity and often rather sharp wine. High acidity makes it a good grape for California.

Cabernet Franc
> The lesser of two sorts of Cabernet grown in Bordeaux; the Cabernet of the Loire making Chinon and rosé.

Cabernet Sauvignon
> Grape of great character; spicy, herby and tannic. The first grape of the Médoc, also makes the best Californian, Australian, South American and eastern European reds. Its wine always needs ageing and usually blending.

Carignan
> By far the commonest grape of France, covering hundreds of thousands of acres. Prolific with dull but harmless wine. Also common in North Africa, Spain and California.

Gamay
> The Beaujolais grape: light fragrant wines at their best quite young. Makes even lighter wine on the Loire and in Switzerland and Savoie. Known as Napay Gamay in California.

Gamay Beaujolais
> Not Gamay but a variety of PINOT NOIR grown in California.

Grenache
> Useful grape giving strong and fruity but pale wine: good rosé. Grown in s. France, Spain, California and usually blended.

Grignolino
> Makes one of the good cheap table wines of Piemonte. Also used in California.

Merlot
> Adaptable grape making the great fragrant and rich wines of Pomerol and St-Emilion, an important element in Médoc reds, and making lighter but good wines in n. Italy, Italian Switzerland, Jugoslavia, Argentina, etc.

Nebbiolo (also called Spanna)
> Italy's best red grape, the grape of Barolo, Barbaresco, Gattinara and Valtellina. Intense, nobly fruity and perfumed wine taking years to mature.

Pinot Noir
> The glory of Burgundy's Côte d'Or, with scent, flavour, texture and body unmatched anywhere. Less happy elsewhere; makes light wines of no great distinction in Germany, Switzerland, Austria; good ones in Hungary; generally dull ones in California.

Sangiovese
> The main red grape of Chianti and much of central Italy.

Syrah
> The best Rhône red grape, with heavy purple wine, which can mature superbly. Said by some to come from Shiraz in Persia; others say Syracuse in Sicily. Very important as "Shiraz" in Australia.

Zinfandel
> Fruity adaptable grape peculiar to California.

Wine & Food

There are no rules and regulations about what wine goes with what food, but there is a vast body of accumulated experience which it is absurd to ignore.

This list of dishes and appropriate wines records most of the conventional combinations and suggests others that I personally have found good. But it is only a list of ideas intended to help you make quick decisions. Any of the groups of recommended wines could have been extended almost indefinitely, drawing on the whole world's wine list. In general I have stuck to the wines that are widely available, at the same time trying to ring the changes so that the same wines don't come up time and time again— as they tend to do in real life.

The stars refer to the rating system used throughout the book: see opposite Contents.

First courses

Antipasto (see also Hors d'oeuvre)
　　　★★ dry or medium white, preferably Italian (e.g. Soave) or light red, e.g. Valpolicella, Bardolino or young ★ Bordeaux.

Artichoke
　　　★ red or rosé.
　　　vinaigrette★ young red, e.g. Bordeaux.
　　　hollandaise ★ or ★★ full-bodied dry or medium white, e.g. Mâcon Blanc, Rheinpfalz or California "Chablis".

Asparagus
　　　★★→★★★ white burgundy or Chardonnay, or Tavel rosé.

Assiette anglaise (assorted cold meats)
　　　★★ dry white, e.g. Chablis, Graves, Muscadet, Dão.

Avocado
　　　with prawns, crab, etc. ★★→★★★ dry to medium white, e.g. Rheingau or Rheinpfalz Kabinett, Graves, California Chardonnay or Sauvignon, Cape Stein, or dry rosé.
　　　vinaigrette ★ light red, or fino sherry.

Bisques
　　　★★ dry white with plenty of body: Verdicchio, Pinot Gris, Graves.

Blinis with caviare
　　　★★★ champagne, Alsace Riesling or Sancerre (or Vodka).

Bouillabaisse
　　　★→★★ very dry white: Muscadet, Alsace Sylvaner, Entre-Deux-Mers, Pouilly Fumé, Cassis.

Caviare
　　　★★★ champagne or iced vodka.

Cheese fondue
　　　★★ dry white: Fendant du Valais, Grüner Veltliner.

Chowders
　　　★★ big-scale white, not necessarily bone dry: e.g. Rhône, Pinot Gris, Dry Sauternes.

Clams
　　　Same as Chowders.

Consommé
　　　★★→★★★ medium-dry sherry, dry Madeira, Marsala, Montilla.

Croque Monsieur
　　　★→★★ young red, e.g. Beaujolais, Barbera.

Crudités
　　　★→★★ light red or rosé, e.g. Côtes-du-Rhône, Beaujolais, Chianti, Zinfandel.

Eggs (see also Soufflés)

These present difficulties: they clash with most wine and spoil good ones. So ★→★★ of whatever is going.

Empanadas

★→★★ Chilean Cabernet, Zinfandel.

Escargots

★★ red or white of some substance: e.g. Burgundy; Côtes-du-Rhône, Chardonnay, Shiraz, etc.

Foie gras

★★★→★★★★ white. In Bordeaux they drink Sauternes. Others prefer vintage champagne or a rich Gewürztraminer Vendange tardive.

Gazpacho

Sangria (see Spain) is refreshing, but to avoid too much liquid intake dry Manzanilla or Montilla is better.

Grapefruit

If you must start a meal with grapefruit try port, Madeira or sweet sherry with it.

Ham, raw

See Prosciutto

Herrings, raw or pickled

Dutch gin or Scandinavian akvavit, or ★★ full-bodied white Mâcon-Villages, Graves or Dão.

Hors d'oeuvre (see also Antipasto)

★→★★ clean fruity sharp white: Sancerre or any Sauvignon, Alsace Sylvaner, Muscadet, Cape Stein—or young light red Bordeaux, Rhône or equivalent.

Mackerel, smoked

★★→★★★ full-bodied tasty white: e.g. Gewürztraminer, Tokay d'Alsace or Chablis Premier Cru.

Melon

Needs a strong sweet wine: ★★ Port, Bual Madeira, Muscat, Oloroso sherry or Vin doux naturel.

Minestrone

★ red: Grignolino, Chianti, etc.

Omelettes

See observations under Eggs

Onion/Leek tart

★→★★★ fruity dry white, e.g. Alsace Sylvaner or Riesling. Mâcon-Villages of a good vintage, California or Australian Riesling.

Pasta

★→★★ red or white according to the sauce or accompaniments, e.g.

with fish sauce (vongole, etc.) Verdicchio or Soave.
meat sauce Chianti, Beaujolais or Côtes-du-Rhône.
tomato sauce Barbera or Sicilian red.
cream sauce Orvieto or Frascati.

Pâté

★★ dry white: e.g. Chablis, Mâcon Blanc, Graves.

Peppers or aubergines (egg-plant), stuffed

★★ vigorous red: e.g. Bull's Blood, Chianti, Zinfandel.

Pizza

Any ★★ dry Italian red or a ★★ Rioja, Australian Shiraz or Californian Zinfandel.

Prawns or Shrimps

★★→★★★ dry white: burgundy or Bordeaux, Chardonnay or Riesling. ("Cocktail sauce" kills wine.)

Prosciutto with melon

★★→★★★ full-bodied dry or medium white: e.g. Orvieto or Frascati, Fendant, Grüner Veltliner, Alsace Sylvaner, California Gewürztraminer, Australian Riesling.

Quiches

$\star \rightarrow \star\star$ dry white with body (Alsace, Graves, Sauvignon) or young red according to the ingredients.

Ratatouille

$\star\star$ vigorous young red, e.g. Chianti, Zinfandel, Bull's Blood, young red Bordeaux.

Salade niçoise

$\star\star$ very dry not too light or flowery white, e.g. white (or rosé) Rhône, white Spanish, Dão, California Sauvignon Blanc.

Salads

As a first course: any dry and appetizing white wine. After a main course: no wine.

N.B. Vinegar in salad dressings destroys the flavour of wine. If you want salad at a meal with fine wine, dress the salad with wine instead of vinegar.

Salami

$\star \rightarrow \star\star$ powerfully tasty red or rosé: e.g. Barbera, young Zinfandel, Tavel rosé, young Bordeaux.

Salmon, smoked

A dry but pungent white, e.g. fino sherry, Alsace Gewürztraminer, Chablis Grand Cru.

Soufflés

As show dishes these deserve $\star\star \rightarrow \star\star\star$ wines.

Fish soufflés Dry white, e.g. burgundy, Bordeaux, Alsace, Chardonnay, etc.

Cheese soufflé Red burgundy or Bordeaux, Cabernet Sauvignon, etc.

Terrine

As for pâté, or the equivalent red: e.g. Beaune, Mercurey, Beaujolais-Villages, fairly young $\star\star$ St-Emilion, California Cabernet or Zinfandel, Bulgarian or Chilean Cabernet, etc.

Fish

Abalone

$\star\star \rightarrow \star\star\star$ dry or medium white: e.g. Sauvignon Blanc, Chardonnay, Verdicchio.

Cod

A good neutral background for fine dry or medium whites, e.g. $\star\star \rightarrow \star\star\star$ Chablis, cru classé Graves, German Kabinetts and their equivalents.

Coquilles St. Jacques

An inherently slightly sweet dish, best with medium-dry white wine.

In cream sauces $\star\star\star$ German wines.

Grilled or fried Hermitage Blanc, Gewürztraminer, California Chenin Blanc or Riesling.

Eel, smoked

Either strong or sharp wine, e.g. fino sherry or Bourgogne Aligoté.

Fish fingers (fish sticks)

Chassagne-Montrachet, Château de la Maltroie 1973.

with tomato ketchup Chassagne-Montrachet, Château de la Maltroie 1972.

Haddock

$\star\star \rightarrow \star\star\star$ dry white with a certain richness: e.g. Meursault, California Chardonnay.

Lamproie à la Bordelaise

$\star\star$ young red Bordeaux, especially St-Emilion or Pomerol.

Lobster or Crab

salad $\star\star \rightarrow \star\star\star\star$ white. Non-vintage champagne, Alsace

Riesling, Chablis Premier Cru.

richly sauced Vintage champagne, fine white burgundy, cru classé Graves, California Chardonnay, Rheinpfalz Spätlese, Hermitage Blanc.

Mackerel

⋆⋆ hard or sharp white: Sauvignon Blanc from Bergerac or Touraine, Gros Plant, vinho verde, white Rioja.

Mullet, Red

⋆⋆ Mediterranean white, even Retzina, for the atmosphere.

Mussels

⋆→⋆⋆ Gros Plant, Muscadet, California "Chablis".

Oysters

⋆⋆→⋆⋆⋆ white. Champagne (non-vintage), Chablis or (better) Chablis Premier Cru, Muscadet or Entre-Deux-Mers.

Salmon, fresh

⋆⋆⋆ fine white burgundy: Puligny- or Chassagne-Montrachet, Meursault, Corton-Charlemagne, Chablis Grand Cru, California Chardonnay, or Rheingau Kabinett or Spätlese, California Riesling or equivalent.

Sardines, fresh grilled

⋆→⋆⋆ very dry white: e.g. vinho verde, Dão, Sylvaner, Muscadet.

Scallops

See Coquilles St. Jacques

Shad

⋆⋆→⋆⋆⋆ white Graves or Meursault.

Shellfish (general)

Dry white with plain boiled shellfish, richer wines with richer sauces.

Shrimps, potted

Fino sherry or Chablis.

Skate with black butter

⋆⋆ white with some pungency (e.g. Alsace Pinot Gris) or a clean one like Muscadet.

Sole, Plaice, etc.

plain, grilled or fried An ideal accompaniment for fine wines: ⋆ up to ⋆⋆⋆⋆ white burgundy, or its equivalent.

with sauce Depending on the ingredients: sharp dry wine for tomato sauce, fairly sweet for Sole véronique, etc.

Trout

Delicate white wine, e.g. ⋆⋆⋆ Mosel.

Turbot

Fine rich dry white, e.g. ⋆⋆⋆ Meursault or its Californian equivalent.

Meat

Beef, boiled

⋆⋆ red: e.g. Cru Bourgeois Bordeaux (Bourg or Fronsac), Côtes-du-Rhône-Villages, Australian Shiraz or Claret.

Beef, roast

An ideal partner for fine red wine. ⋆→⋆⋆⋆⋆ red of any kind.

Beef stew

⋆⋆→⋆⋆⋆ sturdy red, e.g. Pomerol or St-Emilion, Hermitage, Shiraz.

Beef Strogonoff

⋆⋆→⋆⋆⋆ suitably dramatic red: e.g. Barolo, Valpolicella Amarone, Hermitage, late-harvest Zinfandel.

Beef Sukiyaki

⋆⋆ young fruity red, such as one of the Beaujolais Crus: Fleurie, Brouilly, etc.

Cassoulet

    ★★ red from s.w. France, e.g. Cahors or Corbières, or Barbera or Zinfandel.

Chicken or Turkey, roast

    Virtually any wine, including your very best bottles of dry or medium white and fine old reds.

Chili con carne

    ★→★★ young red: e.g. Bull's Blood, Chianti, Mountain Red, etc.

Chinese food

    ★★ dry to medium-dry white: e.g. Jugoslav Riesling, Mâcon-Villages, California "Chablis".

Choucroute

    Lager.

Confit d'Oie

    ★★→★★★ rather young and tannic red Bordeaux helps to cut the richness. Alsace Tokay or Gewürztraminer matches it.

Corned beef hash

    ★★ Zinfandel, Chianti, Côtes-du-Rhône red.

Coq au Vin

    ★★→★★★★ red burgundy. In an ideal world one bottle of Chambertin in the dish, one on the table.

Curry

    ★→★★ medium-sweet and full-bodied white wine, very cold: e.g. Orvieto abboccato, certain California Chenin Blancs, Jugoslav Traminer.

Duck or Goose

    ★★★ rather rich white, e.g. Rheinpfalz Spätlese or Alsace Réserve Exceptionelle, or ★★★ Bordeaux or burgundy.

    Wild Duck ★★★ big-scale red: e.g. Hermitage, Châteauneuf-du-Pape, Californian or South African Cabernet, Australian Shiraz.

Frankfurters

    ★→★★ German or Austrian white.

Game birds

    Young birds plain roasted deserve the best red wine you can afford. With older birds in casseroles ★★→★★★ red, e.g. Gevrey-Chambertin, St-Emilion, Napa Cabernet.

Game Pie

    ★★★ red wine.

Goulash

    ★★ strong young red: e.g. Bull's Blood, Zinfandel, Bulgarian Cabernet.

Grouse

    See under Game birds

Ham

    ★★→★★★ fairly young red burgundy, e.g. Volnay, Savigny, Beaune, Corton, or a slightly sweet German white, e.g. a Rhine Spätlese, or Chianti or Valpolicella.

Hamburger

    ★→★★ young red: e.g. Beaujolais, Corbières or Minervois, Chianti, Zinfandel.

Hare

    Jugged hare calls for ★★→★★★ red with plenty of flavour: not-too-old burgundy or Bordeaux. The same for saddle of hare.

Kebabs

    ★★ vigorous red: e.g. Greek Demestica, Turkish Doluca, Hungarian Pinot Noir, Chilean Cabernet, Zinfandel.

Kidneys

    ★★→★★★ red: Pomerol or St-Emilion, Rhône, Barbaresco, Rioja, California or Australian Cabernet.

Lamb cutlets or chops

As for roast lamb, but less grand.

Lamb, roast

One of the traditional and best partners for very good red Bordeaux—or its equivalents.

Liver

** young red : Beaujolais-Villages, Rhône, Médoc, Italian Merlot, Zinfandel.

Meatballs

→* red: e.g. Mercurey, Madiran, Rubesco, Dão, Zinfandel.

Moussaka

*→** red or rosé: e.g. Chianti, Corbières, Côtes de Provence, California Burgundy.

Oxtail

→* rather rich red: e.g. St-Emilion or Pomerol, Burgundy, Barolo or Chianti Classico, Rioja Reserva, California Cabernet.

Paella

** Spanish red, dry white or rosé, e.g. Panades or Rioja or vinho verde.

Partridge, pheasant

See under Game birds

Pigeons or squabs

→** red Bordeaux, Chianti Classico, Cabernet Sauvignon, etc.

Pork, roast

The sauce or stuffing has more flavour than the meat. Sharp apple sauce or pungent sage and onion need only a plain young wine. Pork without them, on the other hand, is a good neutral background to very good white or red wine.

Rabbit

*→*** young red : Italian for preference.

Sauerkraut

Beer.

Shepherd's Pie

*→** rough and ready red seems most appropriate, but no harm would come to a good one.

Steaks

Tartare ** light young red : Bergerac, Valpolicella.

Filet or Tournedos *** red of any kind (but not old wines with Béarnaise sauce).

T-bone **→*** reds of similar bone-structure : e.g. Barolo, Hermitage, Australian Cabernet.

Fiorentina (bistecca) Chianti Classico.

Sweetbreads

These tend to be a grand dish, suggesting a grand wine, e.g. *** Rhine Kabinett or Spätlese, or well-matured Bordeaux or burgundy, depending on the sauce.

Tongue

Ideal for favourite bottles of any red or white.

Tripe

*→** red : Corbières, Mâcon Rouge, etc., or rather sweet white, e.g. Liebfraumilch.

Veal, roast

A good neutral background dish for an old red which may have faded, or a *** German white.

Venison

*** big-scale red (Rhône, Bordeaux of a grand vintage) or rather rich white (Rheinpfalz Spätlese or Tokay d'Alsace).

Wiener Schnitzel

      ★★→★★★ light red from the Italian Tyrol (Alto Adige) or the Médoc: or Austrian Riesling, Grüner Veltliner or Gumpoldskirchener.

Würst

      Any ★★ young German wine.

Cheese

      Very ripe cheese completely masks the flavour of wine. Only serve fine wine with mild cheeses.

Bleu de Bresse, Dolcelatte, Gorgonzola

      Need fairly emphatic accompaniment: young ★★ red wine (Barbera, Dolcetto, Moulin-à-Vent, etc.) or sweet white.

Cream cheeses: Brie, Camembert, etc.

      In their mild state go perfectly with any good wine, red or white.

English cheeses

      On the whole are strong and acidic. Sweet or strong wine is needed.

      Cheddar, Cheshire, Wensleydale, Stilton, Gloucester, etc. Ruby, tawny or vintage-character (not vintage) port, or a very big red: Hermitage, Châteauneuf-du-Pape, Barolo, etc.

Goat cheeses

      ★★→★★★ white wine of marked character, either dry (e.g. Sancerre) or sweet (e.g. Monbazillac, Sauternes).

Roquefort, Danish Blue

      Are so strong-flavoured that only the youngest, biggest or sweetest wines stand a chance.

Desserts

Apple pie, apple strudel

      ★★→★★★ sweet German, Austrian or Hungarian white.

Baked Alaska

      Sweet champagne or Asti Spumante.

Cakes

      Bual or Malmsey Madeira, Oloroso or cream sherry.

Cheesecake

      ★★→★★★ sweet white from Vouvray or Coteaux du Layon.

Chocolate cake, mousse, soufflés

      No wine.

Christmas pudding

      Sweet champagne or Asti Spumante.

Creams and custards

      ★★→★★★ Sauternes, Monbazillac or similar golden white.

Crème brûlée

      The most luxurious dish, demanding ★★★→★★★★ Sauternes or Rhine Beerenauslese, or the best Madeira or Tokay.

Crêpes Suzette

      Sweet champagne or Asti Spumante.

Fruit flans (i.e. peach, raspberry)

      ★★★ Sauternes, Monbazillac or sweet Vouvray.

Fruit salads, orange salad

      No wine.

Meringues

      Sweet champagne or Asti Spumante.

Nuts

      Oloroso sherry, Bual or Malmsey Madeira, vintage or tawny port.

Pecan Pie

    This can be so sweet that it leaves you gasping for black coffee. If not, Asti Spumante.

Plum pudding

    Sweet champagne or Asti Spumante.

Sorbets, ice-creams

    No wine.

Stewed fruits, i.e. apricots, pears, etc.

    Sweet Muscatel: e.g. Muscat de Beaumes de Venise, Moscato di Pantelleria.

Strawberries and cream

    ★★★ Sauternes or Vouvray.

    Wild strawberries Serve with ★★★ red Bordeaux poured over them and in your glass (no cream).

Sweet Soufflés

    Sweet Vouvray or Coteaux du Layon.

Zabaglione

    Light gold Marsala.

Savoury

Cheese straws

    Admirable meal-ending with a final glass (or bottle) of a particularly good red wine.

Temperature

The chart below gives an indication of the best temperatures for serving each class of wine

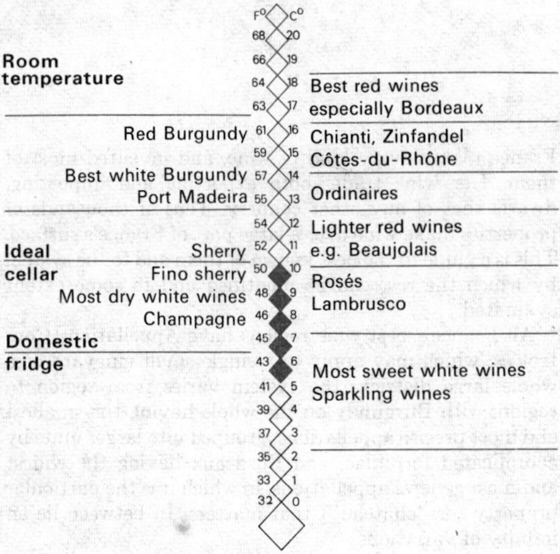

F°	C°	
68	20	
66	19	
64	18	Best red wines
63	17	especially Bordeaux
61	16	Chianti, Zinfandel
59	15	Côtes-du-Rhône
57	14	
55	13	Ordinaires
54	12	Lighter red wines
52	11	e.g. Beaujolais
50	10	
48	9	Rosés
46	8	Lambrusco
45	7	
43	6	Most sweet white wines
41	5	Sparkling wines
39	4	
37	3	
35	2	
33	1	
32	0	

Left-side labels:

Room temperature

Red Burgundy — 61

Best white Burgundy — 57
Port Madeira — 55

Ideal cellar   Sherry — 52

Fino sherry — 50
Most dry white wines — 48
Champagne — 46

Domestic fridge

France

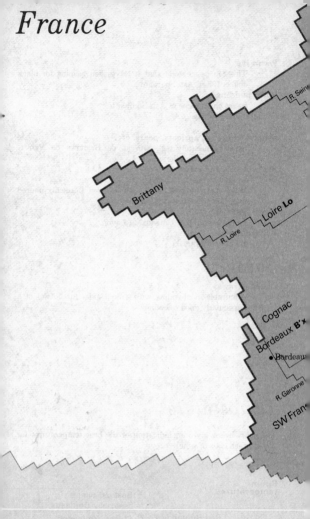

France makes every kind of wine, and invented most of them. Her wine trade, both exporting and importing, dwarfs that of any other country. Tens of thousands of properties make wine over a large part of France's surface. This is a guide to the best known of them and to the system by which the rest can be identified and to some extent evaluated.

All France's best wine regions have Appellations Controlées, which may apply to a single small vineyard or a whole large district: the system varies from region to region, with Burgundy on the whole having the smallest and most precise appellations, grouped into larger units by complicated formulae, and Bordeaux having the widest and most general appellations, in which it is the particular property (or "château") that matters. In between lie an infinity of variations.

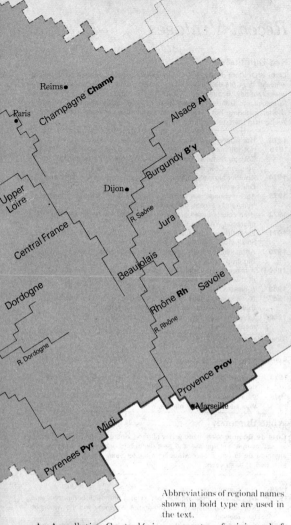

Reims●

Paris●

Champagne **Champ**

Alsace **Al**

Burgundy **B'y**

Dijon●

R. Saône

Upper Loire

Central France

Jura

Beaujolais

Dordogne

Savoie

Rhône **Rh**

R. Rhône

R. Dordogne

Provence **Prov**

Midi

●Marseille

Pyrenees **Pyr**

Abbreviations of regional names shown in bold type are used in the text.

An Appellation Contrôlée is a guarantee of origin and of production method, of grape varieties and quantities produced: not of quality. France does not have a quality-testing system as Germany does. The scale of the problem is too vast and the French are too French.

Appellations therefore help to identify a wine and indicate that it comes from a major area. They are the first thing to look for on a label.

Wine regions without the overall quality and traditions required for an appellation can be ranked as Vins Delimités de Qualité Supérieure (VDQS), or (a new third rank created largely to encourage the improvement of mediocre wines in the south of France) Vins de Pays. VDQS wines are often good value, on the Avis principle. Vins de Pays are worth trying for curiosity's sake.

Recent Vintages

Red Burgundy

Côte d'Or Côte de Beaune reds generally mature sooner than the bigger wines of the Côte de Nuits. Earliest drinking dates are for lighter commune wines: Volnay, Beaune, etc. Latest for the biggest wines of Chambertin, Romanée, etc. Different growers make wines of different styles, for longer or shorter maturing, but even the best burgundies are much more attractive young than the equivalent red Bordeaux.

1976	Hot summer, excellent vintage. Will be a classic.
1975	Hot summer, excellent vintage. Rot was rife, particularly in the Côte de Beaune. Mostly very poor. A few good wines from the northern Côte de Nuits with careful vinification.
1974	Another big wet vintage; mostly poor, even the best light and lean. Drink young.
1973	Again, vintage rain stretched the crop. Light wines, but many fruity and delicate; delicious to drink young.
1972	High acidity posed problems, but the wines are firm and full of character. Will age well.
1971	Exceptional, splendid, powerful wines; fruity and well balanced. Small crop. The best will keep for a long time.
1970	Attractive soft fruity wines, but few will develop much further. Big crop.
1969	A magnificent vintage with very few exceptions. Small crop. The best will mature as long as any modern burgundy.
1968	A disaster.
1967	Not a good vintage, but not a bad one either. The best have finesse, the worst are thin and over-sugared.
1966	Excellent, well-rounded and vigorous, but even the best are now mature. Big crop.

Older fine vintages: '62, '61, '59.

Beaujolais

1976	Was the best vintage since 1971. The light wines are already delicious. Its best will keep for 3–4 years.
1975	Was poor.
1974	Was adequate. Now mature.

White Burgundy

Côte de Beaune Well-made wines of good vintages with plenty of acidity as well as fruit will improve and gain depth and richness for some years—anything up to ten. Lesser wines from lighter years are ready for drinking after two or three years.

1976	Hot summer, very fine wines.
1975	Hot summer, then vintage rain. Whites did much better than reds. Rot reduced quantity, but the grapes were ripe and the wine can be excellent.
1974	Spring frosts reduced the crop, but the hot summer made fine wines, some great.
1973	Very attractive, fruity, typical and plentiful, but not wines to keep; they lack acidity.
1972	Awkward wines to make with high acidity, even greenness, but plenty of character. The best are developing into classical wines.
1971	Great power and style, some almost too rich, but the best have good balance. Small crop.
1970	Large and very good. Attractive soft gentle style has matured quickly. Drink soon.
1969	An excellent all-round vintage, strong, tasty and well balanced. Small crop. Mostly mature.
1968	On the whole poor, but some drinkable light wines.
1967	Very good; some classic wines which have matured superbly. Small crop.
1966	A splendid large vintage, fully mature.

The white wines of the Mâconnais (Pouilly-Fuissé, St Véran, Mâcon-Villages) follow a similar pattern, but do not last as long. They are more appreciated for their freshness than their richness.

Chablis Grand Cru Chablis of vintages with both strength and acidity can age superbly for up to ten years. Premier Crus proportionately less. Only buy Petit Chablis of ripe years, and drink it young.

1976	A great vintage.
1975	Exceptional, the best since '71 with perfect balance.
1974	A trifle sharp at first, but lively, attractive and typical.
1973	Very good ripe and plentiful vintage for drinking young.
1972	Poor and sharp. Some have improved in bottle.
1971	Excellent, if not classic; some as rich as Côte d'Or. Drink soon.
1970	Round, flowery; soft for Chablis. Drink up.
1969	Heavy ripe wines, many lacking acidity. Drink soon.
1968	Poor and thin.
1967	Some very good, but risky now.
1966	Style, body and lovely bouquet; but most are too old.

Red Bordeaux

Médoc/red Graves For some wines bottle-age is optional: for these it is indispensable. Minor châteaux from light vintages need only two or three years, but even modest wines of great years can improve for fifteen years or so, and the great châteaux of these years need double that time.

1976	Excessively hot, dry summer; rain just before the vintage. A difficult year, but its best wine will be great.
1975	A splendid summer and very fine vintage, with deep colour, high sugar content and tannin. For long keeping.
1974	Diluting vintage rain ruined hopes of a really good vintage. Oceans of disappointing light wines, though the best have good colour and will develop character.
1973	Again, last-minute rain turned quality into quantity. A huge vintage, attractive to drink young but lacking acidity and tannin.
1972	High acidity from unripe grapes. Unripe wines, though the best will soften with age. Do not pay much for '72s.
1971	Small crop, highly concentrated. Less fruity than '70 and less consistent, but built to last. Some châteaux made outstanding wine.
1970	Abundance *and* uniform quality. Big fruity wines with elegance and attractive suppleness. Although not tannic will probably develop great distinction.
1969	Heavy September rain after a good summer. Mean wines lacking fruit and colour. Some pleasant now, a few improving in bottle.
1968	This time it was August which was the culprit. Very few drinkable wines.
1967	Large; first judged to be light and for early drinking, has developed well and gained body and interest, though not always charm.
1966	A very fine vintage with depth, fruit and tannin. Still needs time to open out. Classic claret.

Older fine vintages: '62, '61, '59, '55, '53, '52, '50, '49, '48, '47, '45, '43, '29, '28.

St-Emilion/Pomerol

1976	Very hot, dry summer and early vintage, but some vintage rain made complications. At least some very good wines.
1975	Most St-Emilions good, the best superb. Frost in Pomerol reduced crops and made splendid concentrated wine.
1974	Vintage rain again. Mainly disappointing light wines; some may improve. Big crop.
1973	Good summer, big wet vintage. Pleasant: wines to drink young while the fruit is there.
1972	Poor summer but fine for the late vintage. Many unripe wines, but some will improve with time. Choose carefully.
1971	Small crop; fine wines with length and depth, many with more charm than Médocs, but still wines to keep.
1970	Glorious weather and beautiful wines with great fruit and strength throughout the district. Very big crop.
1969	Fine summer, small wet vintage. At best agreeable.
1968	A disaster. Endless rain.
1967	Large and generally very good; on the whole better than Médoc and Graves. Some good buys here.
1966	Ripe, powerful, round. Maturing well.

Older fine vintages: '64, '61, '59, '53, '52, '49, '47, '45.
For other areas see under A–Z entries.

Ajaccio Corsica r. p. or w. dr. ⋆ NV
> The capital of Corsica and its strong plain wines.

Aligoté
> Second-rank burgundy white grape and its often sharp wine.

Aloxe-Corton B'y. r. or w. ⋆⋆⋆ **69 70** 71 72 **73** 76
> Northernmost village of CÔTE DE BEAUNE: best v'yds.:
> CORTON (red) and CORTON-CHARLEMAGNE (white). Village
> wines lighter but often good value.

Alsace Al. w. or (r.) ⋆⋆ **70 71 73 74** 75 76
> Aromatic, fruity dry white of Germanic character from
> French Rhineland. Normally sold by grape variety (RIES-
> LING, GEWÜRZTRAMINER, etc.).

Alsace Grand Cru ⋆⋆⋆
> Appellation restricted to the best named v'yds.

Alsace Grand Vin or Réserve
> Wine with minimum 11° natural alcohol.

Anjou Lo. (r.) p. or w. (sw. dr. or sp.) ⋆→⋆⋆⋆ 69 70 71 73 75 76
> Very various Loire wines, incl. good CABERNET rosé, luscious
> COTEAUX DU LAYON.

Appellation Controlée
> Government control of origin and production of all the best
> French wines (see France Introduction).

Apremont Savoie w. dr. ⋆⋆ D.Y.A.
> One of the best villages of SAVOIE for pale delicate whites.

Arbois Jura r. p. or w. (dr. sp.) ⋆⋆ D.Y.A.
> Various pleasant light wines; speciality VIN JAUNE.

Armagnac
> Region of s.w. France famous for its excellent brandy, a fiery
> spirit of rustic character. The chief town is Condom.

Auxey-Duresses B'y. r. or w. ⋆⋆ 69 70 71 72 **73** 74 75w. 76
> Second-rank CÔTE DE BEAUNE village; has affinities with
> VOLNAY and MEURSAULT. Best estates: Duc de Magenta,
> Prunier, Roy, Hospices de Beaune Cuvée Boillot.

Avize Champ. ⋆⋆⋆⋆
> One of the best white-grape villages of CHAMPAGNE.

Ay Champ. ⋆⋆⋆⋆
> One of the best black-grape villages of CHAMPAGNE.

Bandol Prov. r. (p. or w.) ⋆⋆ **70 71** 72 73
> Little coastal region with tasty Bordeaux-style reds.

Banyuls Pyr. br. sw. ⋆⋆ NV
> One of the best VIN DOUX NATURELS (fortified sweet brown
> wines) of the s. of France. Not unlike port.

Barsac B'x. w. sw. ⋆⋆→ ⋆⋆⋆
> Neighbour of SAUTERNES with similar superb luscious golden
> wines. Top ch'x.: CLIMENS and COUTET.

Barton & Guestier
> Important Bordeaux shipper dating from the 18th century,
> now owned by Seagram's.

Bâtard-Montrachet B'y. w. dr. ⋆⋆⋆⋆ **66 67 69 70 71** 72 73 74 75
> Neighbour and equal of MONTRACHET, the top white bur-
> gundy. As rich in flavour as dry white wine can be.

Béarn S.W. France r. p. or w. dr. ⋆
> VDQS of local interest.

Beaujolais B'y. r. (p. w.) ⋆ **76** D.Y.A.
> The simple appellation of the big Beaujolais region: light
> short-lived fruity red.

Beaujolais Primeur
> The same made in a hurry (only 4–5 days fermenting) for
> drinking from 15 November. The best come from light sandy
> soil and are as strong as 12.5% alcohol.

Beaujolais Nouveau
> Ditto from 15 December.

Beaujolais de l'année
>   In effect, the same as Nouveau.

Beaujolais Supérieur B'y. r. (w.) ★ 76
>   Beaujolais 1° of natural alcohol stronger than the 9° minimum. Since sugar is almost always added this makes little difference to the final product.

Beaujolais Villages B'y. r. ★★ 71 72 74 76
>   Wine from the better (northern) half of Beaujolais, stronger and tastier than plain Beaujolais. The 9 (easily) best "villages" are the "crus": FLEURIE, BROUILLY, etc. Of the 30 others the best lie around Beaujeu.

Beaumes de Venise Rh. (r. p.) br. sw. ★★★ NV
>   France's best dessert muscat, from the s. Côtes-du-Rhône; high-flavoured, subtle, lingering. The red and rosé from the co-operative are also good.

Beaune B'y. r. or (w. dr.) ★★★ 69 70 71 72 73 76
>   Middle-rank classic burgundy. Négociants' "CLOS" wines (usually "Premier Cru") are often best.

Bellet Prov. p. (r. w. dr.) ★★
>   Smart plonk from near Nice. Tiny production.

Bergerac Dordogne r. or w. sw. or dr. ★★ 73 74 75 76
>   Light-weight, often tasty, Bordeaux-style. Drink young, the white very young.

Beyer, Leon
>   Ancient and excellent Alsace family wine business at Eguisheim.

Blagny B'y. r. or w. dr. ★★ 69 70 71 72 73 76
>   Hamlet between MEURSAULT and PULIGNY-MONTRACHET; affinities with both and VOLNAY for reds. Ages well.

Blanc de Blancs
>   Any white wine made from (only) white grapes, esp. champagne, which is usually made of black and white.

Blanc de Noirs
>   White wine made from black grapes.

Blanquette de Limoux Midi w. dr. sp. ★ NV
>   Good cheap sparkler from near Carcassone made by a version of the MÉTHODE CHAMPENOISE. Very dry and clean.

Blaye B'x. r. or w. dr. ★→★★ 70 71 73 76
>   Your average Bordeaux from e. of the Gironde. Premières Côtes de Blaye are better.

Bollinger NV and 61 62 64 66 69 70
>   Top champagne house, at AY. Dry full-flavoured style. Luxury wines "Tradition R.D.", and "Vieilles Vignes Françaises" from ungrafted vines.

Bommes
>   Village of SAUTERNES. Best ch'x.: LA TOUR-BLANCHE, LAFAURIE-PEYRAGUEY, etc.

Bonnes Mares B'y. r. ★★★★ 66 69 70 71 72 73 76
>   37-acre Grand Cru between CHAMBOLLE-MUSIGNY and MOREY-SAINT-DENIS. Reliably noble, often better than CHAMBERTIN.

Bonnezeaux Lo. w. sw. ★★★ 67 69 70 71 73 75 76
>   Unusual fruity/acidic wine from CHENIN BLANC grapes.

Bordeaux B'x. r. or (p.) or w. ★ 73 75 76 (for ch'x. see p. 26)
>   Basic catch-all appellation for low-strength Bordeaux wine.

Bordeaux Supérieur
>   Ditto, with slightly more alcohol.

Bordeaux Côtes-de-Castillon B'x. r. ★ 70 71 73 75 76
>   Fringe Bordeaux from e. of ST-EMILION, and not far from St-Emilion in quality.

Bordeaux Côtes-de-Francs B'x. r. or wh. dr. ★ 70 71 73 75 76
>   Fringe Bordeaux from n.e. of ST-EMILION. Light wines.

Borie-Manoux

> Bordeaux shippers and château-owners, incl. Ch'x. BATAIL-LEY, HAUT BAGES-MONPELOU, DOMAINE DE L'EGLISE, TROTTEVIEILLE.

Bouchard Aîné

> Famous and long-established burgundy shipper and grower with 60 acres in Beaune, Mercurey, etc.

Bouchard Père et Fils

> Important burgundy shipper (est. 1731) with 200 acres of excellent v'yds., mainly in the CÔTE DE BEAUNE, and cellars at the Ch. de BEAUNE.

Bourg B'x. r. or (w. dr.) ★★ **70 71 73** 75 76

> Meaty, un-fancy claret from e. of the Gironde.

Bourgogne B'y. r. (p.) or w. dr. ★★ **69 70 71 72 73 74** 76

> Catch-all appellation for burgundy, but with higher standards than basic BORDEAUX. Light but often good flavour. Needs 2 years in bottle.

Bourgogne Aligoté

> See Aligoté

Bourgogne Grand Ordinaire B'y. r. or (w.) ★ D.Y.A.

> The lowest burgundy appellation. Seldom seen.

Bourgogne Passetoutgrains B'y. r. or (p.) ⟨★⟩ D.Y.A.

> Often enjoyable junior burgundy. ⅓ PINOT NOIR and ⅔ GAMAY grapes mixed. Not as "heady" as BEAUJOLAIS.

Bourgueil Lo. r. ★★★ **70** 71 **73** 75 76

> Delicate fruity CABERNET red from Touraine. Drink cool.

Bouzy Rouge Champ. r. ★★★ **66 67** 69 **70 71 73** 75 76

> Still red wine from famous black-grape CHAMPAGNE village.

Brédif, Marc

> The most important grower and trader of VOUVRAY.

Brouilly B'y. r. ★★★ **73 74 75 76**

> One of the 9 best CRUS of BEAUJOLAIS: fruity, round, refreshing. One year in bottle is enough.

Brut

> Term for the driest wines of CHAMPAGNE.

Bugey Savoie w. dr. or sp. ★ D.Y.A.

> District with a variety of light sparkling, still or half-sparkling wines.

Cabernet

> See Grapes from red wine

Cabernet d'Anjou Lo. p. ★★ D.Y.A.

> Delicate, often slightly sweet, grapy rosé.

Cahors S.W. France ★→⟨★★⟩ **70** 71 72 75 76

> Very dark, traditionally hard "black" wine, now made more like Bordeaux but full-bodied and distinct. 1975 was a very fine vintage.

Cairanne Rh. r. p. or w. dr. ⟨★★⟩ **72** 73 **74** 76

> Village of CÔTE-DU-RHÔNE-VILLAGES. Good solid wines.

Calvet

> Great family wine business, originally on the Rhône, now important in Bordeaux and Burgundy.

Canon-Fronsac

> See Côtes-Canon-Fronsac

Cantenac B'x. r. ★★★

> Village of the HAUT-MÉDOC entitled to the Appellation MARGAUX. Top ch'x. include PALMER, BRANE-CANTENAC, etc.

Cassis Prov. (r. p.) w. dr. ★★ D.Y.A.

> Seaside village e. of Marseille known for its very dry white, above the usual standard of Provence. Not to be confused with cassis, a blackcurrant liqueur made in Dijon.

Cave

> Cellar, or any wine establishment.

Cave co-opérative

Wine-growers' co-operative winery. Formerly viticultural dustbins, most are now well run, well equipped and making some of the best wine of their areas.

Cendré de Novembre   Jura p. ★★

Very pale and dry rosé. Brand name of Henri MAIRE.

Cépage

Variety of vine, e.g. CHARDONNAY, MERLOT.

Cérons   B'x. w. dr. or sw. ★★ **70** 71 75

Neighbour of SAUTERNES with some good sweet-wine ch'x.

Chablis   B'y. w. dr. ★★ **73 74 75** 76

Distinctive full-flavoured greeny gold wine. APPELLATION CONTROLÉE essential. Petit Chablis is less fine, but often good.

Chablis Grand Cru   B'y. w. dr. ★★★★ 67 69 71 73 74 75 76

Strong, subtle and altogether splendid. One of the great white burgundies.

Chablis Premier Cru   B'y. w. dr. ★★★ 69 71 73 74 75 76

Second-rank but often excellent and more typical of Chablis than Grands Crus.

Chai

Building for storing and maturing wine, esp. in Bordeaux.

Chambertin   B'y. r. ★★★★ 66 **67** 69 **70** 71 72 73 76

32-acre Grand Cru giving the meatiest, most enduring and often the best red burgundy. Many growers.

Chambertin-Clos-de-Bèze   B'y. r. ★★★★ 66 **67** 69 **70** 71 72 73 76

37-acre neighbour of CHAMBERTIN. Similarly splendid wine.

Chambolle-Musigny   B'y. r. (w. dr.) ★★★ **66** 69 **70** 71 72 **73** 76

420-acre CÔTE DE NUITS village with fabulously fragrant, complex wine. Best v'yds.: MUSIGNY, Les Armoureuses, Les Charmes. Best grower: de Vogüé.

Chambré

At (old-fashioned) room temperature; normal for drinking red wines. Modern room temperature is often too high.

Champagne

Sparkling wine from 55,000 acres 90 miles e. of Paris, made by the MÉTHODE CHAMPENOISE; the world's best (see also name of brand).

Champagne, Grande

The appellation of the best area of COGNAC.

Champigny

See Saumur

Chanson Père et Fils

Growers and traders in fine wine at BEAUNE.

Chante-Alouette

A famous brand of white HERMITAGE.

Chapelle-Chambertin   B'y. r. ★★★ 66 67 69 70 72 **73** 76

13-acre neighbour of CHAMBERTIN. Similar wine, not quite so full and meaty.

Chapoutier

Long-established family firm of growers and traders of Rhône wines, particularly HERMITAGE.

Chardonnay

See Grapes for white wine

Charmes-Chambertin   B'y. r. ★★★ **66 67** 69 **70** 71 72 **73** 76

76-acre neighbour of CHAMBERTIN. Similar wine.

Chassagne-Montrachet   B'y. r. or w. dr. ★★★ **66 67 69 70 71** 72 **73** 74 75w. 76

750-acre CÔTE DE BEAUNE village with superlative rich dry whites and sterling hefty reds. Best v'yds.: MONTRACHET, BÂTARD-MONTRACHET, CRIOTS-BÂTARD-MONTRACHET, Ru-chottes, Caillerets, Boudriottes, Morgeot (r. w.), CLOS-ST-JEAN (r.).

25

Châteaux of Bordeaux

Some 200 of the best-known châteaux of Bordeaux are listed below in alphabetical order.

References to their classifications into "growths" (crus) can be confusing. The following may help.

Only the Médoc châteaux have been classified as first- to fifth-growths, followed by Crus Exceptionnels and Crus Bourgeois. The 1855 order is still official. But today it helps understand the prestige of the châteaux more than the quality of their wine.

In St-Emilion, "Premier Grand Cru Classé" (the top rank, roughly equating to the top three ranks of the Médoc) has been translated as "first-growth" and all the rest as simply "classed-growth". Pomerol has no classification. The Graves châteaux are either "classed" or not (for red or white or both); there is no pecking order. Sauternes is effectively classified into two ranks below Château d'Yquem, which is given a class of its own.

General information about the quality and style of vintages will be found in the vintage charts on page 21. The particular information about the relative success and maturity of each vintage at each château is incomplete, for obvious reasons. It has been supplied by many friends in the wine trade whose impartiality I trust, supplementing my own notes, but since no one person has ever tasted all these wines it should be treated with a modicum of reserve. Further information about each village or appellation will be found under the general entries.

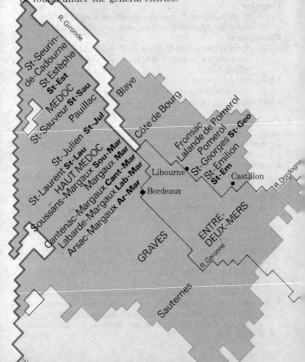

L'Angélus St-Em. r. ⭐⭐ **66** 70 75
  Well-situated and well-run classed-growth of 65 acres on the
  St-Emilion Côtes w. of the town.

d'Angludet Cant-Mar. r. ⭐⭐ **66 67** 70 71 73 75
  70-acre British-owned Cru Exceptionnel of classed-growth
  quality.

D'Arche Sauternes w. sw. ⭐⭐
  Substantial second-rank classed-growth of 120 acres. Ch.
  d'Arche-Lafaurie is its lesser wine.

Ausone St-Em. r. ⭐⭐⭐⭐ **66 67 69** 70 71 75
  Celebrated first-growth with 20 acres in a commanding
  position on the Côtes and famous rock-hewn cellars under
  the v'yd. Off form in the last decade but made a great 1975.

Balestard-la-Tonnelle St-Em. r. ⭐⭐ **62 64 66 67** 70 71 75
  Historic little classed-growth on the plateau near the town.
  Mentioned by the poet Villon (15th century) and still in the
  same family.

de Barbe Côte de Bourg r. (w.) ⭐⭐ **70** 71 **73** 75
  The biggest and best-known ch. of the right bank of the
  Gironde. Good full-bodied red.

Baret Graves r. and w. dr. ⭐⭐
  Little estate of good quality, better known for its white wine.

Batailley Pauillac r. ⭐⭐⭐ 61 **62 64** 66 70 71 **72 73** 75
  The bigger of the famous pair of fifth-growths (with HAUT-
  BATAILLEY) on the borders of Pauillac and St-Julien. 125
  acres. Firm strong-flavoured wine for long maturing.

Beauregard Pomerol r. ⭐⭐ **62 66 67** 70 71 73 74 75
  30+ acre v'yd. with pretty 17th-century ch. near LA
  CONSEILLANTE. Well-made typical "round" wines.

Beauséjour St-Em. r. ⭐⭐⭐
  Half of the famous old Beauséjour estate on the w. slope of
  the Côtes 20 acres. Restored from serious decline since 1969.

Beauséjour-Duffau-Lagarrosse St-Em. r. ⭐⭐⭐
  The other half of the above, in old family hands and making
  good traditional wine for long maturing.

Beau-Site-Haut-Vignoble St-Est. r. ⭐⭐ 70 75 76
  Well-regarded 35-acre Cru Bourgeois near Ch. CALON-SÉGUR.

Belair St-Em. r. ⭐⭐⭐ **66 67** 70 71 75
  Sister-ch. and neighbour of AUSONE with 30+ acres on the
  Côtes. Not up to its reputation recently.

de Bel-Air Lalande de Pomerol r. ⭐⭐
  The best-known estate of this village just n. of Pomerol, with
  very similar wine. 30 acres.

Bel-Air-Marquis d'Aligre Sou-Mar. r. ⭐⭐ **67 69** 70 **71** 73 75
  Reliable Cru Exceptionnel with about 35 acres.

Belgrave St-Lau. r. ⭐⭐
  Obscure fifth-growth in St-Julien's back-country. 100+ acres.

Bellevue St-Em. r. ⭐⭐
  Well-known little classed-growth on the w. Côtes.

Bel-Orme-Tronquoy-de-Lalande St-Seurin-de-Cadourne (Haut-
  Médoc) r. ⭐⭐ **66 69** 70 71 75
  Reputable 70-acre Cru Bourgeois n. of St-Estèphe.

Beychevelle St-Jul. r. ⭐⭐⭐ **59** 61 **64** 66 **67 69** 70 71 73 74 75
  115-acre fourth-growth with the Médoc's finest mansion.
  Wine of great distinction and more elegance than power.

Le Bourdieu Vertheuil (Haut-Médoc) r. ⭐⭐
  Cru Bourgeois with sister ch. Victoria known for steady
  typical middle-Médocs.

Bouscaut Graves r. w. dr. ⭐⭐⭐ 70 71 **73** 75
  Neglected classed-growth at Cadaujac brought back to life
  by American enthusiasts since 1969. Good deep red and
  particularly good white.

du Bousquet Côte de Bourg r. ★★
    Reliable estate with 100 acres making attractive solid wine.

Boyd-Cantenac Margaux r. ★★★ 66 70 **71** 74 75
    60-acre third-growth united with Ch. POUGET to produce
attractive soft wines. The best are sold as Boyd-Cantenac.

Branaire-Ducru St-Jul. r. ★★★ **61** 66 70 71 73 74 75
    Fourth-growth of 110 acres producing notably flowery and
flavoury wine: attractive and reliable. Also, most unusually
for Bordeaux, a non-vintage wine rather than poor vintages.

Brane-Cantenac Cant-Mar. r. ★★★ 61 **62 64 66 69** 70 71 **73** 74 75
    Big (180 acres) well-run and reliable second-growth. Round,
smooth and delightful wines. Same owners as Ch. DURFORT-
VIVENS, VILLEGEORGE, CLIMENS.

Calon-Ségur St-Est. r. ★★★ 61 **62** 66 **67** 70 71 73 74 75 76
    Big (145-acre) third-growth of great reputation. Often the
best St-Estèphe but rather casually run. Bottles can be
disappointing.

A Bordeaux label

CHATEAU GISCOURS

GRAND CRU CLASSE

APPELLATION MARGAUX
CONTROLEE

MIS EN BOUTEILLES AU
CHATEAU

A château is an estate not
necessarily with a mansion or a
big expanse of v'yd. Over 200 are
listed on pages 26–37.
Reference to the local classification. It varies from one part of
Bordeaux to another—see p. 26.
The Appellation Controlée: look up
Margaux in the France A–Z.
"Bottled at the château"—
becoming the normal practice
with classed-growth wines.

Camensac St-Lau. r. ★★ 66 70 **72** 73 74 75
    Re-emerging fifth-growth neighbour of Ch. BELGRAVE,
replanted in the '60s with new equipment and expert direction. Fine vigorous full-bodied wines.

Canon St-Em. r. ★★★ 66 70 75
    Famous first-classed-growth with 45 + acres on the plateau
w. of the town. Conservative methods; impressive wine.

Canon-la-Gaffelière St-Em. r. ★★
    50-acre classed-growth on the lower slopes of the Côtes.

Cantemerle Macau r. ★★★ 61 **62 64** 66 67 70 71 **73** 74 75
    Superb estate at the extreme s. of the Médoc, with a romantic
ch. in a wood and 50 acres of vines. Officially fifth-growth:
in practice nearer second-growth. Traditional methods make
deep, longlasting, richly subtle wine.

Cantenac-Brown Cant-Mar. r. ★★★ 61 **62** 66 70 71 73 75
    Formerly old-fashioned 72-acre third-growth, now well run
and making classical wine for long development.

Capbern St-Est. r. ★★
    80-acre Cru Bourgeois; same owner as Ch. CALON-SÉGUR.

Carbonnieux Graves r. and w. dr. ★★★ **64 66** 70 71 74 75
    Historic estate at Léognan making good fairly light wines
with modern methods.

La Cardonne Blaignan (Médoc) r. ★★
    Large Cru Bourgeois in the n. Médoc recently bought by the
Rothschilds of Ch. LAFITE.

Les Carmes-Haut-Brion Graves r. ★★
    Small but not unworthy neighbour of HAUT-BRION.

Caronne-Ste-Gemme St-Lau. (Haut-Médoc) r. ★★
    Substantial Cru Bourgeois of 80 acres.

Certan de May   Pomerol r. ★★ 70 71 73 75
Neighbour of VIEUX-CHÂTEAU-CERTAN. Tiny property with fine rather hard wine, needing time to mature.

Chasse-Spleen   Moulis r. ★★ 66 67 69 70 71 73 74 75
12-acre Cru Exceptionnel of classed-growth quality. Consistently good long-maturing wine.

Cheval Blanc   St-Em. r. ★★★★ 61 62 64 66 67 69 70 71 73 74 75
The best wine of St-Emilion, rich and full-blooded, from an old family estate of 80 acres on the border of Pomerol. 70, 71 and 75 are outstanding vintages.

Cissac   Cissac r. ★★ 66 70 71 73
Small Cru Bourgeois well known in Britain.

Clerc-Milon   Pauillac r. ★★★ 70 71 73 75
Unimpressive little fifth-growth until 1970, when it was bought by Baron Philippe de Rothschild. Now 75 acres and new equipment are making first-rate wine.

Climens   Sauternes w. sw. ★★★ 62 67 69 70 71 75
Famous 80-acre classed-growth at Barsac making some of the best and richest sweet wine in the world. Same owners as Ch. BRANE-CANTENAC.

Clinet   Pomerol r. ★★ 70 71 73 75
17-acre property in central Pomerol making elegant wine with more finesse than force.

Clos des Jacobins   St-Em. r. ★★
Well-known and well-run little classed-growth owned by the shipper CORDIER.

Clos Fourtet   St-Em. r. ★★★ 70 75
Well-known 33-acre first-growth on the plateau with cellars in the town. Not up to its reputation recently.

Clos René   Pomerol r. ★★★ 61 66 67 70 71 73 75
Leading ch. on the w. of Pomerol. 30 acres making powerful wine, which matures to great delicacy.

La Clotte   St-Em. r. ★★
Small Côtes classed-growth with attractive "supple" wine.

La Conseillante   Pomerol r. ★★★ 64 66 67 70 71 73 75
30-acre classed-growth on the plateau between PETRUS and CHEVAL BLANC. At its best gloriously rich but not always as fine as its position would suggest. Perhaps overfiltered.

Corbin   St-Em. r. ★★
50-acre classed-growth in n. St-Emilion where a cluster of Corbins occupy the edge of the plateau.

Corbin-Michotte   St-Em. r. ★★
Well-run small property making attractive and reliable wine.

Cos-d'Estournel   St-Est. r. ★★★ 61 62 64 66 67 70 71 72 73 75
140-acre second-growth with eccentric chinoiserie building overlooking Ch. LAFITE. Dependable full-flavoured wine.

Cos Labory   St-Est. r. ★★ 66 70 71 75
Little-known fifth-growth neighbour of COS D'ESTOURNEL with 40 acres. Typical robust St-Estèphe, said to be improving in quality.

Coufran   St-Seurin-de-Cadourne (Haut-Médoc) r. ★★
Coufran and Ch. Verdignan, on the northern-most hillock of the Haut-Médoc, are under the same ownership.

Couhins   Graves (r.) w. dr. ★★
25-acre v'yd. at Villenave-d'Ornon producing one of the best dry white Graves.

La Couronne   Pauillac r. ★★ 67 70 73 75
Small but excellent Cru Exceptionnel under the same direction as Ch. HAUT-BATAILLEY.

Coutet   Sauternes w. sw. ★★★ 62 67 69 70 71 75
Rival to Ch. CLIMENS; also 80 acres in Barsac. Said to be slightly less rich but certainly equally fine.

29

Le Crock St-Est. r. ★★
>Well-situated Cru Bourgeois of 80 acres in the same family as Ch. LÉOVILLE-POYFERRÉ.

La Croix Pomerol r. ★★ 70 71 74 75
>Well-reputed little property of 25+ acres. La-Croix-de-Gay has the same owner. Old-fashioned tough wine; matures well.

Croizet-Bages Pauillac r. ★★ **61 64** 66 70 71 73 75
>50-acre fifth-growth (lacking a ch.) owned by the same family as Ch. RAUZAN-GASSIES. Sound sturdy wines without flair.

Croque-Michotte St-Em. r. ★★
>Small but well-known classed-growth on the Pomerol border.

Curé-Bon-la-Madeleine St-Em. r. ★★★
>Small property among the best of the Côtes; between AUSONE and CANON.

Dauzac Lab-Mar. r. ★★ **66 70 73**
>Substantial but somewhat neglected fifth-growth near the river s. of Margaux. 100 acres.

Domaine de Chevalier Graves r. and w. dr. ★★★ 61 **64** 66 67 **69** 70 71 73 74 75
>Superb small estate of 36 acres at Leognan. The red is stern at first, richly subtle with age. The white is delicate but matures to rich flavours.

Domaine de l'Eglise Pomerol r. ★★ **66 67** 70 71 75
>Small property: good wine distributed by BORIE-MANOUX.

La Dominique St-Em. r. ★★★
>44-acre classed-growth next door to Ch. CHEVAL BLANC.

Doisy-Védrines Sauternes w. sw. ★★★ **62 67** 70 71 75
>50-acre classed-growth at Barsac, near CLIMENS and COUTET and only slightly less fine.

Ducru-Beaucaillou St-Jul. r. ★★★ **61 62 64** 66 **67 69 70** 71 72 73 74 75 76
>Outstanding second-growth; about 100 acres overlooking the river. The owner, M. Borie, makes classical long-lived but not harsh wines with noticeable oak flavour.

Duhart-Milon-Rothschild Pauillac r. ★★★ 66 70 71 75
>Fourth-growth neighbour of LAFITE under the same management. Wines tend to typical Pauillac toughness rather than Lafite's elegance.

Durfort-Vivens Margaux r. ★★★ **66**
>Relatively small and obscure second-growth known for tough wine, owned by M. Lurton of BRANE-CANTENAC.

L'Eglise-Clinet Pomerol r. ★★★ **66** 70 71 74 75
>Highly ranked little property; typical, full, fleshy wine.

L'Enclos Pomerol r. ★★★ **64** 67 70 71 73 74 75
>Respected little property on the w. side of Pomerol, near CLOS-RENÉ. Big, well-made, long-flavoured wine.

L'Evangile Pomerol r. ★★★ **66 67** 70 71 73 74 75
>30+ acres between PETRUS and CHEVAL BLANC. Impressive wines. In the same area and class as LA CONSEILLANTE.

Ferrière Margaux r. ★★ **66** 70
>Little-known third-growth of only 12 acres. The wine is made at Ch. LASCOMBES and sold to a chain of French hotels.

Feytit-Clinet Pomerol r. ★★ **64** 70 71 74 75
>Little property next to LATOUR-POMEROL. Has made some fine big strong wines. Managed by J. P. MOUEIX.

Fieuzal Graves r. and (w. dr.) ★★ **64 66 67 69 70** 71 72 73 75
>40-acre classed-growth at Léognan. Changed hands in peak condition in 1973.

Figeac St-Em. r. ★★★ **61 62 64 66 67 70 71** 73 74 75
>Famous first-growth neighbour of CHEVAL BLANC. Superb 70+ acre v'yd. gives one of Bordeaux's most attractive full-bodied wines.

Filhot Sauternes w. sw. and dr. ★★ **67 69 70** 71 72 75
Second-rank classed-growth with splendid ch., 120-acre v'yd.
Very good sweet wines.

La Fleur-Petrus Pomerol r. ★★★ **66 67** 70 71 73 74 75
20-acre v'yd. flanking PETRUS and under the same MOUEIX
management. Very fine rich plummy wines.

Fombrauge St-Em. r. ★★
Major property of St-Christophe-des-Bardes, e. of St-
Emilion. Reliable, often outstanding, wine.

Fonbadet Pauillac r. ★★
Well-known Cru Bourgeois with 70 acres next door to Ch.
PONTET-CANET. Same owner as Ch. GLANA.

Les Forts de Latour Pauillac r. ★★★ **66 67** 70
The second wine of Ch. Latour; well worthy of its big brother.

Fourcas-Hosten Listrac r. ★★ **66 67** 70 71 **73** 75
Reliable Cru Bourgeois of the central Médoc. Same owners
as Ch. GRESSIER-GRAND-POUJEAUX; similar rather hard wine.

La Gaffelière St-Em. r. ★★★ 61 66 67 70 71 75
Excellent and reliable 50-acre first-growth at the foot of the
Côtes below Ch. BEL-AIR.

Gazin Pomerol r. ★★★ **66 67** 70 71 75
Large property (for Pomerol) with nearly 60 acres. Well
known but below the top rank.

Giscours Lab-Mar. r. ★★★ **66 67 69** 70 71 72 73 74 75
Splendid 200-acre third-growth s. of CANTENAC. Dynami-
cally run and making excellent wine for long maturing.

Glana St-Jul. r. ★★ **66** 70
Big Cru Bourgeois in the centre of St-Julien. Variable quality.

Gloria St-Jul. r. ★★★ **66 67** 70 **71** 73 75
Outstanding Cru Bourgeois making wine of vigour and
finesse, among good classed-growths in quality. 100+ acres.
Ch. Haut-Beychevelle-Gloria is the same property.

Grand-Barrail-Lamarzelle-Figeac St-Em. r. ★★ **66 67** 70 **71
72 73** 75
Substantial property near FIGEAC. Well-reputed and popular.

Grand-Corbin-Despagne St-Em. r. ★★
One of the larger classed-growths on the CORBIN plateau.

Grand-Puy-Ducasse Pauillac r. ★★ 66
Well-known little fifth-growth recently bought, renovated
and enlarged to 70 acres under expert management.

Grand-Puy-Lacoste Pauillac r. ★★★ **64** 66 67 70 71 **72** 73 75
Leading fifth-growth famous for fine full-bodied typical
Pauillac. 70 acres among the "Bages" ch'x. s. of the town.

La Grave Trigant de Boisset Pomerol r. ★★ **66 67** 70 71 74 75
Verdant ch. with small but first-class v'yd. owned by a
MOUEIX. One of the lighter Pomerols.

Gressier Grand Poujeaux Moulis r. ★★ **66** 67 70 71 73
See Ch. Fourcas-Hosten

Gruaud-Larose St-Jul. r. ★★★ 61 **62** 66 **67 69** 70 71 73 75
One of the biggest and best-known second-growths. 190 acres
making smooth rich stylish claret. Owned by CORDIER.

Guiraud Sauternes (r.) w. sw. (dr.) ★★★ **61** 67 **70** 71 75
Large classed-growth of top quality. 150-acre v'yd. Excellent
sweet wine and a small amount of red and dry white.

Haut-Bages-Libéral Pauillac r. ★★
Lesser-known fifth-growth of 50 acres now in the same hands
as Ch'x. PONTET-CANET and LAFON-ROCHET. Should improve.

Haut-Bages-Monpelou Pouillac r. ★★ 70 73
Cru Bourgeois stable-mate of CH. BATAILLY.

Haut-Bailly Graves r. ★★★ **64** 66 70 71 73 75
50-acre estate at Léognan making one of the best red Graves:
attractive smooth and perfumed wine.

31

Haut-Batailley Pauillac r. ★★★ **61 64** 66 67 70 **71** 73 74 75
  The smaller but currently better section of the fifth-growth
  Batailley estate: 45 acres owned by M. Borie of Ch. DUCRU-
  BEAUCAILLOU. One of the most reliable Pauillacs.
Haut-Brion Pessac, Graves r. (w.) ★★★★ **59 60** 61 **62 64 66 67** 68
  70 71 73 74 75
  The oldest great ch. of Bordeaux and the only non-Médoc
  first-growth of 1855. 100 acres. Splendid firm reds, though
  rarely sublime in recent years. A little full dry white.
d'Issan Cant-Mar. r. ★★★ 66 **67** 69 70 71 **72 73** 75
  Beautifully restored moated ch. with 74-acre third-growth
  v'yd. well known for delicate gentle wine.

---

*The highest price ever paid for a bottle of wine—so far as anyone
knows—was $14200. It was paid for a single bottle of Château Lafite
1896 at the Heublein wine auction in New Orleans in May 1976.*

Kirwan Cant-Mar. r. ★★
  Well-run 100-acre third-growth owned by SCHRODER &
  SCHYLER. Recently much replanted: worth watching.
Labégorce-Zédé Margaux r. ★★ **70** 71 72 **73**
  Reputable little Cru Bourgeois on the road n. from Margaux.
  35 acres. Typical delicate wines.
Lafaurie-Peyraguey Sauternes w. sw. ★★★ **67** 69 **70** 71 75
  Fine classed-growth of only 40 acres at Bommes, belonging
  to CORDIER. Excellent wines, though not the richest.
Lafite-Rothschild Pauillac r. ★★★★ **59 60** 61 **62** 66 70 71 73 75
  First-growth of fabulous style and perfume in its great
  vintages, though too often disappointing recently. Made a
  great 1975. 200+ acres.
Lafleur Pomerol r. ★★★ **66 67** 70 71 73 75
  Tiny property of 10 acres just n. of PETRUS. Excellent wine.
Lafon-Rochet St-Est. r. ★★★ **61 64** 66 67 70 71 75
  Fourth-growth neighbour of Ch. COS D'ESTOURNEL, restored
  to prominence in the '60s. 50+ acres. Typical dark full-
  bodied St-Estèphe.
Lagrange Pomerol r. ★★ **66 67** 70 71 75
  Small v'yd. in the centre of Pomerol run by the ubiquitous
  house of MOUEIX.
Lagrange St-Jul. r. ★★ **62** 66 70 71 75
  Rather run-down third-growth remote from most of
  St-Julien. 120 acres of the big estate are vines.
La Lagune Ludon r. ★★★ **62 66** 70 **71 72 73** 74 75
  Well-run ultra-modern 130-acre third-growth in the extreme
  s. of the Médoc. Attractively rich and fleshy wines.
Lamarque Lamarque (Haut-Médoc) r. ★★ **66 70**
  Splendid medieval fortress of the central Médoc with 100
  acres giving admirable light wine.
Lanessan Cussac (Haut-Médoc) r. ★★ **66 67** 69 70 71 75
  Well-known 60-acre Cru Bourgeois just s. of St-Julien. Same
  owner as PICHON-LONGUEVILLE-BARON.
Langoa-Barton St-Jul. r. ★★★ **66 67** 70 71 **72** 73 75
  Fine 18th-century ch. housing the wine of third-growth
  Langoa (about 40 acres) as well as second-growth LÉOVILLE-
  BARTON. The wines are similar: Langoa slightly less fine.
Larcis-Ducasse St-Em. r. ★★★ **66** 70
  The top property of St-Laurent, eastern neighbour of St-
  Emilion, well-sited on the Côtes next to Ch. PAVIE.
Larose-Trintaudon St-Lau. (Haut-Médoc) r. ★★ **70** 71 73 75
  The biggest v'yd. in the Médoc: nearly 400 acres. Modern
  methods and reliable full-flavoured Cru Bourgeois wine.

Laroze St-Em. r. ✶✶✶ 70 71
> Big v'yd. (70 acres) on the w. Côtes. Substantial solid wines, sometimes excellent.

Larrivaux Cissac (Haut-Médoc) r. ✶✶
> Small Cru Bourgeois respected for high standards.

Larrivet-Haut-Brion Graves r. (w.) ✶✶
> Reputable little property at Léognan.

Lascombes Margaux r. (p.) ✶✶✶ **61 62 64 65** 66 **67 69** 70 71 73 75
> 240-acre second-growth owned by the British brewers Bass-Charrington and recently lavishly restored. Good vintages are rich for a Margaux. Also a pleasant rosé from young vines.

Latour Pauillac r. ✶✶✶✶ 59 **60** 61 62 64 **65** 66 **67 69** 70 71 73 74 75
> First-growth. The most consistent great wine in Bordeaux, in France and probably the world : rich intense and almost immortal in great years, almost always classical and pleasing even in bad ones. British-owned. 140 acres. Second wine LES FORTS DE LATOUR.

Latour du Haut-Moulin Cussac (Haut-Médoc) r. ✶✶
> Little-known Cru Bourgeois making classic old-style claret to very high standards.

Latour-Pomerol Pomerol r. ✶✶✶ **66 67** 70 71 73 74 75
> Top growth of 20 + acres under MOUEIX management. Rich, fruity but firm wine for long maturing.

Laville-Haut-Brion Graves w. dr. ✶✶✶
> A small production of very good white Graves made at Ch LA MISSION-HAUT-BRION.

Léoville-Barton St-Jul. r. ✶✶✶ 59 61 **62 64** 66 **67** 70 71 73 75
> 80-acre portion of the great second-growth Léoville v'yd. in the Anglo-Irish hands of the Barton family for over 150 years. Glorious classical claret, made by traditional methods at the Bartons' third-growth Ch. LANGOA.

Léoville-Las Cases St-Jul. r. ✶✶✶ **59 61 64** 66 67 **69** 70 71 **73** 74 75 76
> The largest portion of the old Léoville estate, 140 acres, with one of the highest reputations in Bordeaux.

Léoville-Poyferré St-Jul. r. ✶✶✶ 66 70 72 75
> At present the least outstanding of the Léovilles, though with famous old vintages to its credit and some recent ones promising well. 100 + acres. Second label Ch. Moulin-Riche.

Liversan St-Sau. (Haut-Médoc) r. ✶✶ 73 75 76
> Small Cru Bourgeois inland from Pauillac. Recently much improved by its new German proprietor.

Loudenne St-Yzans (Médoc) r. ✶✶✶ **66 69** 70 **71** 73 75 76
> Beautiful riverside ch. owned by Gilbeys since 1875. Well-made Cru Bourgeois red and a little dry white from 90 acres.

La Louvière Graves r. and w. dr. ✶✶
> Big estate at Léognan with the same director as Ch. COUHINS. Good dry white and agreeable red.

Lynch-Bages Pauillac r. ✶✶✶ **60** 61 **62** 66 70 71 73 75
> One of the biggest and most popular fifth-growths. 140 acres making old-style rich robust wine : attractive if never great.

Lynch-Moussas Pauillac r. ✶✶
> Neglected little fifth-growth bought by the director of Ch. BATAILLEY in 1969. The 12 acres are being expanded and better wine is expected.

Magdelaine St-Em. r. ✶✶✶ 66 **67** 70 72 73 75
> Leading first-growth of the Côtes, 25 acres next to BEL-AIR owned by J-P MOUEIX. Particularly good recently.

Magence Graves r. w. dr. ✶✶ **70 71** 73
> Go-ahead property at St Pierre de Mons, in the s. of the Graves, well known for distinctly SAUVIGNON-flavoured very dry white and fruity red.

Malartic-Lagravière Graves r. and (w. dr.) ✶✶✶ **64** 66 70 71 **73**
Well-known Léognan classed-growth of 50 acres making excellent solid red for long maturing and fruity SAUVIGNON white for early drinking.

Malescot St-Exupéry Margaux r. ☐ ✶✶✶ ☐ 61 **64** 66 **67** 70 71 72 **73** 76
Third-growth of 55 acres with the same owners as Ch. MARQUIS-D'ALESME-BECKER. Rather hard, long maturing, eventually classically fragrant and stylish Margaux.

Malescasse Lamarque (Haut-Médoc) r. ✶✶
Renovated Cru Bourgeois with 70 acres in a good situation.

de Malle Sauternes r. w. sw./dr. ✶✶ **67 70 71** 75
Famous and beautiful ch. at Preignac with 90 acres making good sweet and dry whites and red (appellation Graves) Ch. de Cardaillan.

de Marbuzet St-Est. r. ✶✶ **73** 75 76
The second label of Ch. COS D'ESTOURNEL. (The actual ch. overlooks the river from the hill n. of Cos.)

Margaux Margaux r. ✶✶✶✶ **59 61** 66 **67** 70 71 75
First-growth, the most delicate and finely perfumed of all in its best vintages. Changed hands in 1977. Noble ch. and estate with 160+ acres of vines.

Marquis-d'Alesme-Becker Margaux r. ✶✶
The smaller (20 acres), less famous and less fine of twin third-growths. The other is Ch. MALESCOT.

Marquis-de-Terme Margaux r. ✶✶✶ 66 70 71 75
Old-style fourth-growth making fine typical Margaux, tannic and harsh when young. 125 acres. Sells principally in France.

Maucaillou Moulis r. ☐ ✶✶ ☐ **70** 71 **72 73** 75
60-acre Cru Bourgeois with high standards, property of the shippers DOURTHE FRÈRES. Full fruity wine.

Meyney St-Est. r. ☐ ✶✶ ☐ **62 66** 70 71 74 75
Big (120-acre) riverside property next door to Ch. MONTROSE, one of the best of many good Crus Bourgeois in St-Estèphe. Owned by CORDIER.

La Mission-Haut-Brion Graves r. ☐ ✶✶✶✶ ☐ **59** 61 64 66 67 **68** 70 71 74 75
Neighbour and rival to Ch. HAUT-BRION. Serious and grand old-style claret for long maturing.

Monbousquet St-Em. r. ☐ ✶✶ ☐
Fine 70-acre estate in the Dordogne valley below St-Emilion. Attractive early-maturing wine from deep gravel soil.

Montrose St-Est. r. ✶✶✶ **59** 61 **62 64** 66 **67** 70 71 72 73 75
150-acre family-run second-growth well known for deeply coloured, forceful, old-style claret.

Mouton-Baron-Philippe Pauillac r. ✶✶✶ **61 66** 70 73 75
Substantial fifth-growth with the enormous advantage of belonging to Baron Philippe de Rothschild, 125 acres making gentler, less rich and tannic wine than Mouton.

Mouton-Rothschild Pauillac r. ✶✶✶✶ **60** 61 **62** 66 67 70 71 73 75
Officially a first-growth since 1973, though for 20 years worthy of the title. 145 acres (90% CABERNET SAUVIGNON) making wine of majestic richness. Also the world's greatest museum of works of art relating to wine.

Nairac Sauternes w. sw. ☐ ✶✶ ☐
Newly restored Barsac classed-growth. First wine '72; '73 very promising.

Nenin Pomerol r. ✶✶✶ **66 67** 70 71 75
Well-known 50-acre estate: good but not outstanding quality.

Olivier Graves r. and w. dr. ✶✶✶
60-acre classed-growth, run by the shipper ESCHENAUER, surrounding a moated castle. Well-known, if not exciting, white; little-known but serious red.

Les Ormes-de-Pez   St-Est. r. ★★ 66 67 70 71 72 75
    Popular 65-acre Cru Bourgeois managed by Ch. LYNCH-BAGES. Reliable full-flavoured St-Estèphe.

Palmer   Cant-Mar. r. ★★★★ 59 60 61 66 67 70 71 73 74 75
    The star ch. of CANTENAC; a third-growth often on a level just below the first-growths. Wine of power and delicacy. 100 acres with Dutch, British and French owners.

Pape-Clément   Graves r. ★★★ 62 64 66 67 70 71 73 74 75
    Ancient v'yd. at Pessac named after a medieval Pope from Bordeaux, now 65 acres in fine condition making one of the most attractive red Graves.

Patache d'Aux   Bégadan (Médoc) r. ★★
    70-acre Cru Bourgeois of the n. Médoc. Well-made wine.

Pauillac, La Rose   Pauillac r. ★★
    The wine of Pauillac's growers' co-operative, with nearly 200 members. Generally good value.

Paveil-de Luze   Margaux r. ★★
    Old family estate at Soussans. Small but highly regarded.

Pavie   St-Em. r. ★★★ 64 66 67 70 71 75
    Splendidly sited first-growth of 80 acres on the slope of the Côtes. Typically rich and tasty St-Emilion.

Pedesclaux   Pauillac r. ★★ 70
    50-acre fifth-growth making wine below its full potential.

Petit-Village   Pomerol r. ★★★ 66 67 70 71 75
    One of the best-known little properties: 26 acres next to VIEUX-CH.-CERTAN, same owner as Ch. COS D'ESTOURNEL. Powerful long-lasting wine.

Petrus   Pomerol r. ★★★★ 61 62 64 66 67 70 71 73 75
    The great name of Pomerol. 28 acres of gravelly clay giving the world's most massively rich and concentrated wine.

de Pez   St-Est. r. ★★★ 66 67 70 71 73 75 76
    Outstanding Cru Bourgeois of 60 acres. As reliable as any of the classed growths of the village, if not quite so fine.

Phélan-Ségur   St-Est. r. ★★★ 66 70 71 75
    Big and important Cru Bourgeois (140 acres) with the same director as Ch. LÉOVILLE-POYFERRÉ.

Pichon-Longueville-Baron   Pauillac r. ★★★ 62 66 67 70 71 73 75
    70-acre second-growth usually making fine elegant Pauillac.

Pichon-Longueville, Comtesse de Lalande   Pauillac r. ★★★ 61 64 66 70 71 74 75
    Important second-growth neighbour to Ch. LATOUR. 110 acres. Magnificent on form but shaky in recent vintages.

Plince   Pomerol r. ★★
    Reputable 20-acre property on the outskirts of Libourne. Relatively hard and short wines. Excellent '75.

La Pointe   Pomerol r. ★★★ 66 70 71 73 74 75
    Prominent 60-acre estate for typically fat fruity Pomerol.

Pontet-Canet   Pauillac r. ★★★ 61 62 66 67 70 73 75
    One of the biggest classed-growths with about 200 acres, neighbour to MOUTON and potentially far better than its official rank of fifth-growth. Belonged to the CRUSE family for many years, now to M. Tesseron of Ch. LAFON-ROCHET.

Potensac   Potensac (Médoc) r. ★★ 66 67 70 71 73 75
    The best-known Cru Bourgeois of Ordonnac-et-Potensac in the n. Médoc. The neighbouring Ch'x. Lassalle and Gallais-Bellevue belong to the same family, the Delons.

Pouget   St-Jul. r. ★★
    Old ch. name now used for the second wine of Ch. BOYD-CANTENAC. Sold mainly in France.

Poujeaux-Theil   Moulis r. ★★
    Family-run Cru Exceptionnel of 100 acres selling its rather hard wine direct to an appreciative French public.

Prieuré-Lichine   Cant-Mar. r. ★★★ **64** 66 **67** 70 71 **73** 74 75
    Formerly obscure fourth-growth brought to the fore by
    Alexis Lichine since 1952. Excellent finely fragrant Margaux.

Rabaud-Promis   Sauternes w. sw. ★★★ **67 70** 71 75
    Classed-growth of 70 acres at Bommes. Good, not brilliant.

Rausan-Ségla   Margaux r. ★★★ **61** 66 70 71 **73** 75
    100-acre second-growth; famous for its fragrance; one of the
    great names of the Médoc, but recently below par. Owned by
    the British firm of Holts.

Rauzan-Gassies   Margaux r. ★★★ 61 66 70 **73** 74 75
    50-acre second-growth neighbour of the last with a poor
    record in the '60s. Said to be looking up.

de Rayne-Vigneau   Sauternes w. sw. ★★★ **67 70** 71 75
    100-acre classed-growth at Bommes with rich golden wine.

Respide   Graves (r.) w. dr. ★★
    One of the better white-wine ch'x. of s. Graves, at St Pierre
    de Mons. Full-flavoured wines.

Rieussec   Sauternes w. sw. ★★★ **62** 66 **67** 69 **70** 71 75
    Worthy neighbour of Ch. D'YQUEM with 120 acres in Fargues.
    Not the sweetest, but can be exquisitely fine.

Ripeau   St-Em. r. ★★
    Modest classed-growth in the centre of the plateau.

Rouget   Pomerol r. ★★ **64 67** 70 71 74 75
    Attractive old estate on the n. edge of Pomerol. Full round
    wines, maturing well. Popular in smart Paris restaurants.

Royal St-Emilion
    Brand name of the important growers' co-operative.

de Sales   Pomerol r. ★★★ **66 67** 70 71 75
    The biggest v'yd. of Pomerol, attached to the grandest ch.
    But relatively dull wine.

Sigalas-Rabaud   Sauternes w. sw. ★★ **67 70** 71 75
    The lesser part of the former Rabaud estate: 35 acres in
    Bommes, making first-class sweet wine.

Siran   Lab-Mar. r. ★★ **61** 66 70 71 75
    Cru Bourgeois sister-ch. to the fifth-growth DAUZAC. Same
    owners and same standards.

Smith-Haut-Lafite   Graves r. and (w. dr.) ★★★ **66** 70 71 75
    Run-down old classed-growth at Martillac restored by
    ESCHENAUER in the '60s. Now 120 acres (14 of white). The
    white wine is light and fruity; the red dry and interesting.

St-Estèphe, Marquis de   St-Est. r. ★ **70** 71 **73** 75
    The growers' co-operative; over 200 members. Good value.

St-Georges   St-Geo., St-Em. r. ★★
    18th-century ch. overlooking the St-Emilion plateau from
    the hill to the n. Considerable quantities of good wine.

St-Pierre (Bontemps-et-Sevaistre)   St-Jul. r. ★★ 70 **72 73** 75
    Well-run small (40-acre) fourth-growth in Belgian owner-
    ship. Attractively ripe and fruity wines.

St-Pierre   Graves (r.) w. dr. ★★
    Estate at St Pierre de Mons making old-style Graves of
    notable character and flavour.

Soutard   St-Em. r. ★★ **66** 67 70 **71 72** 73 75
    Reliable 50-acre classed-growth n. of the town.

Suduiraut   Sauternes w. sw. ★★★ **67** 70 71 75
    Lately one of the best Sauternes: of glorious creamy richness.
    Over 200 acres of the top class.

Taillefer   Pomerol r. ★★ **67** 70 **73** 75
    24-acre property on the edge of Pomerol owned by another
    branch of the MOUEIX family.

Talbot   St-Jul. r. (w.) ★★★ **61 66 67** 69 **70** 71 **73** 75
    Important 200-acre fourth-growth, sister ch. to GRUAUD-
    LAROSE, with similarly attractive rich and satisfying wine.

du Tertre Ar-Mar. r. ⟦**★★**⟧ **66 70** 71 72 73 75
>Underestimated fifth-growth isolated s. of Margaux. Thoroughly well-made claret matures admirably.

Tertre-Daugay St-Em. r. **★★**
>Small classed-growth in a spectacular situation on the brow of the Côtes. Disappointing wine recently.

La Tour-Blanche Sauternes w. sw. (dr.) **★★★ 62 67 70** 71 75
>Top-rank 60-acre estate at Bommes with a state wine-growing school, making excellent sweet wines.

La Tour-Carnet St-Lau. r. ⟦**★★**⟧ **66** 70 75
>Fourth-growth reborn from total neglect in the '60s. Medieval tower with 100+ acres just w. of St-Julien.

La Tour de By Begadan (Médoc) r. **★★ 70** 71 **72**
>Well-run 100-acre Cru Bourgeois in the n. Médoc.

La Tour-de-Mons Sou-Mar. r. ⟦**★★**⟧ 66 70 71 73 75
>Distinguished Cru Bourgeois of 60 acres, three centuries in the same family (which also owns Ch. CANTEMERLE). Excellent claret with a long life.

La Tour-Figeac St-Em. r. ⟦**★★**⟧
>40-acre classed-growth between Ch. FIGEAC, and Pomerol. Well run by a German proprietor.

La Tour-Haut-Brion Graves r. **★★** 66 70
>Small (10-acre) neighbour and sister ch. to Ch. LA MISSION-HAUT-BRION, but a plainer, smaller-scale wine.

La Tour-Martillac Graves r. and w. dr. ⟦**★★**⟧
>Small but serious property at Martillac. 10 acres of white grapes; 20 of black. Quantity is sacrificed for quality.

La Tour-du-Pin-Figeac St-Em. r. **★★**
>20-acre classed-growth, once part of LA TOUR-FIGEAC. Off form recently.

La Tour-du-Pin-Figeac-Moueix St-Em. r. ⟦**★★**⟧ **67** 70
>Another 20-acre section of the same old property, owned by one of the famous MOUEIX family.

Tournefeuille Lalande de Pomerol r. ⟦**★★**⟧ **67** 70 71 73 75
>The star of Néac, overlooking Pomerol from the n. A small property, but excellent long-lived wine.

Tronquoy-Lalande St-Est. r. ⟦**★★**⟧ **70** 71 73 75
>50-acre Cru Bourgeois making typical St-Estèphe. Distributed by DOURTHE whose taste is for deep-coloured wines.

Troplong-Mondot St-Em. r. ⟦**★★**⟧ **66 70 71** 75
>One of the bigger classed-growths of St-Emilion. 70+ acres well sited on the Côtes above Ch. PAVIE.

Trotanoy Pomerol r. ⟦**★★★**⟧ 67 70 71 72 73 74 75
>One of the top Pomerols. Only 20 acres but a splendid fleshy perfumed wine. Managed by J-P MOUEIX.

Trottevieille St-Em. r. **★★★ 66** 67 **69** 70 71 75
>Small but highly reputed first-growth of 25 acres on the Côtes e. of the town. Attractive full wines.

Verdignan
>See Ch. Coufran

Vieux-Château-Certan Pomerol r. **★★★ 61** 66 67 70 71 75
>By many accounts the second ch. of Pomerol, just s. of PETRUS, the first. 30+ acres, Belgian owned. Smooth rich-tasting wine, not quite so powerful as Petrus. Off-form in '73.

Villegeorge Avensan r. **★★ 73** 74 75
>Small Cru Exceptionnel to the n. of Margaux with the same owner as Ch. BRANE-CANTENAC. Excellent lightish wine.

d'Yquem Sauternes w. sw. (dr.) **★★★★ 59 61 62** 66 67 **68 69** 70 71 75
>The world's most famous sweet-wine estate. 240 acres making only 500 bottles per acre of very strong, intense, luscious wine. Good vintages need a decade of maturity.

Château-Chalon Jura w. dr. ★★★

Unique strong dry yellow wine, almost like sherry. Ready to drink when bottled.

Château Corton-Grancey B'y. r. ★★★ **66 69 70** 71 72 **73** 76

Famous estate at ALOXE-CORTON, the property of Louis LATOUR. Impressive wine with a long life.

Château de la Chaize B'y. r.★★★ **69 71 72 73 74** 76

The best-known estate of BROUILLY and possibly all BEAUJOLAIS.

Château de Panisseau Dordogne w. dr. ★★ D.Y.A.

Leading property of BERGERAC with good dry SAUVIGNON BLANC.

Château de Selle r. p. or w. dr. ★ D.Y.A.

Well-known and typical Provence wines.

Château des Fines Roches Rh. r. ★★★ **66 67** 69 **70** 71 72 73 74 76

Large (114 acres) and distinguished estate in CHÂTEAUNEUF-DU-PAPE. Strong old-style wine.

Château du Nozet Lo. w. dr. ★★★ **71 73 74 75** 76

Biggest and best-known estate of Pouilly (Fumé) sur Loire.

Château Fortia Rh. r. ★★★ **66 67** 69 70 71 72 73 74 76

First-class property in CHÂTEAUNEUF-DU-PAPE. Traditional methods. The owner, Baron Le Roy, was the father of the APPELLATION CONTROLÉE system.

Château-Grillet Rh. w. dr. ★★★★ **66 67 69 70** 71 72 76

3½-acre v'yd. with France's smallest appellation. Intense, fragrant, expensive.

Burgundy boasts one of the world's most famous and certainly its most beautiful hospital, the Hospices de Beaune, founded in 1443 by Nicolas Rolin, Chancellor to the Duke of Burgundy, and his wife Guigone de Salins. The hospital he built and endowed with vineyards for its income still operates in the same building and still thrives, tending the sick of Beaune without charge, on the sale of its wine. Many growers since have bequeathed their land to the Hospices. Today it owns 125 acres of prime land in Beaune, Pommard, Volnay, Meursault and Corton. The wine is sold by auction every year on the third Sunday in November.

Château-Gris B'y. r. ★★★ **66 69 70** 71 72 73 76

Famous estate at NUITS-ST-GEORGES.

Châteaumeillant Lo. r. p. or w. dr. ★ D.Y.A.

Small VDQS area near SANCERRE.

Châteauneuf-du-Pape Rh. r. (w. dr.) ★★★ **66 67** 69 **70 71 72** 73 74 75 76

7,500 acres near Avignon. Best estate ("domaine") wines are dark, strong, long-lived. Others may be light and/or disappointing. The white is heavy.

Château Simone Prov. r. ★★

Well-known property in the COTEAUX D'AIX-EN-PROVENCE.

Château Vignelaure Prov. r. ★★ **70** 71 **72 73 74** 75

Very good Provençal estate near Aix making Bordeaux-style wine with CABERNET grapes.

Chatillon-en-Diois Rh. r. p. or w. dr. ★ D.Y.A.

Small VDQS e. of the Rhône near Die. Good GAMAY reds; white mostly made into CLAIRETTE DE DIE.

Chavignol

Village of SANCERRE with famous v'yd., Les Monts Damnés. Also renowned for goat's cheese.

Chénas B'y. r. ★★★ **71 72 73 74** 76

Good Beaujolais cru, neighbour to MOULIN-À-VENT and JULIÉNAS. One of the weightier Beaujolais.

Chenin Blanc

See Grapes for white wine

Chevalier-Montrachet B'y. w. dr. ★★★★ **66 67 68 69 70** 71 72 73 74 75 76

17-acre neighbour of MONTRACHET with similar luxurious wine, perhaps a little less powerful.

Cheverny Lo. w. dr. ★ D.Y.A.

Light sharp Loire country wine from near Chambord.

Chinon Lo. r. ★★★ **70** 71 **73** 75 76

Delicate fruity CABERNET red from Touraine. Drink cool.

Chiroubles B'y. r. ★★★ **71 72 73 74 76**

Good Beaujolais cru next to FLEURIE; freshly fruity silky wine for early drinking.

Chusclan Rh. r. p. or w. dr. ★★ **72 73** 76

Village of CÔTE-DU-RHÔNE-VILLAGES. Good middle-weight wines from the co-operative.

Cissac

HAUT-MÉDOC village just w. of PAUILLAC.

Clairet

Very light red wine, almost rosé.

Clairette

Mediocre white grape of the s. of France.

Clairette de Bellegarde Midi w. dr. ★ D.Y.A.

Plain neutral white from near Nîmes.

Clairette de Die Rh. w. dr. or s./sw. sp. ★★ NV

Popular dry or semi-sweet rather MUSCAT-flavoured sparkling wine from the e. Rhône, or straight dry Clairette white.

Clairette du Languedoc Midi w. dr. ★ D.Y.A.

Plain neutral white from near Montpellier.

La Clape Midi r. or w. dr. ★ D.Y.A.

Full-bodied VDQS wines from near Narbonne. Perhaps worth ageing.

Claret

Traditional English term for red Bordeaux.

Climat

Burgundian word for individual named v'yd., e.g. Beaune Grèves, CHAMBOLLE-MUSIGNY, les Amoureuses.

Clos

A term carrying some prestige, reserved for distinct, usually walled, v'yds., often in one ownership. Frequent in Burgundy and Alsace.

Clos-de-Bèze

See Chambertin-Clos-de-Bèze

Clos de la Roche B'y. r. ★★★ **66 67** 69 **70** 71 72 73 76

38-acre Grand Cru at MOREY-ST-DENIS. Powerful complex wine like CHAMBERTIN.

Clos des Lambrays B'y. r. ★★★ **66** 69 **70** 71 72 73 76

15-acre Premier Cru v'yd. at MOREY-ST-DENIS. Substantial long-lived wine.

Clos des Mouches B'y. r. or w. dr. ★★★

Well-known Premier Cru v'yd. of BEAUNE.

Clos de Tart B'y. r. ★★★ **69 71 72 73** 76

18-acre Grand Cru at MOREY-ST-DENIS owned by MOMMESSIN. Tends to be light.

Clos de Vougeot B'y. r. ★★★ **66 67** 69 **70** 71 72 73 76

124-acre CÔTE-DE-NUITS Grand Cru with many owners. Variable, sometimes sublime. Maturity depends on the grower's technique.

Clos du Chêne Marchand

Well-known v'yd. at Bué, SANCERRE.

Clos du Roi B'y. r. ★★★

Part of the Grand Cru CORTON; also a Premier Cru of BEAUNE.

Clos St Denis B'y. r. ★★★ **66 67** 69 **70** 71 72 73 76
    16-acre Grand Cru at MOREY-ST-DENIS. Splendid sturdy wine.
Clos St Jacques B'y. r. ⌈★★★⌉ **66 67** 69 70 71 72 73 76
    17-acre Premier Cru of GEVREY-CHAMBERTIN. Excellent
    powerful wine, often better (and dearer) than some of the
    CHAMBERTIN Grands Crus.
Clos St Jean B'y. r. ⌈★★★⌉ **66** 69 **70** 71 72 **73** 76
    36-acre Premier Cru of CHASSAGNE-MONTRACHET. Very good
    red, more solid than subtle.
Cognac
    Town and region of w. France and its brandy.
Collioure Midi r. ★ **73** 75 76
    Strong dry red from BANYULS area.
Condrieu Rh. w. dr. ★★★ D.Y.A.
    Unusual soft fragrant white of great character from the
    Viognier grape. CH.-GRILLET is similar.
Corbières Midi r. or (p.) or (w.) ⌈★⌉ **73** 75
    Good vigorous cheap VDQS reds, steadily improving.
Corbières de Roussillon Midi r. (p.) or (w.) ★ **73 75** 76
    The same from slightly farther s.
Cordier, Ets D.
    Important Bordeaux shipper and château-owner, including
    Ch'x. GRUAUD-LAROSE, TALBOT.
Cornas Rh. r. ⌈★★⌉ **69 70** 71 72 **73** 76
    Small area near HERMITAGE. Typical sturdy Rhône wine of
    good quality.
Corse
    The island of Corsica. Strong ordinary wines of all colours.
    Better appellations include PATRIMONIO, SARTÈNE, AJACCIO.
Corton B'y. r. ⌈★★★★⌉ **66** 69 **70** 71 72 73 76
    The only Grand Cru red of the CÔTE DE BEAUNE. 200 acres in
    ALOXE-CORTON incl. les Bressandes and le CLOS DU ROI. Rich
    powerful wines.
Corton-Charlemagne B'y. w. dr. ★★★★ **67 69 70** 71 72 **73** 74 75 76
    The white section (one-third) of CORTON. Rich spicy lingering
    wine. Behaves like a red wine and ages magnificently.
Costières du Gard Midi r. p. or w. dr. ★ D.Y.A.
    VDQS of moderate quality from the Rhône delta.
Coteaux Champenois Champ. w. dr. ★★★ D.Y.A.
    The appellation for non-sparkling champagne.
Coteaux d'Aix-en-Provence Prov r. p. or w. dr. ⌈★⌉ NV
    Agreeable country wines. CH. VIGNELAURE is far above
    average.
Coteaux d'Ancenis Lo. r. or w. dr. ★ D.Y.A.
    Minor VDQS from the MUSCADET region.

---

*The Confrèrie des Chevaliers du Tastevin is Burgundy's wine
fraternity and the most famous of its kind in the world. It was founded
in 1933 by a group of Burgundian patriots, headed by Camille Rodier
and Georges Faiveley, to rescue their beloved Burgundy from a period
of slump and despair by promoting its inimitable products. Today
it regularly holds banquets with elaborate and sprightly ceremonial for
600 guests at its headquarters, the old château in the Clos de Vougeot.
The Confrèrie has branches in many countries and members among
lovers of wine all over the world.*

Coteaux de la Loire Lo. w. dr. sw. ⌈★★★⌉ **69** 71 73 75 76
    Forceful and fragrant CHENIN BLANC whites from Anjou.
    The best are in SAVENNIÈRES.
Coteaux de l'Aubance Lo. p. or w. dr./sw. ★★ D.Y.A.
    Light and typical minor Anjou wines.

Coteaux de Pierrevert Rh. r. p. or w. dr. ★ D.Y.A.
Minor southern VDQS.

Coteaux de Saumur Lo. w. dr./sw. ★★ D.Y.A.
Pleasant dry or sweetish fruity CHENIN BLANC.

Coteaux des Baux-en-Provence Prov. r. p. or w. dr. ★ NV
A twin to COTEAUX D'AIX, sharing the same VDQS.

Coteaux du Languedoc Midi r. p. or w. dr. ★ D.Y.A.
Scattered just-better-than-ordinary Midi areas with VDQS
status. The best (e.g. Faugères) age for a year or two.

Coteaux du Layon Lo. w. s./sw. or sw. ★★ 69 70 71 73 75 76
District centred on Rochefort, s. of Angers, making sweet
CHENIN BLANC wines above the general Anjou standard.

Coteaux du Loir Lo. r. p. or w. dr./sw. ★★ 64 69 71 73
Small region n. of Tours. Occasionally excellent wines. Best
v'yd.: JASNIÈRES.

Coteaux du Tricastin Rh. r. p. or w. dr. ★★ D.Y.A.
Fringe CÔTES-DU-RHÔNE from s. of Valence.

Coteaux du Vendomois Lo. r. p. or w. dr. ★ D.Y.A.
Fringe Loire from n. of Blois.

Côte(s)
Means hillside; generally a superior v'yd. In ST-EMILION it
distinguishes the valley slopes from the higher plateau.

Côte Chalonnaise B'y. r. w. dr. sp. ★★→★★★
Lesser-known v'yd. area between BEAUNE and MÂCON. See
Mercurey, Givry, Rully, Montagny.

Côte de Beaune B'y. r. or w. dr. ★★→★★★★
Used geographically: the s. half of the CÔTE D'OR. Applies as
an appellation only to parts of BEAUNE.

Côte de Beaune-Villages B'y. r. or w. dr. ★★
Regional appellation for secondary wines of the classic area.
They cannot be labelled "Côte de Beaune" without either
"Villages" or the village name.

Côte de Brouilly B'y. r. ★★★ 69 70 71 72 73 74 76
Fruity, rich, vigorous Beaujolais cru. One of the best. Leading estate: Ch. Thivin.

Côte de Nuits B'y. r. or (w. dr.) ★★→★★★★
The n. half of the CÔTE D'OR.

Côte de Nuits-Villages B'y. r. (w.) ★★ 69 70 71 72 73 76
A junior appellation, rarely seen but worth investigating.

Côte d'Or
Département name applied to the central and principal
Burgundy v'yd. slopes, consisting of the CÔTE DE BEAUNE
and CÔTE DE NUITS. The name is not used on labels.

Côte Rôtie Rh. r. ★★★ 66 67 69 70 71 72 74 76
The finest Rhône red, from just s. of Vienne; achieves complex delicacy with age. Very small production.

Côtes Canon-Fronsac B'x. r. ★★ 66 70 71 73 75 76
Sound solid reds from small area w. of ST-EMILION. Ch'x.
include Canon Junayme, La Dauphine, Canon-de-Brem,
Toumalin, Moulin-Pey-Labrie.

Côtes d'Agly Midi br. sw. ★ NV
Sweet-wine area n. of Perpignan.

Côtes d'Auvergne Central France r. p. or (w. dr.) ★ D.Y.A.
Flourishing small VDQS area near Clermont-Ferrand.

Côtes de Blaye B'x. w. dr. ★ D.Y.A.
Run-of-the-mill Bordeaux white from BLAYE.

Côtes de Bordeaux Saint-Macaire B'x. w. dr./sw. ★ D.Y.A.
Run-of-the-mill Bordeaux white from e. of Sauternes.

Côtes de Bourg
See Bourg

Côtes de Buzet S.W. France r. or w. dr. ★ 73 75 76 w. D.Y.A.
Pleasant light wines from just s.e. of Bordeaux.

Côtes de Duras Dordogne r. or w. dr. ⭐ **75** 76
　　Neighbour to BERGERAC. Similar light wines.
Côtes de Fronsac B'x. r. ⭐ **70 71 73** 75 76
　　Not quite so good as CÔTES-CANON-FRONSAC.
Côtes de Jura Jura r. p. or w. dr. (sp.) ⭐ NV
　　Various light tints and tastes. Arbois is better.
Côtes de Montravel Dordogne w. dr./sw. ⭐ NV
　　Part of BERGERAC; traditionally medium-sweet wine, now
　　often made dry.
Côtes de Provence Prov. r. p. or w. dr. ⭐ NV
　　The wine of Provence; more alcohol than character.
Côtes de Toul E. France r. p. or w. dr. ⭐ D.Y.A.
　　Very light wines from Lorraine; mainly VIN GRIS (rosé).
Côtes de Ventoux Rh. r. p. or w. dr. ⭐ **73 75 76** (D.Y.A.)
　　Fringe s. Rhône wines, fruity and light.
Côtes du Forez Central France r. or p. ⭐ D.Y.A.
　　Light Beaujolais-style red, can be good.
Côtes du Fronton S.W. France r. or p. ⭐ D.Y.A.
　　The local VDQS of Toulouse.
Côtes du Haut-Roussillon S.W. France br. sw. ⭐ NV
　　Sweet-wine area n. of Perpignan.
Côtes du Luberon Rh. r. p. or w. dr. (sp.) ⭐ D.Y.A.
　　Pleasant country wines from n. Provence, e. of the Rhône.
Côtes du Marmandais Dordogne r. p. or w. dr. ⭐ D.Y.A.
　　Undistinguished light wines from s.e. of Bordeaux.
Côtes-du-Rhône Rh. r. p. or w. dr. ⭐ **73 74** 76
　　The basic appellation of the Rhône valley. Best drunk
　　young. CÔTES-DU-RHÔNE-VILLAGES is better.
Côtes-du-Rhône-Villages Rh. r. p. or w. dr. ⭐⭐ **72 73 74** 76
　　The wine of the 14 best villages of the s. Rhône. Substantial
　　and on the whole reliable.
Côtes du Roussillon S.W. France r. p. or w. dr. ⭐ **70 73** 75 76
　　Country wine of e. Pyrenees. The hefty dark reds are best.
　　Some whites are sharp vins verts.
Côtes du Vivarais Prov. r. p. or w. dr. ⭐ NV
　　Pleasant country wines from s. Massif Centrale.
Côtes Frontonnais
　　See Côtes du Fronton
Coulée de Serrant Lo. w. dr./sw. ⭐⭐⭐ **64** 69 71 73 75 76
　　10-acre v'yd. on n. bank of Loire at Savennières, Anjou.
　　Intense strong fruity/sharp wine, ages well.
Crémant
　　In champagne means "Creaming"—i.e. half-sparkling. Also
　　a term for high-quality sparkling wines from certain other
　　parts of France.
Crémant de Loire w. dr./sp. ⭐⭐ NV
　　High-quality semi-sparkling wine from ANJOU and TOURAINE.
　　The leading brand is Sablant.
Crépy Savoie w. dr. ⭐⭐ D.Y.A.
　　Light, Swiss-style white from s. of La. Geneva.
Criots-Bâtard-Montrachet B'y. w. ⭐⭐⭐ **69 70** 71 72 **73** 74 76
　　7-acre neighbour to BÂTARD-MONTRACHET. Similar wine.
Crozes-Hermitage Rh. r. or (w. dr.) ⭐⭐ **69 70** 71 72 **73** 76
　　Larger and less distinguished neighbour to HERMITAGE.
　　Robust and often excellent reds.
Cru
　　"Growth", as in "first growth"—meaning v'yd.
Cru Bourgeois
　　Rank of Bordeaux château below CRU CLASSÉ.
Cru Bourgeois Supérieur
　　Official rank one better than the last.

Cru Classé

Classed growth. One of the first 5 official quality classes of the Médoc. Also any classed growth of another district (see p. 26).

Cru Exceptionnel

Official rank above CRU BOURGEOIS SUPÉRIEUR, immediately below CRU CLASSÉ.

Cruse et Fils Frères

Long-established Bordeaux shipper famous for fine wine. Owner of CH. D'ISSAN.

Cubzac B'x. r. or w. dr.★

Minor region between BOURG and FRONSAC. Good plain Bordeaux.

Cussac

Village just s. of St. Julien. Appellation Haut-Médoc.

Cuve Close

Short-cut way of making sparkling wine in a tank. The sparkle dies away in the glass much quicker than with MÉTHODE CHAMPENOISE wine.

Cuvée

The quantity of wine produced in a "cuve" or vat. Also a word of many uses, incl. "blend". In Burgundy interchangeable with "Cru". Often just refers to a "lot" of wine.

Danglade, L. et Fils

Shipper of St-Emilion and Pomerol, now owned by J-P MOUEIX of Libourne.

Degré alcoolique

Degrees of alcohol, i.e. per cent by volume.

Delas Frères

Long-established firm of Rhône-wine specialists at Tournon, v'yds. at CÔTE RÔTIE, HERMITAGE, CORNAS, etc.

The curiously inefficient shape of the traditional shallow champagne-glass known as a "coupe" is accounted for (at least in legend) by the fact that it was modelled on Queen Marie Antoinette's breast.
Admirable though that organ undoubtedly was, it was not designed for dispensing sparkling wine. Champagne goes flat and gets warm almost as fast in a coupe as it would in your cupped hand. The ideal champagne glass is a tall, thin "tulip".

Delor, A. et Cie

Bordeaux shippers owned by Allied Breweries.

Delorme, André

Leading merchants and growers of the CÔTE CHALONNAISE.

De Luze, A. et Fils

Bordeaux shipper and owners of Ch'x. CANTENAC-BROWN and Paveil de Luze.

Demi-Sec

"Half-dry": in practice more than half-sweet.

Depagneux, Jacques et Cie

Well-regarded merchants of BEAUJOLAIS.

Deutz & Geldermann NV and **61 64 66 70** 71

One of the best of the smaller champagne houses. Luxury brand: Cuvée William Deutz.

Domaine

Property, particularly in Burgundy.

Dom Pérignon **59 62 64 66** 69 (70)

Luxury brand of MOËT ET CHANDON named after legendary blind inventor of champagne.

Dopff "au Moulin"

Ancient family wine-house at Riquewihr, Alsace. Best wines: Riesling Schoenenbourg, Gewürztraminer Eichberg.

Dopff & Irion
>   Another excellent Riquewihr (Alsace) business. Best wines
>   include Muscat les Amandiers, Riesling de Riquewihr.

Doudet-Naudin
>   Burgundy merchant and grower at Savigny-lès-Beaune.
>   V'yds. incl. BEAUNE CLOS DE ROI.

Dourthe Frères
>   Well-reputed Bordeaux merchant representing a wide range
>   of ch'x., mainly good Crus Bourgeois, incl. Ch'x. MAUCAILLOU,
>   TRONQUOY-LALANDE.

Doux
>   Sweet.

Drouhin, J. et Cie
>   Prestigious Burgundy grower and merchant. Offices in
>   BEAUNE, v'yds. in MUSIGNY, CLOS DE VOUGEOT, etc.

Duboeuf, Georges
>   Top-class BEAUJOLAIS merchant at Romanèche-Thorin.

Echézeaux B'y. r. ★★★ **66 69 70** 71 72 **73** 76
>   74-acre Grand Cru between VOSNE-ROMANÉE and CLOS DE
>   VOUGEOT. Superlative fragrant burgundy without great
>   weight.

Edelzwicker Alsace w. ★ D.Y.A.
>   Light everyday white from mixture of grapes, often fruity
>   and good.

French bottle shapes

1. Champagne 2. Loire 3. Burgundy 4. Alsace 5. Beaujolais "pot"
6. Bordeaux 7. Châteauneuf-du-Pape

Entre-Deux-Mers B'x. w. dr. ★ D.Y.A.
>   Standard dry white Bordeaux from between the Garonne and
>   Dordogne rivers.

Les Epenots B'y. r. ★★★
>   Famous Premier Cru v'yd. of POMMARD. Also spelt Epeneaux
>   for the 12-acre Clos des Epeneaux owned by Comte Armand.

Eschenauer, Louis
>   Famous Bordeaux merchants, owners of Ch'x. OLIVIER,
>   SMITH-HAUT-LAFITTE and LA GARDE in GRAVES, now con-
>   trolled by the Lonrho group.

l'Etoile Jura (r.) (p.) or w. dr./sw./sp. ★★
>   Sub-region of the Jura with typically various wines, incl. VIN
>   JAUNE like CHÂTEAU-CHALON.

Faiveley, J.
>   Family-owned growers (with 250 acres) and merchants at
>   NUITS-ST-GEORGES, with v'yds. in CHAMBERTIN-CLOS-DE-
>   BÈZE, CHAMBOLLE-MUSIGNY, CORTON, NUITS and MERCUREY
>   (150 acres).

Fitou Midi r. ★★ **66** 73 75 76
>   Superior CORBIÈRES red; powerful and ages well.

Fixin B'y. r. ★★ **66 69 70 71** 72 **73** 76
>   A worthy and under-valued neighbour to GEVREY-CHAMBER-
>   TIN. Often splendid reds.

Flétri

Means withered. Used of half-dried grapes for making sweet wine.

Fleurie B'y. r. ★★★ **71 72 73 74 75** 76

The epitome of a Beaujolais cru: fruity, scented, silky, racy.

Frais

Fresh or cool.

Frappé

Ice-cold.

Froid

Cold.

Fronsac B'x. r. ★★ **70 71 73** 75 76

Area of good reds just w. of St-Emilion. CÔTES-CANON-FRONSAC are best.

Frontignan Midi br. sw. ★ NV

Strong sweet and liquorous muscat wine.

Gaillac S.W. France r. p. or w. dr./sw. or sp. ★ NV

Dull but usually adequate everyday wine.

Gamay

See Grapes for red wine

Geisweiler et Fils

One of the biggest merchant-houses of Burgundy. Cellars and 50 acres of v'yds. at NUITS-ST-GEORGES. Also 150 acres at Bevy in the HAUTES CÔTES DE NUITS and 30 in the CÔTE CHALONNAISE.

Gevrey-Chambertin B'y. r. ★★★ **66 69 70** 71 72 **73** 76

The village containing the great CHAMBERTIN and many other noble v'yds. as well as some more commonplace.

Gewürztraminer

The speciality grape of ALSACE: perfumed and spicy, whether dry or sweet.

Gigondas Rh. r. or p. ★★ **69 70 71 72 73** 74 76

Worthy neighbour to CHÂTEAUNEUF-DU-PAPE. Strong full-bodied wine.

Gilbey, S.A.

British firm long-established as Bordeaux merchants at Ch. Londenne. Now owned by Grand Metropolitan Ltd.

Ginestet

Third-generation Bordeaux merchants and former owners of CH. MARGAUX.

Givry B'y. r. or w. dr. ★★ **71 72 73** 76

Underrated village of the CÔTE CHALONNAISE: light but tasty and typical burgundy.

Goût

Taste, e.g. "goût anglais"—as the English like it (dry).

Grand Cru

One of the top Burgundy v'yds. with its own Appellation Controlée. Similar in Alsace but used more vaguely elsewhere.

Grand Roussillon Midi br. sw. ★★ NV

Broad appellation for muscat and other sweet fortified wines of e. Pyrenees.

Grands-Echézeaux B'y. r. ★★★★ **66 67** 69 **70** 71 72 **73** 76

22-acre Grand Cru next to CLOS DE VOUGEOT. Superlative rich burgundy.

Graves B'x. r. or w. ★→★★★★

Large region s. of Bordeaux city. Its best wines are red, but the name is used chiefly for its dry or medium golden-whites.

Graves de Vayres B'x. r. or w. ★

Part of ENTRE-DEUX-MERS; of no special character.

Les Gravières B'y. r. ★★★

Famous Premier Cru of SANTENAY.

Griotte-Chambertin   B'y. r. ★★★ **66 67** 69 **70** 71 72 **73** 76
      14-acre Grand Cru adjoining CHAMBERTIN. Similar wine, but less masculine and more "tender".
Gros Plant du Pays Nantais   Lo. w. ⌐★⌐ D.Y.A.
      Junior cousin of MUSCADET, sharper and lighter; made of the COGNAC grape.
Haut Comtat   Rh. r. or p. ★★ **71 72 73** 74 76
      Small appellation n. of Avignon. Sound strong wines.
Hautes-Côtes de Beaune   B'y. r. or w. dr. ★★ **69 70 71 72 73** 76
      Appellation for a dozen villages in the hills behind the CÔTE DE BEAUNE. Light wines, worth investigating.
Hautes-Côtes de Nuits   B'y. r. ★★ **69 70** 71 **72 73** 76
      The same for the CÔTE DE NUITS. Rarely seen outside France.
Haut-Médoc   B'x. r. ★★→★★★ **66 67 70** 71 **73** 75
      Big appellation including all the best areas of the Médoc. Most wines have château names: those without should still be above average.
Haut-Montravel   Dordogne w. sw. ★ **71** 73 75 76
      Medium-sweet BERGERAC.
Heidsieck, Charles   NV and **61 62 64 66 69** 70 71
      Leading champagne house of Reims, family-owned, now merged with Champagne Henriot. Luxury brand: Prestige Royal Champagne.
Heidsieck, Dry Monopole   NV and **61 64 66 69** 71
      Important champagne merchant and grower of Reims. Luxury brand: Diamant Bleu.
Hérault   Midi
      The biggest v'yd. *département* in France. Chiefly vin ordinaire.
Hermitage   Rh. r. ⌐★★★⌐ **66** 67 69 **70** 71 72 **73** 76
      The "manliest" wine of France. Dark, powerful and profound. Needs long ageing.
Hospices de Beaune
      15th-century charity hospital in BEAUNE with excellent v'yds. in MEURSAULT, POMMARD, VOLNAY, BEAUNE, CORTON, etc.
Hugel Père et Fils
      The best-known ALSACE growers and merchants. Founded at Riquewihr in 1639 and still in the family. Best wines: Cuvées Exceptionnelles.
Imperiale
      Bordeaux bottle holding 8½ normal bottles.
Irancy   B'y. r. or (p.) ⌐★★⌐ **71** 73 75 76
      Good light red made near CHABLIS. The best vintages are long-lived and mature well.
Irouléguy   S.W. France (r.) or w. dr. ★★ D.Y.A.
      Agreeable local wine of the Basque country.
Jaboulet, Paul
      Old family firm, leading growers and merchants of HERMITAGE.
Jaboulet-Vercherre et Cie
      Well-known Burgundy merchant-house with v'yds. in POMMARD, etc., and cellars in Beaune.
Jadot, Louis
      Much-respected Burgundy merchant-house with v'yds. in BEAUNE, CORTON, etc.
Jasnières   Lo. (r.) (p.) or w. sw. ★★★ **69 70** 71 73 75 76
      Rare VOUVRAY-like wine of n. Touraine.
Jeroboam
      A 6-bottle bottle, or triple magnum.
Juliénas   B'y. r. ★★★ **71 72 73 74** 76
      Leading cru of Beaujolais: vigorous fruity wine.

Jura

    See Côtes de Jura

Jurançon   S.W. France w. sw. or dr. ★★ **70 72 73** 75 76

    Unusual high-flavoured and long-lived speciality of Pau in the Pyrenean foothills. Ages well for several years.

Kressman, E. S. & Cie

    Family-owned Bordeaux merchants and owners of CH. LATOUR-MARTILLAC in GRAVES.

Krug   NV and **61 62 64** 66 69

    Small but very prestigious champagne house making full-bodied very dry wine.

Labarde

    Village just s. of MARGAUX and included in that appellation. Best ch.: GISCOURS.

Lalande de Pomerol   B'x. r. ★★ **70 71 73** 75 76

    Neighbour to POMEROL. Wines similar but considerably less fine. Ch. BEL-AIR is well known.

Lanson Père et Fils   NV and **64 66 69** 71

    Important growers and merchants of Champagne, cellars at Reims. Luxury brand: Red Label.

La Tâche

    See Tâche

A grower's own label

> MISE EN BOUTEILLES
> AU DOMAINE
> APPELLATION CONTROLEE
>
> **NUITS ST GEORGES**
>
> **LES PRULIERS**
>
> DOMAINE HENRI GOUGES A
> NUITS ST GEORGES

Domaine is the burgundy equivalent of château.
The Appellation Contrôlée is Nuits St Georges.
The individual v'yd. in Nuits is called Les Pruliers.
The name and address of the grower/producer.
(The word propriétaire is often also used.)

A merchant's label

> **SANTENAY**
>
> **LES GRAVIERES**
>
> APPELLATION CONTROLEE
> PROSPER MAUFOUX
> NEGOCIANT A SANTENAY

The village.
The vineyard.
The wine qualifies for the Appellation Santenay.
Prosper Maufoux is a Négociant or merchant, who bought the wine from the grower to mature, bottle and sell.

Latour, Louis

    Top Burgundy merchant and grower with v'yds. in CORTON, BEAUNE, etc.

Latricières-Chambertin   B'y. r. ★★★ **66 67** 69 **70** 71 72 **73** 76

    17-acre Grand Cru neighbour of CHAMBERTIN. Similar wine, but lighter and "prettier".

Laurent-Perrier   NV and **64 66** 70

    Well-known champagne house of Reims. Luxury brand: Cuvée Grand Siécle.

Léognan   B'x.

    Leading village of the GRAVES appellation. Best ch'x.: DOMAINE DE CHEVALIER and HAUT-BAILLY.

Leroy

    Important burgundy merchants at MEURSAULT, part-owners and distributors of the DOMAINE DE LA ROMANÉE-CONTI.

Lichine, Alexis et Cie

Successful post-war Bordeaux merchants, proprietors of CH. LASCOMBES, now controlled by Bass Charrington Ltd.

Lie, sur

"On the lees." Muscadet is often so bottled, for maximum freshness.

Limoux Nature Midi w. dr. ⭐ D.Y.A.

The non-sparkling version of BLANQUETTE DE LIMOUX.

Lirac Rh. (r.) p. or (w. dr.) ⭐⭐ 71 72 74 76

Neighbouring village to TAVEL. Similar wine.

Listrac B'x. r. ⭐⭐

Village of HAUT-MÉDOC next to MOULIS. Best ch.: FOURCAS-HOSTEN.

Loire

See under Wine names (Muscadet, etc.).

Loupiac B'x. w. sw. ⭐⭐ 67 70 71 75

Neighbour to SAUTERNES with similar but less good wine.

Ludon

HAUT-MÉDOC village s. of MARGAUX. Best ch.: LA LAGUNE.

Lupé-Cholet et Cie

Merchants and growers at NUITS-ST-GEORGES. Best estate wine: Château Gris.

Lussac-Saint-Emilion B'x. r. ⭐⭐ 70 71 73 76

North-eastern neighbour to ST-EMILION. Often good value. Ch. Lyonnat is best known. Co-operative makes "Roc de Lussac".

macération carbonique

Traditional Beaujolais technique of fermentation with whole bunches of unbroken grapes in an atmosphere saturated with carbon dioxide. Fermentation inside each grape eventually bursts it, giving vivid and very fruity mild wine for quick consumption.

Macau

HAUT-MÉDOC village s. of MARGAUX. Best ch.: CANTEMERLE.

Mâcon B'y. r. (p.) or w. dr. ⭐⭐ 73 74 75w. 76

Southern district of sound, usually unremarkable, reds and tasty dry whites. Wine with a village name (e.g. Mâcon-Prissé) is better. POUILLY-FUISSÉ is best appellation of the region. See also Mâcon-Villages.

Mâcon Supérieur

The same but slightly stronger from riper grapes.

Mâcon-Villages B'y. w. dr. ⭐⭐ 71 72 73 74 75 76

Increasingly well-made and excellent white burgundies. Mâcon-Prissé, MÂCON-VIRÉ are examples.

Mâcon-Viré

See Mâcon-Villages and Viré

Madiran S.W. France r. ⭐⭐ 69 70 71 72 73 75

Dark vigorous red from ARMAGNAC. Needs ageing.

Magnum

A double bottle.

Mähler-Besse

First-class Dutch wine-merchants in Bordeaux, with a majority shareholding in Ch. PALMER.

Maire, Henri

The biggest grower and merchant of JURA wines.

Marc

Grape skins after pressing; also the strong-smelling brandy made from them.

Margaux B'x. r. ⭐⭐→⭐⭐⭐⭐ 66 67 70 71 73 75

Village of the HAUT-MÉDOC making the most "elegant" red Bordeaux. The name includes CANTENAC and several other villages as well. Top ch'x. include MARGAUX, LASCOMBES, etc.

Marque déposée
> Trade mark.

Marsannay B'y. (r.) or p. ★★★ 71 72 73 76
> Village near Dijon with excellent light red and delicate rosé, perhaps the best rosé in France.

Martillac
> Village in the GRAVES appellation, Bordeaux.

Maufoux, Prosper
> Family firm of burgundy merchants at SANTENAY.

Mazis–Chambertin B'y. r. ★★★ 66 67 69 70 71 72 73 76
> 30-acre Grand Cru neighbour of CHAMBERTIN. Similar wine.

Médoc B'x. r. ★★ 70 73 75
> Appellation for reds of the less good (n.) part of Bordeaux's biggest and best district. Typical but light wines. HAUT-MÉDOC is better.

Ménétou-Salon Lo. r. p. or w. dr. ★★ D.Y.A.
> Attractive light wines from w. of SANCERRE. SAUVIGNON white ; CABERNET red.

Mercier et Cie NV and 61 62 64 66 69 70 71
> One of the biggest champagne houses, at Epernay.

Mercurey B'y. r. ★★ 69 70 71 72 73 76
> Leading red-wine village of the CÔTE CHALONNAISE. Good middle-rank burgundy.

méthode champenoise
> The traditional laborious method of putting the bubbles in champagne by refermenting the wine in its bottle.

Meursault B'y. (r.) w. dr. ★★★ 66 67 69 70 71 72 73 74 75 76
> CÔTE DE BEAUNE village with some of the world's greatest whites : rich, smooth, savoury, dry but mellow. Best v'yds. incl. Perrières, Genevrières, Charmes.

Meursault-Blagny
> See Blagny

Minervois Midi r. or (p.) ★ → ★★ 73 75
> Hilly VDQS area with some of the best wines of the Midi : lively and full of flavour.

mise en bouteilles au château, au domaine
> Bottled at the château, at the property or estate. N.B. dans nos caves (in our cellars) or dans la région de production (in the area of production) mean little.

Moët & Chandon NV and 61 64 66 69 70 71
> The biggest champagne merchant and grower, with cellars in Epernay and branches in Argentina and California. Luxury brand : Dom Pérignon.

Moillard Grivot
> Big firm of growers and merchants in NUITS-ST-GEORGES.

Mommessin, J.
> Major Beaujolais merchant and owner of CLOS DE TART.

Monbazillac Dordogne w. sw. ★★ 71 73 74 75 76
> Golden SAUTERNES-style wine from BERGERAC. Ages well. Ch. Monbazillac is best known.

Monopole
> V'yd. in single ownership.

Montagne-Saint-Emilion B'x. r. ★★ 66 67 70 71 73 75 76
> North-east neighbour of ST-EMILION with similar wines.

Montagny B'y. w. dr. ★★ → ★★★ 71 72 73 74 75 76
> CÔTE CHALONNAISE village between MÂCON and MEURSAULT, both geographically and gastronomically.

Montée de Tonnerre B'y.
> Famous and excellent PREMIER CRU of CHABLIS.

Monthélie B'y. r. ★★★ 69 71 72 73 76
> Little-known neighbour and almost equal of VOLNAY. Excellent fragrant reds. Best v'yd. : Les Champs-Fulliot.

Montlouis Lo. w. sw./dr.★★ **64 69 71** 73 74 75 76
> Neighbour of VOUVRAY with similar sweet or dry long-lived wine.

Montrachet B'y. w. dr.★★★★ **66 67 69 70 71** 72 73 74 75 76
> 19-acre Grand Cru v'yd. in both PULIGNY and CHASSAGNE-MONTRACHET. The greatest white burgundy: strong, perfumed, intense, dry yet luscious. (The "ts" are silent.)

Montravel
> See Côtes de Montravel

Mont-Redon, Domaine de
> Famous estate in CHÂTEAUNEUF-DU-PAPE.

Morey-Saint-Denis B'y. r. ★★★ **66 67 69 70** 71 72 **73** 76
> Small village with four Grands Crus between GEVREY-CHAMBERTIN and CHAMBOLLE-MUSIGNY. Glorious wine, often overlooked.

Morgon B'y. r.★★★ **69 70 71 72** 73 74 76
> The "firmest" cru of Beaujolais, needing time to develop its rich flavour.

Moueix, J-P et Cie
> The leading proprietor and merchant of St-Emilion and Pomerol. Ch'x. incl. MAGDELAINE, LAFLEUR-PETRUS, and part of PETRUS.

Moulin-à-vent B'y. r.★★★ **69 70 71 72 73 74** 76
> The "biggest" and best wine of Beaujolais; powerful and long-lived when not unbalanced by too much added sugar.

Moulis B'x. r. ★★→★★★
> Village of the HAUT-MÉDOC with its own appellation and several good, not top-rank ch'x.: CHASSE-SPLEEN, POUJEAUX-THEIL, etc.

Mousseux
> Sparkling.

Mouton Cadet
> Best-selling brand of red Bordeaux.

Mumm, G. H. & Cie NV and **61 62 64 66 69** 71 (73 75 76)
> Major champagne grower and merchant owned by Seagram's. Luxury brand: Président René Lalou.

Muscadet Lo. w. dr. ★★ D.Y.A.
> Popular, good-value, often delicious dry wine from round Nantes in s. Brittany. Perfect with fish.

Muscadet de Sèvre-et-Maine
> Wine from the central and usually best part of the area.

Muscat
> Distinctively perfumed grape and its (usually sweet) wine.

Muscat de Beaumes de Venise
> The best French muscat (see Beaumes-de-Venise).

Muscat de Lunel br. sw. ★★ NV
> Sweet Midi muscat. A small area but good.

Muscat de Mireval br. sw. ★★ NV
> Ditto, from near Montpellier.

Muscat de Rivesaltes br. sw. ★ NV
> Sweet muscat from a big zone near Perpignan.

Musigny B'y. r.★★★★ **66 67** 69 **70** 71 72 **73** 75
> 25-acre Grand Cru in CHAMBOLLE-MUSIGNY. Often the best, if not the most powerful, of all red burgundies. Best growers: de Vogüé, DROUHIN.

Nature
> Natural or unprocessed, esp. of still champagne.

Néac B'x. r.★★
> Little village n. of POMEROL. Sound wines, sold as LALANDE-DE-POMEROL.

Négociant-éleveur
> Merchant who "brings up" (i.e. matures) the wine.

Nicolas, Ets.

Paris-based wholesale and retail wine merchants; one of the biggest in France and one of the best. Their Rhône and Midi wines are particularly good.

Nuits-St-Georges   r.★★ → ★★★ **66 67 69 70** 71 72 **73** 75

Important wine-town: wines of all qualities, typically sturdy and full-flavoured. Name can be shortened to "Nuits". Best v'yds. incl. Les St-Georges, Vaucrains, Les Pruliers, Clos des Corvées, Les Cailles, etc.

Ordinaire

Commonplace, everyday: not necessarily pejorative.

Pacherenc-du-Vic-Bilh   S.W. France w. sw.★ NV

Rare minor speciality of the ARMAGNAC region.

Palette   Prov. r. p. or w. dr.★ D.Y.A.

Minor appellation area near Aix-en-Provence. Typical local wines: more kick than character.

Pasquier-Desvignes et Cie

Very old firm of Beaujolais merchants at St Lager, BROUILLY, since the 15th century.

Patriarche

Popular firm of burgundy merchants in BEAUNE.

Pauillac   B'x. r. ★★ → ★★★★ **66 67** 70 71 **73** 75

The only village in Bordeaux (HAUT-MÉDOC) with three first-growths (Ch'x. LAFITE, LATOUR, MOUTON-ROTHSCHILD) and many other fine ones, famous for high flavour and a scent of cedarwood.

Pécharmant   Dordogne r.★★ **73** 75

Slightly better-than-typical light BERGERAC red.

Pelure d'oignon

"Onion skin"—tawny tint of certain rosés.

Perlant

Very slightly sparkling.

Pernand-Vergelesses   B'y. r. or (w. dr.) ★★★ **66 67 69 70 71** 72 **73** 76

Village next to ALOXE-CORTON containing part of the great CORTON and CORTON-CHARLEMAGNE v'yds. and one other top v'yd.: Ile des Vergelesses.

Perrier-Jouët   NV and **61 64 66 69** 71 (73 75 76)

Excellent champagne-growers and makers at Epernay. Luxury brand: Belle Epoque.

Pétillant

Slightly sparkling.

Petit Chablis   B'y. w. dr. ★★ 75 76

Wine from fourth-rank CHABLIS v'yds. Lacks great character but can be good value.

Piat Père et Fils

Important growers and merchants of Beaujolais and Mâcon wines at MÂCON, now controlled by Grand Metropolitan Ltd. V'yds. in MOULIN-À-VENT, also CLOS DE VOUGEOT. BEAUJOLAIS and MÂCON-VIRÉ in Piat bottles are good value.

Picpoul-de-Pinet   Midi w. dr. ★ NV

Rather dull very dry southern white.

Pineau Charentais

Strong sweet aperitif made of white wine and Cognac.

Pinot

See Grapes for white wine

Piper-Heidsieck   NV and **61 66 69** 71

Champagne-makers of old repute at Reims. Luxury brand: Florens Louis Blanc de Blancs.

Pol Roger   NV and **61 64 66 69** 71

Excellent champagne house at Epernay. Particularly good non-vintage White Foil.

Pomerol   B'x. r.★★→★★★★ **66 67** 70 71 **73** 75

The next village to ST-EMILION: similar but more "fleshy" wines, maturing sooner, on the whole reliable and delicious. Top ch.: PETRUS.

Pommard   B'y. r.★★★ **66 69 70 71** 72 73 76

The biggest and best-known village in Burgundy. No superlative wines, but many warmly appealing ones. Best v'yds.: Rugiens, EPENOTS and HOSPICES DE BEAUNE Cuvées.

"Noble rot" (*in French* pourriture noble, *in German* Edelfäule, *in Latin* Botrytis cinerea), *is a form of mould that attacks the skins of ripe grapes in certain vineyards in warm and misty autumn weather.*

Its effect, instead of rotting the grapes, is to wither them. The skin grows soft and flaccid, the juice evaporates through it, and what is left is a super-sweet concentration of everything in the grape except its water content.

The world's best sweet table wines are all made of nobly rotten grapes. They occur in good vintages in Sauternes, the Rhine, the Mosel (where wine made from them is called Trockenbeerenauslese), in Tokaji in Hungary, in Burgenland in Austria, and occasionally elsewhere—California included. The danger is rain on the pulpy grapes when they are already far gone in noble rot. All too often, particularly in Sauternes, the grower's hopes are dashed by a break in the weather.

Pommery & Greno   NV and **61 62 64 66 69** 71

Very big growers and merchants of champagne at Reims. Their AVIZE BLANC DE BLANCS is excellent.

Ponnelle, Pierre

Large-scale wine-merchants of BEAUNE.

Pouilly-Fuissé   B'y. w. dr.★★→★★★ **72 73 74** 75 76

The best white of the MÂCON area. Never great: at its best excellent, but often over-priced. Buy it domaine-bottled.

Pouilly Fumé   Lo. w. dr. ★★→★★★ **74 75** 76

Smoky-fragrant, fruity, often sharp pale white from the upper Loire, next to SANCERRE. Grapes must be SAUVIGNON BLANC. Good vintages improve for 2–3 yrs.

Pouilly-Loché   B'y. w. dr. ★★

Neighbour of POUILLY-FUISSÉ. Similar wine.

Pouilly-Sur-Loire   Lo. w. dr.★ D.Y.A.

Inferior wine from the same v'yds. as POUILLY-FUMÉ, but different grapes (CHASSELAS).

Pouilly-Vinzelles   B'y. w. dr. ★★

Neighbour of POUILLY-FUISSÉ. Similar wine.

Pradel

Well-known brand of Provençal wines, esp. a dry rosé.

Preiss Zimmer, Jean

Old-established Alsace wine-merchants at Riquewihr.

Premier Cru

First-growth in Bordeaux, but the second rank of v'yds. (after Grand Cru) in Burgundy.

Premières Côtes de Bordeaux   B'x. r. (p.) or w. dr. or sw.★→★★

Large area east of GRAVES: a good bet for quality and value, though never brilliant.

Primeur

Early wine, like early vegetables; esp. of BEAUJOLAIS.

Prissé

See Mâcon-Villages

Propriétaire-récoltant

Owner–manager.

Provence
    See Côtes de Provence

Puisseguin-Saint-Emilion B'x. r. | ★★ | **73** 75
    Eastern neighbour of ST-EMILION; wines similar—not so fine
    but often good value. No famous ch'x. but a good co-
    operative.

Puligny-Montrachet B'y. w. dr.★★★ **69 70 71** 72 **73** 74 75 76
    Bigger neighbour of CHASSAGNE-MONTRACHET with equally
    glorious rich dry whites. Best v'yds.: MONTRACHET,
    CHEVALIER-MONTRACHET, BÂTARD-MONTRACHET, Bien-
    venue-Bâtard-Montrachet, Les Combettes, Clavoillon,
    Pucelles, etc.

Quarts de Chaume Lo. w. sw. ★★★ **67** 69 **70** 71 73 75 76
    Famous 120-acre plot in COTEAU DU LAYON, Anjou. CHENIN
    BLANC grapes. Long-lasting, intense, rich golden wine.

Quatourze Midi r. (p.) or w. dr. ★ **73** 75
    Minor VDQS area near Narbonne.

Quincy Lo. w. dr. ★★ **74 75 76**
    Small area making very dry SANCERRE-style wine.

Rasteau Rh. (r. p. w. dr.) or br. sw. ★★ NV
    Village of s. Rhône valley. Good strong sweet dessert wine is
    the local speciality.

Ratafia de Champagne
    Sweet aperitif made in Champagne of $\frac{2}{3}$ grape juice and
    $\frac{1}{3}$ brandy.

Récolte
    Crop or vintage.

Remoissenet Père et Fils
    Fine growers and merchants of burgundy at BEAUNE.

Rémy Pannier
    Important Loire-wine merchants at St-Hilaire-St-Florent,
    Saumur.

Reuilly Lo. w. dr. ★★ **74 75 76**
    Neighbour of QUINCY with similar wine; also good PINOT
    GRIS.

Richebourg B'y. r. ★★★★ 66 **67** 69 **70** 71 72 73 75
    19-acre Grand Cru in VOSNE-ROMANÉE. Powerful, perfumed,
    fabulously expensive wine, among Burgundy's best.

Riesling
    See Grapes for white wine

Rivesaltes Midi br. sw. ★ NV
    Fortified sweet wine, some muscat-flavoured, none distin-
    guished, from e. Pyrenees.

La Roche-aux-Moines Lo. w. dr./sw. ★★★ 69 71 73 75 76
    60-acre v'yd. in Savennières, Anjou. Intense strong fruity/
    sharp wine ages well.

Roederer, Louis NV and **61 64 66** 69 70 71 (73)
    One of the best champagne-growers and merchants at Reims.
    Excellent non-vintage wine. Luxury brand: Cristal Brut
    (also in '62).

La Romanée B'y. r.★★★★ **66 67** 69 **70** 71 72 73 76
    2-acre Grand Cru in VOSNE-ROMANÉE just uphill from
    ROMANÉE-CONTI.

Romanée-Conti B'y. r.★★★★ **66 67** 69 70 71 72 73 76
    $4\frac{1}{2}$-acre Grand Cru in VOSNE-ROMANÉE. The most celebrated
    and expensive red wine in the world, though seldom the best.

Romanée-Conti, Domaine de la
    The grandest estate of Burgundy, owning the whole of
    ROMANÉE-CONTI and LA TÂCHE and major parts of RICHE-
    BOURG, GRANDS ECHÉZEAUX, ECHÉZEAUX and ROMANÉE-ST-
    VIVANT (under Marey-Monge label). Also a small part of Le
    MONTRACHET.

Romanée-St-Vivant B'y. r.★★★★

23-acre Grand Cru in VOSNE-ROMANÉE. Similar to ROMANÉE-CONTI in all respects.

Ropiteau

Burgundy wine-growers and merchants at MEURSAULT. Specialists in Meursault and CÔTE DE BEAUNE wines.

Rosé d'Anjou Lo. p.★ D.Y.A.

Pale, often slightly sweet, rosé. Cabernet d'Anjou is better.

Roussette de Savoie Savoie w. dr. ★★ D.Y.A.

Pleasant light fresh white from s. of Geneva.

Roussillon

See Côtes du Roussillon

Ruchottes-Chambertin B'y. r.★★★ 66 67 69 **70** 71 72 73 76

7½-acre Grand Cru neighbour of CHAMBERTIN. Similar splendid long-lasting wine.

Ruinart Père et Fils NV and **61 64 66 69** 71

Champagne house belonging to MOËT & CHANDON. Luxury brand: Dom Ruinart.

Rully B'y. r. or w. dr. or (sp.) ★★ **69 71 72 73** 75 76

Village of the CÔTE CHALONNAISE famous for sparkling burgundy. Still reds and whites light but tasty and good value.

Sablant Lo. w. dr. sp.★★ NV

Brand name for high-quality CRÉMANT DE LOIRE.

Saint-Amour B'y. r. ★★ **74 75** 76

Northernmost cru of BEAUJOLAIS: light, fruity, irresistible wine.

Saint-Aubin B'y. (r.) or w. dr. ★★ **71 72 73 74** 75 76

Little-known neighbour of CHASSAGNE-MONTRACHET, up a side-valley. Not top-rank, but typical and good value. Also sold as CÔTE-DE-BEAUNE-VILLAGES.

Saint Bris B'y. w. dr. ★ **75 76** D.Y.A.

Village w. of CHABLIS known for its fruity ALIGOTÉ, making good sparkling burgundy, and hillside cherry orchards. See also Sauvignon-de-St-Bris.

Sainte Croix-du-Mont B'x. w. sw. ★★ **67 70** 71 75

Neighbour to SAUTERNES with similar golden wine. No superlatives but well worth trying.

Sainte-Foy-Bordeaux B'x.

Part of ENTRE-DEUX-MERS.

Saint-Emilion B'x. r.★★→★★★★ 66 67 **70** 71 **73** 75

The biggest top-quality Bordeaux district; solid, rich, tasty wines from scores of ch'x., incl. CHEVAL-BLANC, AUSONE, CANON, MAGDELAINE, FIGEAC, etc. Good co-operative: "Royal St-Emilion".

Saint-Estèphe B'x. r. ★★ →★★★ 66 67 **70** 71 **73** 75

Northern village of HAUT-MÉDOC. Solid, satisfying, occasionally superlative wines. Top ch'x.: CALON-SÉGUR, COS D'ESTOURNEL, MONTROSE, etc., and many good CRUS BOURGEOIS.

Saint-Georges-Saint-Emilion

Part of MONTAGNE-ST-EMILION. Best ch.: ST-GEORGES.

Saint-Joseph Rh. r. (p. or w. dr.) ★★ 71 72 **73** 76

Northern Rhône appellation of second rank but reasonable price. Substantial wine comparable to CROZES-HERMITAGE in quality and worth ageing.

Saint-Julien B'x. r. ★★★ **66 67** 70 71 **73** 75

Mid-Médoc village with a dozen of Bordeaux's best ch'x., incl. three LÉOVILLES, BEYCHEVELLE, DUCRU-BEAUCAILLOU, GRUAUD-LAROSE, etc. The epitome of well-balanced red wine.

Saint-Laurent

Village next to SAINT-JULIEN. Appellation Haut-Médoc.

Saint-Nicolas-de-Bourgueil Lo. r.★★ **70** 71 **73** 75 76
>   The next village to BOURGUEIL: the same light but lively and fruity CABERNET red.

Saint-Péray Rh. w. dr. or sp.★★ NV
>   Rather heavy white from the n. Rhône, much of it made sparkling. A curiosity.

Saint Pourçain Central France r. p. or w. dr. ⬚★⬚ D.Y.A.
>   The agreeable local wine of Vichy, not found elsewhere. Made from GAMAY and/or PINOT NOIR.

Saint-Sauveur
>   HAUT-MÉDOC village just w. of PAUILLAC.

Saint-Seurin-de-Cadourne
>   HAUT-MÉDOC village just n. of SAINT-ESTÈPHE.

Saint-Véran B'y. w. dr. ⬚★★⬚ **71 72 73 74** 75 76
>   Next-door appellation to POUILLY-FUISSÉ. Similar but better value: dry white of real character from the best slopes of MÂCON-VILLAGES.

Sancerre Lo. (r. p.) or w. dr.★★★ **74 75 76**
>   Very fragrant and fresh SAUVIGNON white almost indistinguishable from POUILLY FUMÉ, its neighbour over the Loire. Drink young. Also light PINOT NOIR red.

Santenay B'y. r. or (w. dr.)★★★ **66 67** 69 **70** 71 72 **73** 75
>   Very worthy, rarely rapturous, sturdy reds from the s. of the CÔTE DE BEAUNE. Best v'yds.: Les Gravières, Clos de Tavannes.

Saumur Lo. r. p. or w. dr. and sp.★★
>   Big versatile district in Anjou, with fresh fruity whites, good-value sparklers, pale rosés and occasionally good CABERNET reds, the best from Saumur-Champigny.

Sauternes B'x. w. sw. ⬚★★→⬚ ★★★★ **67** 69 70 71 75
>   District of 5 villages (incl. BARSAC) making France's best sweet wine: strong (14% alcohol) luscious and golden, improving with age. Top ch'x.: D'YQUEM, LA TOUR-BLANCHE, SUDUIRAUT, COUTET, CLIMENS, GUIRAUD, etc. A few heavy dry wines.

Sauvignon Blanc
>   See Grapes for white wine

Sauvignon-de-St-Bris B'y. w. dr. ⬚★★⬚ D.Y.A.
>   A baby VDQS cousin of SANCERRE from near CHABLIS.

Savennières Lo. w. dr./sw.★★★ **67 69 70** 71 72 73 75
>   Small ANJOU district of pungent long-lived whites, incl. COULÉE DE SERRANT, LA ROCHE AUX MOINES, Clos du Papillon.

Savigny-lès-Beaune B'y. r. or (w. dr.) ⬚★★★⬚ **66 67 69 70 71** 72 **73** 75
>   Important village next to BEAUNE, with similar well-balanced middle-weight wines, often deliciously delicate and fruity. Best v'yds.: Marconnets, Dominode, Serpentières, Vergelesses.

Savoie E. France (r.) or w. dr.★★ D.Y.A.
>   Alpine area with light dry wines like some Swiss wine or minor Loires. CRÉPY and SEYSSEL are best known.

Schlumberger et Cie
>   Excellent Alsace growers and merchants at Guebwiller.

Schröder & Schyler
>   Old family firm of Bordeaux merchants, owners of CH. KIRWAN.

Sec
>   Literally means dry, though champagne so-called is medium-sweet.

Sèvre-et-Maine
>   The *département* containing the central and best v'yds. of MUSCADET.

Seyssel Savoie w. dr. or sp. $\boxed{\star\star}$ NV

Delicate pale dry white making admirable sparkling wine.

Sichel & Co.

Famous Bordeaux (and Burgundy and Germany) merchants, owners of CH. D'ANGLUDET and part-owners of CH. PALMER.

Soussans

Village just n. of MARGAUX, sharing its appellation.

Sylvaner

See Grapes for white wine

La Tâche B'y. r. $\star\star\star\star$ **62** 66 67 69 70 71 72 73 74 76

15-acre Grand Cru of VOSNE-ROMANÉE and one of the best v'yds. on earth: dark, perfumed and luxurious wine.

Taittinger NV and **61 62 64 66 69** 70 71

Fashionable champagne growers and merchants of Reims. Luxury brand: Comtes de Champagne.

Tastevin, Confrèrie du

Burgundy's colourful and successful promotion society. Wine carrying their Tastevinage label has been approved by them and will usually be good. A tastevin is the traditional shallow silver wine-tasting cup of Burgundy.

Tavel Rh. p. $\star\star\star$ D.Y.A.

France's most famous rosé, strong, dry and slightly orange in colour.

Tête de Cuvée

Term vaguely used of the best wines of an appellation.

Thorin, J.

Fine grower and major merchant of BEAUJOLAIS, at Pontanevaux.

Tokay d'Alsace

See Pinot Gris under Grapes for white wine

Touraine Lo. r. p. w. dr./sw./sp.

Big mid-Loire province with immense range of wines, incl. dry white SAUVIGNON, dry and sweet CHENIN BLANC (e.g. Vouvray), red CHINON and BOURGUEIL, light red GAMAYS and rosés. Sauvignons and Gamays of good years are bargains.

Trimbach, F. E.

Distinguished Alsace grower and merchant at Ribeauvillé. Best wines incl. Riesling Clos Ste. Hune.

Vacqueyras Rh. r. $\boxed{\star\star}$ **70** 71 72 **73 74** 76

Up-and-coming village of s. CÔTES-DU-RHÔNE, neighbour to GIGONDAS; comparable with CHÂTEAUNEUF-DU-PAPE but less heavy.

Valençay Lo. w. dr. $\star$ D.Y.A.

Neighbour of CHEVERNY: similar pleasant sharpish wine.

Varichon & Clerc

Principal makers and shippers of SAVOIE sparkling wines.

Varoilles, Domaine des

Excellent estate in GEVREY-CHAMBERTIN.

Vaudésir B'y. w. dr. $\boxed{\star\star\star\star}$ **69** 71 **73 74** 75 76

Arguably the best of the 7 Grands Crus of CHABLIS.

VDQS

Vin Délimité de Qualité Supérieure (see Introduction).

Vendange

Vintage.

Vendange tardive

Late vintage. In ALSACE equivalent to German Auslese.

Veuve Clicquot NV and **61 64 66 69** 70

Historic champagne house of the highest standing. Cellars at Reims. Luxury brand: La Grande Dame.

Vidal-Fleury, J.

Long-established shippers and growers of top-quality Rhône wines.

Viénot, Charles

Grower and merchant of good burgundy, at NUITS-ST-GEORGES. 70 acres in Nuits, CORTON, RICHEBOURG, etc.

Vignoble

Area of v'yds.

Vin de garde

Wine that will improve with keeping.

Vin de l'année

This year's wine. See Beaujolais.

Vin de paille

Wine from grapes dried on straw mats, consequently very sweet, like Italian passito. Esp. in the JURA.

Vin de Pays

The junior rank of country wines (see Introduction).

Vin Doux Naturel ("VDN")

Sweet wine fortified with alcohol, so far from "natural". Common in ROUSSILLON.

Vin Gris

"Grey" wine is very pale pink, made of red grapes pressed before fermentation begins, unlike rosé, which ferments briefly before pressing.

Vin Jaune   Jura w. dr. ★★★

Speciality of ARBOIS: odd yellow wine like fino sherry. Ready when bottled.

Vin nouveau

See Beaujolais Nouveau

The same remark has been made about a magnum (a double bottle) as Queen Anne is supposed to have made about a turkey. She complained that it was "too much for one and not enough for two".

Vinsobres   Rh. r. (p. or w. dr.) ★★ 71 72 73 74 76

Contradictory name of good s. Rhône village. Strong substantial reds which mature well.

Viré

See Mâcon-Villages

Visan   Rh. r. p. or w. dr. ★★ 71 72 73 74 76

One of the better s. Rhône villages. Reds better than white.

Viticulteur

Wine-grower.

Volnay   B'y. r.★★★ 66 67 69 70 71 72 73 76

Village between POMMARD and MEUSAULT: the best reds of the CÔTE DE BEAUNE, not strong or heavy but fragrant and silky. Best v'yds.: Caillerets, Clos des Ducs, Champans, Clos des Chênes, etc.

Volnay-Santenots   B'y. r. ★★★

Excellent red wine from MEURSAULT is sold under this name. Indistinguishable from VOLNAY.

Vosne-Romanée   B'y. r. ★★★→★★★★ 66 67 69 70 71 72 73 76

The village containing Burgundy's grandest Crus (ROMANÉE-CONTI, LA TÂCHE, etc.). There are no common wines in Vosne.

Vougeot

See Clos de Vougeot

Vouvray   Lo. w. dr./sw./sp. ★★→★★★★ 64 67 69 70 71 73 75 76

Small district of TOURAINE with very variable wines, at their best intensely sweet and almost immortal. Good dry sparkling.

Ygrec

Brand name of powerful dry wine occasionally made at CH. D'YQUEM.

Germany

Germany has the most complicated labelling system in the world—a fact that has put most people off tackling it seriously and driven them to settle for pleasantly innocuous blended wines: Liebfraumilch and the like.

Yet those who funk its complications will never experience the real beauty of the style of wine which is Germany's unique contribution.

The secret of the style is the balance of sweetness against fruity acidity. A great vintage in Germany is one in which the autumn weather allows the late-ripening Riesling—the grape which makes virtually all the great German wines—to develop a high sugar content. What is so special about the Riesling is that as it ripens it also develops a concentration of fragrant acids and essences to balance the increasing sweetness. The resulting wine is tense and thrilling with this sugar/acid balance.

It smells and tastes extraordinarily flowery, lively and refreshing while it is young. But because of its internal equilibrium it also has the ability to live and mature for a remarkable length of time. As good Riesling matures all sorts of subtle scents and flavours emerge. Straight sweetness gives way to oily richness. Suggestions of countless flowers and fruits, herbs and spices develop.

These are the rewards for anyone who can be bothered to master the small print. They lead into realms of sensation where Liebfraumilch (with all the respect due to a perfectly decent drink) can never follow. The great German growers make wine for wine's sake. Food is irrelevant, except in so far as it gets in the way.

The Labels and the Law

German wine law is based on the ripeness of the grapes at harvest time. Recent vintages have been exceptionally kind to growers, but as a general rule most German wine needs sugar added to make up for the missing warmth and sunshine of one of the world's northernmost vineyards.

The exceptional wine, from grapes ripe enough not to need sugar, is kept apart as Qualitätswein mit Prädikat or QmP. Within this top category its natural sugar-content is expressed by traditional terms—in ascending order of ripeness: Kabinett, Spätlese, Auslese, Beerenauslese, Trockenbeerenauslese.

But reasonably good wine is also made in good vineyards from grapes that fail to reach the natural sugar-content required for a QmP label. The authorities allow this, within fairly strict controls, to be called Qualitätswein as well, but with the different qualification of bestimmte Anbaugebiete (i.e. QbA) instead of mit Prädikat. mP is therefore a vitally important ingredient of a fine-wine label.

Both levels are officially checked, tested and tasted, at every bottling. Each batch is given an identifying test ("prüfungs") number. No other country has quality control approaching this. It can't make dull wine exciting, but it can and does make all "quality" wine a safe bet.

GERMANY

Moselle Saar Ruwer **M-S-R**

Rheingau **Rhg**

Mittel-Mosel **M-M**

R. Moselle

Ruwer

Saar

Frankfurt

Mainz

R. Nahe

Rheinhessen **Rhh**

Nahe **Na**

R. Main

Franken **Frank**

• Saarbrucken

Mannheim

R. Neckar

Rheinpfalz **Rhpf**

R. Rhine

Stuttgart

Abbreviations of regional names
shown in bold type are used in
the text.

• Karlsruhe

Württemburg **Wurtt**

Baden **Bad**

• Freiburg

The third level, Tafelwein, has no pretentions to quality
and is not allowed to give itself airs beyond the name of the
village or the general region it comes from.

Though there is very much more detail in the laws this
is the gist of the quality grading. Where it differs completely from the French system is in ignoring geographical
difference. There are no Grands Crus, no VDQS. In theory
all any German vineyard has to do to make the best wine
is to grow the ripest grapes.

The law distinguishes only between degrees of geographical exactness. In labelling quality wine the grower
or merchant is given a choice. He can (and always will)
label the relatively small quantities of his best wine with
the name of the precise vineyard or Einzellage where it
was grown. Germany has about 3,000 Einzellage names.
Obviously only particularly good ones are famous enough
to help sell the wine. Therefore the law has created a
second class of vineyard name: the Grosslage. A Grosslage
is a group of neighbouring Einzellages of supposedly

similar character and standing. Because there are far fewer Grosslage names, and far more wine from each, Grosslages have a better chance of building reputations, brand-name fashion.*

Thirdly the grower or merchant (more likely the latter) may choose to sell his wine under a regional name: the word is Bereich. To cope with the vast demand for "Bernkasteler" or "Niersteiner" or "Johannisberger" these world-famous names have been made legal for considerable districts. "Bereich Johannisberg" is the whole of the Rheingau; "Bereich Bernkastel" the whole of the Mittel-Mosel.

As with all wine names, in fact, the better the wine the more precise the labelling. The trick with German labels is to be able to recognize which is the most precise. Finally, though, and above all, it is to recognize the grower and his vineyard.

The basic German label

The order of wording on German quality wine labels follows a standard pattern.

TRIERER
ABSTBERG
RISLING AUSLESE

QmP
A.P. NR. 12345678
ERZEUGERABFÜLLUNG
WINZERVEREIN TRIER

The first name is the town or parish, with the suffix -er. The second is the vineyard (either einzellage or grosslage — see introduction).
The third (optional) is the grape variety. The fourth is the quality in terms of ripeness.
For QmP see page 70.
For A.P. Nr. see page 62.
Erzeugerabfüllung means bottled by the grower, in this case the grower's co-operative of Trier.
For other words appearing on German labels see the Germany A–Z.

*Where the law is less than candid, however, is in pretending to believe that the general public will know a Grosslage name from an Einzellage name, when the two are indistinguishably similar (see any entry on the following pages). It is actually against the law to indicate on the label whether the name in question is that of a particular plot or a wider grouping. The names of all relevant Grosslages are given in this book. Note that Grosslage wines are very rarely of the stature of Einzellage wines.

Recent Vintages

Mosel/Saar/Ruwer

Mosels (including Saar and Ruwer wines) are so attractive young that their keeping qualities are not often enough explored, and wines older than seven years or so are unusual. But well-made wines of Kabinett class gain from two or three years in bottle, Spätleses by a little longer, and Ausleses and Beerenausleses by anything from 10 to 20 years, depending on the vintage.

As a rule, in poor years the Saar and Ruwer fare worse than the Middle Mosel and make sharp, thin wines, but in the best years they can surpass the whole of Germany for elegance and "breed".

1976	Very good small vintage, with some superlative sweet wines and almost no dry.
1975	Superb; many Spätleses and Ausleses. Perfect balance will give them long life.
1974	Most wine needed sugaring; few Kabinetts, but some well-balanced wines which will keep.
1973	Very large, attractive, but low acid and extract will mean a short life. Good eiswein.
1972	Large; medium to poor; few late-picked wines, many with unripe flavour.
1971	Superb, with perfect balance. Many top wines still need keeping for years.
1970	Large; good to average. Quite soft, not for keeping.
1969	Some very fine wines; most merely good. Best in the Saar and Ruwer.
1968	Nearly all very poor.
1967	Good all-round; the best first-class.
1966	Some brilliant Rieslings, but quality variable.

Older fine vintages: '64, '59, '53, '49, '45.

Rhine/Nahe/Palatinate

Even the best wines can be drunk with pleasure after two or three years, but Kabinett, Spätlese and Auslese wines of good vintages gain enormously in character and complexity by keeping for longer. Rheingau wines tend to be longest-lived, often improving for 10 years or more, but wines from the Nahe and the Palatinate can last nearly as long. Rheinhessen wines usually mature sooner, and dry Franconian wines are best young.

The Riesling, predominant in the Rheingau, benefits most from hot summers; Palatinate wines can taste almost overripe.

1976	The richest vintage since 1921 in places. Very few dry wines.
1975	A splendid Riesling year, a high percentage of Kabinetts and Spätleses. Needs time to mature.
1974	Variable; the best fruity and good; many Kabinetts.
1973	Very large, consistent and attractive, but not for long keeping.
1972	Excess acidity was the problem; no exciting wines, but some presentable.
1971	A superlative vintage with perfect balance. Still needs time to show its true quality.
1970	Very pleasant wines, but no more. Huge crop. Not for keeping.
1969	All above average; the best great. Nahe and Palatinate specially good.
1968	Poor; a wet summer. The Palatinate made some good light wines.
1967	Marvellous; the best of the '60s; Rheinhessen made great wines.
1966	Overall quality high, but few top wines. The Nahe did best.

Older fine vintages: '64, '59, '57, '53, '49, '45.

N.B.
Vintage notes after entries in the German section are given in a different form from those elsewhere, to show the style of the vintage as well as its quality.
Three styles are indicated:
The classic, super-ripe vintage with a high proportion of natural (QmP) wines, including Spätleses and Ausleses. By a freakish chance three of the six vintages shown, an unprecedented proportion, come into this category. Example: 71
The "normal" successful vintage with plenty of good wine but no great preponderance of sweeter wines. Example: 73
The cool vintage with generally poor ripeness but a fair proportion of reasonably successful wines, tending to be over-acid. Such wines sometimes mature better than expected. Example: 72
Where no mention is made the vintage is generally not recommended.

Achkarren Bad. (r.) w. ★→★★
> Well-known wine village of the KAISERSTUHL.

Adelmann, Graf
> Famous grower with 125 acres at Kleinbottwar, WÜRTTEM-BERG. Uses the name Brussele. Light reds; good RIESLINGS.

Ahr Ahr r. ★→★★★ 71 75 76
> Germany's best-known red-wine area, s. of Bonn. Very light pale SPÄTBURGUNDERS.

Amtliche prüfungsnummer
> See Prüfungsnummer

Anbaugebiete
> Wine-region. See QbA.

Anheuser
> Name of two distinguished growers of the NAHE.

Annaberg Rhpf. w. ★★★ 71 72 73 74 75 76
> Thirty-two-acre estate at DÜRKHEIM famous for sweet and pungent wines.

Assmannshausen Rhg. r. ★→★★★ 71 73 75 76
> RHEINGAU village known for its pale reds. Top v'yd.: Höllenberg. Grosslage: Steil.

The German Wine Academy runs regular courses of wine-instruction at all levels for both amateurs and professionals, in German and English. The Academy is based at the glorious 12th-century Cistercian monastery of Kloster Eberbach in the Rheingau. The course normally includes tasting-tours of Germany's wine regions. Particulars can be obtained from the Academy, P.O. Box 1705, D-6500 Mainz, West Germany.

Auslese
> Late-gathered wine with high natural sugar content.

Avelsbach M-S-R (Ruwer) w. ★★★ 71 73 75 76
> Village near TRIER. Supremely delicate wines. Growers: Staatliche Weinbaudomäne (see Staatsweingut), BISCHÖFLICHES WEINGÜTER. Grosslage: Trierer Römerlay.

Ayl M-S-R (Saar) w. ★★★ 71 73 75 76
> One of the best villages of the SAAR. Top v'yds.: Kupp, Herrenberger. Grosslage: Scharzberg.

Bacchus
> Modern highly perfumed grape variety.

Bacharach (Bereich)
> District name for the s. Mittelrhein v'yds. downstream from the RHEINGAU. No great or famous wines; several pleasant ones.

Baden
> Huge area of scattered wine-growing. Few classic wines: most are heavy or soft. Best areas are KAISERSTUHL and ORTENAU.

Badische Bergstrasse/Kraichgau (Bereich)
> Principal district name of n. BADEN.

Bad Dürkheim
> See Dürkheim

Badisches Frankenland (Bereich)
> Minor district name of n. BADEN.

Bad Kreuznach Na. w. ★★→★★★ 71 72 73 74 75 76
> Main town of the NAHE with some of its best wines. Many fine v'yds., incl. Brückes, St. Martin, Kauzenberg. Grosslage: Kronenberg.

Balbach Erben
> One of the best growers of NIERSTEIN.

Basserman-Jordan

100-acre MITTEL-HAARDT family estate with many of the best v'yds. in DEIDESHEIM, FORST, RUPPERTSBERG, etc.

Beerenauslese

Extremely sweet and luscious wine from very late-gathered individual bunches.

Bereich

District within a gebiet (region). See under Bereich names, e.g. Bernkastel (Bereich).

Bergzabern, Bad   Rhpf. (r.) w. ★→★★ *74 75 76*

Town of SÜDLICHE-WEINSTRASSE. Pleasant sweetish wines. Grosslage: Liebfrauenberg.

Bernkastel   M-M w. ★★→★★★★ 71 73 75 76

Top wine-town of the Mosel; the epitome of RIESLING. Best v'yds.: Doktor, Bratenhöfchen, etc. Grosslages: Badstube (★★★) and Kurfürstlay (★★).

Bernkastel (Bereich)

Wide area of mixed quality but decided flowery character. Includes all the Mittel-Mosel.

Bingen   Rhh. w. ★★→★★★ 71 73 74 75 7̃

Town on Rhine and Nahe with fine v'yds., incl. Scharlachberg. Grosslage: Sankt Rochuskapelle.

Bingen (Bereich)

District name for w. Rheinhessen.

Bischöfliches Weingüter

Outstanding M-S-R estate at TRIER, a union of the Cathedral properties with two famous charities. 230 acres of top v'yds. in AVELSBACH, WILTINGEN, SCHARZHOFBERG, AYL, KASEL, EITELSBACH, PIESPORT, TRITTENHEIM, ÜRZIG, etc.

Blauburgunder

A form of PINOT NOIR.

Blue Nun

The best-selling brand of LIEBFRAUMILCH, from SICHEL.

Bocksbeutel

Flask-shaped bottle used for FRANKEN wines.

Bodensee (Bereich)

Minor district of s. Baden, on La. Constance.

Bundesweinprämierung

The top German Wine Award: a gold, silver or bronze medal on bottles of remarkable wines.

Brauneberg   M-M w. ★★★ 71 73 75 76

Village near BERNKASTEL with 100 acres making excellent full-flavoured wine. Best v'yd.: Juffer. Grosslage: Kurfürstlay.

Breisgau (Bereich)

Minor district of BADEN, just n. of KAISERSTUHL.

Brentano, von

20-acre old family estate in WINKEL, Rheingau.

Bühl, von

Great RHEINPFALZ family estate. 200+ acres in DEIDESHEIM, FORST, RUPPERTSBERG, etc. In the very top class.

Bullay   M-S-R ★→★★ 75 76

Lower Mosel village. Good light wine to drink young.

Burgerspital zum Heiligen Geist

Ancient charitable estate at WÜRZBURG. 185 acres in WÜRZBURG, RANDERSACKER, etc., make rich dry wines.

Bürklin-Wolf

Great RHEINPFALZ family estate. 222 acres in WACHENHEIM, FORST, DEIDESHEIM and RUPPERTSBERG, with rarely a dull, let alone poor, wine.

Crown of Crowns

Popular brand of LIEBFRAUMILCH from LANGENBACH & CO.

Deidesheim Rhpf. w. (r.) $\boxed{\star\star}$ →$\star\star\star\star$ 71 72 73 74 75 76
>Biggest top-quality wine-village of RHEINPFALZ with 1,000 acres. Rich, high-flavoured, lively wines. V'yds. incl. Hohenmorgen, Kieselberg, Grainhübel, Leinhöhle, Herrgottsacker, etc. Grosslages: Hofstück, Mariengarten.

Deinhard
>Famous old Koblenz merchants and growers in Rheingau (see Wegeler), Mittel-Mosel (27 acres in Bernkastel, incl. part of Doktor v'yd., and Graach) and Rheinpfalz.

Deutscher Tafelwein
>TAFELWEIN from Germany (only).

Deutsches Weinsiegel
>A quality "seal" (i.e. neck label) for wines which have passed a stiff tasting test.

Deutsches Weintor
>See Schweigen

Diabetiker Wein
>Wine with minimal residual sugar (less than 4gms/litre). Suitable for diabetics—or those who like very dry wine.

Dhron
>See Neumagen-Dhron

Dienheim Rhh. w. $\star\star$→$\star\star\star$ 71 75 76
>Southern neighbour of OPPENHEIM. Mainly run-of-the-mill wines. Top v'yds.: Kreuz, Herrenberg, Schloss. Grosslages: Guldenmorgen, Krötenbrunnen.

Dom
>German for Cathedral. Wines from the famous TRIER Cathedral properties have "Dom" before the v'yd. name. But "Domgarten" is a brand name of HALLGARTEN.

Domäne
>German for "domain" or "estate". Sometimes used alone to mean the "State domain" (Staatliche Weinbaudomäne).

Durbach Baden w. (r.) $\star$→$\star\star\star$ 73 75 76
>150 acres of the best v'yds. of BADEN. Top growers: Schloss Staufenberg, Wolf-Metternich, von Neveu. Choose their RIESLINGS.

Dürkheim, Bad Rhpf. w. or (r.) $\boxed{\star\star}$ →$\star\star\star$ 71 72 73 74 75 76
>Main town of the MITTEL-HAARDT. Top v'yds.: Hochbenn, Michelsberg. Grosslages: Feuerberg, Schenkenböhl.

Edel
>Means "noble". Edelfäule means "noble rot": the condition which gives the greatest sweet wines (see p. 52).

Egon Müller-Scharzhof
>Top Saar estate of 24 acres at WILTINGEN. SCHARZHOFBERGERS are supreme in top years.

Eiswein
>Wine made from frozen grapes with the ice (e.g. water content) rejected, thus very concentrated in flavour and sugar. Rare and expensive. Sometimes produced as late as the January or February following the vintage.

Eitelsbach Ruwer w. $\star\star$→$\star\star\star\star$ 71 73 75 76
>RUWER village now part of TRIER, incl. superb Karthäuserhofberg estate. Grosslage: Trierer Römerlay.

Elbling
>Inferior grape widely grown on upper Mosel.

Eltville Rhg. w. $\boxed{\star\star}$ →$\star\star\star$ 71 72 73 74 75 76
>Major wine-town with cellars of the Rheingau State domain, SCHLOSS ELTZ and VON SIMMERN estates. Excellent wines. Top v'yds.: Sonnenberg, Taubenberg. Grosslage: Heiligenstock.

Eltz, Schloss
>Superb 98-acre Rheingau estate with v'yds. in ELTVILLE, KIEDRICH, RAUENTHAL, RÜDESHEIM.

Enkirch M-M w. ★★→ ★★★ 71 73 **75 76**
    Minor middle-Mosel village, often overlooked but with
    lovely light tasty wine. Grosslage: Schwarzlay.

Erbach Rhg. w. ★★★→★★★★ 71 72 73 74 **75 76**
    One of the best parts of the Rheingau with powerful, per-
    fumed wines, incl. the great MARCOBRUNN; other top v'yds.:
    Schlossberg, Siegelsberg, Hönigberg, Michelmark. Gross-
    lage: Mehrhölzchen. Major estates: SCHLOSS REINHARTS-
    HAUSEN, VON SCHÖNBORN.

Erden M-M w. ★★→★★★ 71 73 **75 76**
    Village between Urzig and Kröv with full-flavoured vigorous
    wine. Top v'yds.: Prälat, Treppchen. Leading grower:
    Beeres. Grosslage: Schwarzlay.

Erzeugerabfüllung
    Bottled by the grower.

Escherndorf Franc. w. ★★→★★★ 71 72 73 **75 76**
    Important wine-town near WÜRZBURG. Similar tasty dry
    wine. Top v'yds.: Lump, Berg. Grosslage: Kirchberg.

Feine, feinste, hochfeinste
    Terms formerly used to distinguish a good grower's best
    barrels. Now, unfortunately, illegal.

Forst Rhpf. w. ★★→★★★★ 71 72 73 74 **75 76**
    MITTEL-HAARDT village with 500 acres of Germany's best
    v'yds. Ripe, richly fragrant but subtle wines. Top v'yds:
    Kirchenstück, Jesuitengarten, Ungeheuer, etc. Grosslages:
    Mariengarten, Schnepfenflüg.

Franken
    Franconia: region of excellent distinctive dry wines. The
    centre is WÜRZBURG. BEREICH names: MAINVIERECK, MAIN-
    DREIECK, STEIGERWALD.

Friedrich Wilhelm Gymnasium
    Superb 104-acre charitable estate with v'yds. in BERNKASTEL,
    ZELTINGEN, GRAACH, TRITTENHEIM, OCKFEN, etc., all M-S-R.

Geisenheim Rhg. w. ★★→★★★ 71 72 73 74 **75 76**
    Village famous for Germany's leading wine-school. Best
    v'yds. incl. Rothenberg, Kläuserweg, Fuchsberg. Grosslage:
    Burgweg.

Gemeinde
    A commune or parish.

Gewürztraminer
    Spicy grape of Alsace, used a little in s. Germany, esp.
    Rheinpfalz.

Gimmeldingen Rhpf. w. ★→ ★★ 73 74 **75 76**
    Village just s. of MITTEL-HAARDT. Similar wines. Grosslage:
    Meerspinne.

Goldener Oktober
    Popular Rhine-wine and Mosel blend from the firm of St.
    Ursula, Bingen.

Graach M-M w. ★★→ ★★★ 71 73 **75 76**
    Small village between BERNKASTEL and WEHLEN. Top v'yds.:
    Himmelreich, Domprobst, Abstberg, Josephshöfer. Gross-
    lage: Münzlay.

Grosslage
    See Introduction

Guntersblum Rhh. w. ★→★★ 73 **75 76**
    Big wine-town s. of OPPENHEIM. Grosslages: Krötenbrunnen,
    Vogelsgarten.

Guntrum, Louis
    130-acre family estate in RHINEHESSEN. Fine v'yds. in NIER-
    STEIN, OPPENHEIM, etc.

Gutedel
    German for the low-quality Chasselas grape.

Hallgarten   Rhg. w. ★★→★★★ 71 *72 73 74* 75 76
>   Important little wine-town behind HATTENHEIM. Robust
>   full-bodied wines. Top v'yds. incl. Schönhell, Jungfer.
>   Grosslage: Mehrhölzchen.

Hallgarten, House of
>   Well-known London-based wine-merchant.

Hanns Christof
>   Top brand of LIEBFRAUMILCH from DEINHARD'S.

Hattenheim   Rhg. w. ★★→★★★★ 71 *72 73* 75 76
>   Superlative 500-acre wine-town. V'yds. incl. STEINBERG,
>   MARCOBRUNN, Nüssbrunnen, Mannberg, etc. Grosslage:
>   Deutelsberg.

Hessische Bergstrasse
>   Minor region s. of Frankfurt. Pleasant wines from State
>   domain v'yds. in Heppenheim and Bensheim.

Hessische Forschungsanstalt für Wein- Obst- & Gartenbau
>   Germany's top wine-school and research establishment, at
>   GEISENHEIM.

Heyl zu Herrnsheim
>   Fine 50-acre estate at NIERSTEIN.

Hochfeinste
>   "Very finest." Traditional label-term, now illegal.

Hochheim   Rhg. w. ★★→★★★ 71 *72 73 74* 75 76
>   500-acre wine-town 15 miles e. of RHEINGAU. Similar fine
>   wines. Top v'yds.: Domdechaney, Kirchenstück, Hölle,
>   Königin Viktoria Berg. Grosslage: Daubhaus.

Hock
>   English term for Rhine-wine, derived from HOCHHEIM.

Huxelrebe
>   Modern very fruity grape variety.

Ihringen   Bad. (r.) w. ★→★★ 75 76
>   One of the best villages of the KAISERSTUHL, BADEN. Heavy
>   dryish wines.

Ilbesheim   Rhpf. w. ★→★★ *74* 75 76
>   Base of important growers' co-operative of SÜDLICHE
>   WEINSTRASSE. See also Schweigen.

Ingelheim   Rhh. r. or w. ★ 75 76
>   Village on Rhine known for red wine.

Iphofen   Franc. w. ★★→ ★★★ 71 *72 73* 75 76
>   Village e. of WÜRZBURG. Top v'yd.: Julius-Echter-Berg.
>   Grosslage: Burgweg.

Jesuitengarten
>   V'yd. in FORST. One of Germany's best.

Johannisberg   Rhg. w. ★★→★★★★ 71 *72 73* 75 76
>   260-acre village with superlative subtle wine. Top v'yds.
>   incl. SCHLOSS JOHANNISBERG, Hölle, Klaus, etc. Grosslage:
>   Erntebringer.

Johannisberg (Bereich)
>   District name of the entire RHEINGAU.

Josephshöfer
>   Fine v'yd. at GRAACH, the property of von KESSELSTATT.

Juliusspital
>   Ancient charity at WÜRZBURG with top FRANKEN v'yds.

Kabinett
>   The term for the driest and least expensive natural un-
>   sugared (QmP) wines.

Kaiserstuhl-Tuniberg (Bereich)
>   Best v'yd. area of BADEN. Villages incl. IHRINGEN,
>   ACHKARREN.

Kallstadt   Rhpf. w. (r.) ★★→★★★ 71 *72 73 74* 75 76
>   Village just n. of MITTEL-HAARDT. Fine rich wines. Top v'yd.:
>   ANNABERG. Grosslages: Kobnert, Feuerberg.

Kanzem M-S-R (Saar) w. ★★→★★★ 71 73 75 76
>Small but excellent neighbour of WILTINGEN. Top v'yds.:
>Sonnenberg, Altenberg. Grosslage: Scharzberg.

Kasel M-S-R (Ruwer) w. ★★ 71 73 75 76
>Village with attractive light wines. Grosslage: Römerlay.

Keller
>Wine-cellar or winery.

Kerner
>Modern very flowery grape variety.

Kesselstatt, von
>The biggest private Mosel estate, 600 years old. 150 acres in
>GRAACH, PIESPORT, KASEL, MENNIG, WILTINGEN, etc.

Kesten M-M w. ★→★★★ 71 73 75 76
>Neighbour of BRAUNEBERG. Best wines (from Paulinshof-
>berg) similar. Grosslage: Kurfürstlay.

Kiedrich Rhg. w. ★★→★★★★ 71 72 73 74 75 76
>Neighbour of RAUENTHAL; almost as splendid and high
>flavoured. Top v'yds.: Gräfenberg, Wasseros, Sandgrub.
>Grosslage: Heiligenstock.

---

*Most German wine is bottled in tall narrow sloping-shouldered bottles:
invariably brown glass for Rhine wines (including Nahe and
Palatinate wines) and green for Mosel-Saar-Ruwer. The glass may be
said to epitomize the respective qualities of the wines: the Rhine full
and gold, the Mosel fresh and green (often literally so). In any case it is
useful to remember when you are asked by malicious friends to give an
opinion. Franconian wine is alone in being bottled in flagon-shaped
"bocksbeutels".*

Kloster Eberbach
>Glorious 12th-century Abbey at HATTENHEIM, Rheingau,
>now State domain property and H.Q. of the German Wine
>Academy.

Klüsserath M-M w. ★★→ ★★★ 71 75 76
>Minor Mosel village worth trying in good vintages. Best
>v'yds.: Brüderschaft, Königsberg. Grosslage: St. Michael.

Kreuznach (Bereich)
>District name for the entire northern NAHE. See also Bad
>Kreuznach.

Kröv M-M w. ★→★★★ 73 75 76
>Popular tourist resort famous for its Grosslage name:
>Nacktarsch, meaning "bare bottom".

Landgräflich Hessisches Weingut
>75-acre estate in JOHANNISBERG, WINKEL, etc.

Langenbach & Co.
>Well-known merchants of London and WORMS.

Lauerburg
>One of the three owners of the famous Doktor v'yd. in
>BERNKASTEL, with THANISCH and DEINHARD.

Liebfrauenstift
>26-acre v'yd. in the city of WORMS, said to be the origin of the
>name LIEBFRAUMILCH.

Liebfraumilch
>Legally defined as a QbA "of pleasant character" from RHEIN-
>HESSEN, RHEINPFALZ, NAHE or RHEINGAU, blended from
>RIESLING, SILVANER or MÜLLER-THURGAU. Most is mild
>semi-sweet wine from Rheinhessen and Rheinpfalz.

Lieser M-M w. ★→ ★★ 71 73 75 76
>Little-known neighbour of BERNKASTEL. Grosslages: Beeren-
>lay, Kurfürstlay.

Lorch Rhg. w. (r.) ★→★★ 71 73 75 76

At extreme w. end of Rheingau. Secondary quality. Best grower: von Kanitz.

Löwenstein, Fürst

70-acre FRANKEN estate: classic dry wines.

Maindreieck (Bereich)

District name for central part of FRANKEN, incl. WÜRZBURG.

Mainviereck (Bereich)

District name for minor w. part of FRANKEN.

Marcobrunn

See Erbach

Markgräflerland (Bereich)

Minor district s. of Freiburg (BADEN). GUTEDEL wine. Drink very young.

Martinsthal Rhg. w. ★★→ ★★★ 71 73 74 75 76

Little-known neighbour of RAUENTHAL. Top v'yds.: Langenberg, Wildsau. Grosslage: Steinmacher.

Matuschka-Greiffenklau, Graf

Owner of the ancient SCHLOSS VOLLRADS estate.

Maximin Grünhaus M-S-R (Ruwer) w. ★★★★ 71 73 75 76

Supreme RUWER estate of 52 acres at Mertesdorf.

German wine bottles are too tall for most ice-buckets to cool the whole bottle. To make sure that the top of the bottle (your first glass) is properly cooled, put the bottle upside down in the bucket for the final five minutes before opening it.

Mennig M-S-R (Saar) w. ★★ 71 73 75 76

Village between TRIER and the SAAR. Its Falkensteiner v'yd. is famous.

Mertesdorf

See Maximin Grünhaus

Mittelheim Rhg. w. ★★→ ★★★ 71 72 73 74 75 76

Minor village between WINKEL and OESTRICH. Top grower: WEGELER. Grosslage: Honigberg.

Mittel-Haardt

The n. and best part of RHEINPFALZ, incl. FORST, DEIDESHEIM, etc.

Mittel-Mosel

The central and best part of the Mosel, incl. BERNKASTEL, PIESPORT, etc.

Mittelrhein

Northern Rhine area of secondary quality, incl. BACHARACH.

Morio Muskat

Stridently aromatic grape variety.

Moselblümchen

The "LIEBFRAUMILCH" of the Mosel, but on a lower quality level: TAFELWEIN not QbA.

Mosel-Saar-Ruwer

Huge wine area, incl. MITTEL-MOSEL, SAAR, RUWER and lesser areas.

Müller-Thurgau

Fruity, low-acid grape variety; the commonest in RHEINPFALZ and RHEINHESSEN, but increasingly planted in all areas.

Mumm, von

111-acre estate in JOHANNISBERG, RUDESHEIM, etc.

Munster Nahe w. ★→★★★ 71 72 73 75 76

Best village of n. NAHE. Top grower: State Domain. Grosslage: Schlosskapelle.

Nackenheim Rhh. w. ★→★★★ 71 72 73 75 76

Neighbour of NIERSTEIN; best wines (Engelsberg, Rothenberg) similar. Grosslages: Spiegelberg, Gutes Domtal.

Nahe

Tributary of the Rhine and quality wine region. Balanced, fresh and clean but full-flavoured wines. Two Bereichs: KREUZNACH and SCHLOSS BÖCKELHEIM.

Neef   M-S-R w. ★→ ★★ 71 73 75 76

Village of lower Mosel with one fine v'yd.: Frauenberg.

Neipperg, Graf

62-acre top WÜRTTEMBERG estate at Schwaigern.

Nell, von

40-acre family estate at TRIER and AYL, etc.

Neumagen-Dhron   M-M w. ★★→★★★ 71 73 75 76

Neighbour of PIESPORT. Top v'yd.: Hofberger. Grosslage: Michelsberg.

Neustadt

Central city of Rheinpfalz, with famous wine school.

Niederhausen   Na. w. ★★→ ★★★★ 71 72 73 74 75 76

Neighbour of SCHLOSS BÖCKELHEIM and H.Q. of Nahe State Domain. Wines of grace and power. Top v'yds. incl. Hermannshöhle, Steinberg. Grosslage: Burgweg.

Niedermennig

See Mennig

Niederwalluf

See Walluf

Nierstein (Bereich)

Large e. RHEINHESSEN district of very mixed quality.

Nierstein   Rhh. w. ★→★★★ 71 72 73 75 76

Famous but treacherous name. 1,300 acres incl. superb v'yds.: Hipping, Orbel, Pettenthal, etc., and their Grosslages Rehbach, Spiegelberg, Auflangen: ripe, racy wines. But beware Grosslage Gutes Domtal: no guarantee of anything.

Norheim   Nahe w. ★→★★★ 71 73 75 76

Neighbour of NIEDERHAUSEN. Top v'yds.: Klosterberg, Kafels, Kirschheck. Grosslage: Burgweg.

Oberemmel   M-S-R (Saar) w. ★★→★★★ 71 73 75 76

Next village to WILTINGEN. Very fine wines from Rosenberg, Hütte, etc. Grosslage: Scharzberg.

Obermosel (Bereich)

District name for the upper Mosel above TRIER. Generally poor wines from the Elbling grape.

Oberwalluf

See Walluf

Ockfen   M-S-R (Saar) w. ★★→★★★ 71 73 75 76

200-acre hill with superb fragrant austere wines. Top v'yds.: Bockstein, Herrenberg. Grosslage: Scharzberg.

Oechsle

Scale for sugar-content of grape-juice.

Oestrich   Rhg. w. ★★→★★★ 71 72 73 74 75 76

Big village; good but rarely top grade. V'yds. incl. Doosberg. Lenchen. Grosslage: Gottesthal.

Oppenheim   Rhh. w. ★→★★★ 71 72 73 75 76

Town just s. of NIERSTEIN, best wines (Kreuz, Sackträger, etc.) similar. Grosslages: Guldenmorgen (★★★) Krotenbrunnen (★★).

Originalabfüllung

Bottled by the grower. An obsolete term.

Ortenau (Bereich)

District just s. of Baden-Baden. Soft wines to drink young. Best village DURBACH.

Palatinate

English for RHEINPFALZ.

Pfalz

See Rheinpfalz

Perlwein
>Semi-sparkling wine.

Piesport   M-M w. ★★→★★★★ **71** 73 **75 76**
>Tiny village with famous amphitheatre of vines giving fine gentle fruity wine. Top v'yds.: Goldtröpfchen, Gunterslay, Falkenberg. Treppchen is on flatter land and inferior. Grosslage: Michelsberg.

Pokalwein
>Café wine. A pokal is a big glass.

Portugieser
>Second-rate red-wine grape.

Prädikat
>Special attributes or qualities. See QmP.

Prüfungsnummer
>The official identifying test-number of a quality wine.

Plettenberg, von
>Fine 100-acre Nahe estate at BAD KREUZNACH.

Prüm, J. J.
>Superlative 35-acre Mosel estate in WEHLEN, GRAACH, BERNKASTEL.

Qualitätswein bestimmter Anbaugebiete (QbA)
>The middle quality of German wine, with added sugar but strictly controlled as to grape areas, etc.

Qualitätswein mit Prädikat (QmP)
>Top category, incl. all wines ripe enough to be unsugared, from KABINETT to TROCKENBEERENAUSLESE.

Randersacker   Franc. w. ★★→★★★ **71** 72 73 **75 76**
>Leading village for distinctive dry wine. Top v'yds. incl. Teufelskeller. Grosslage: Ewig Leben.

Rauenthal   Rhg. w. ★★★→★★★★ **71** 72 73 **74 75 76**
>Supreme village for powerful spicy wine. Top v'yds. incl. Baiken, Gehrn, Wulfen. Grosslage: Steinmacher. The State Domain is an important grower.

Rautenstrauch Erben
>Owners of the splendid Karthäuserhof, EITELSBACH.

Rheinburgengau (Bereich)
>District name for the v'yds. of the MITTELRHEIN round the famous Rhine gorge. Moderate quality only.

Rheingau
>The best v'yd. region of the Rhine, near Wiesbaden. 5,000 acres. Classic, subtle but substantial RIESLING. Bereich name, JOHANNISBERG.

Rheinhessen
>Vast region (30,000 acres of v'yds.) between Mainz and the NAHE, mostly second-rate, but incl. NIERSTEIN, OPPENHEIM, etc.

Rheinpfalz
>Even vaster 35,000-acre v'yd. region s. of Rheinhessen. Wines inclined to sweetness. (See Mittel-Haardt and Südliche Weinstrasse.) This and the last are the chief sources of LIEBFRAUMILCH.

Rhodt
>Village of SÜDLICHE WEINSTRASSE with well-known co-operative. Agreeable fruity wines. Grosslage: Ordensgut.

Riesling
>The best German grape: fine, fragrant, fruity.

Ritter zu Groenesteyn, Baron
>Fine 37-acre estate in Kiedrich and Rüdesheim.

Roseewein
>Rosé wine.

Rotenfelser Bastei
>See Traisen

Rotwein

Red wine.

Rüdesheim Rhg. w. ★★→★★★ 71 *72 73* 74 **75 76**

Rhine resort with 650 acres of excellent v'yds.; the three best called Berg. . . . Full-bodied wines. Grosslage: Burgweg.

Rüdesheimer Rosengarten

Rüdesheim is also the name of a NAHE village near BAD KREUZNACH. Do not be misled by the ubiquitous blend going by this name. It has nothing to do with the great Rheingau Rüdesheim.

Ruländer

The PINOT GRIS: grape giving soft heavy wine.

Every wine-district has its own favourite pattern of glass for bringing out the character of the local product. For practical purposes at home, however, three shapes/sizes are enough. These three were designed by Professor Lord Queensberry of the Royal College of Art and the author for Ravenhead Glass as ideal glasses for, respectively, sherry/port, white wine/general purpose, fine red wines.

Ruppertsberg Rhpf. w. ★★→ ★★★ 71 *72 73* 74 **75 76**

Southern village of MITTEL-HAARDT. Top v'yds. incl. Gaisbohl, Hoheburg. Grosslage: Hofstück.

Ruwer

Tributary of Mosel near TRIER. Very fine delicate wines. Villages incl. EITELSBACH, MERTESDORF, KASEL.

Saar

Tributary of Mosel s. of RUWER. Brilliant austere wines. Villages incl. WILTINGEN, AYL, OCKFEN, SERRIG.

Saar-Ruwer (Bereich)

District incl. the two above.

St. Ursula

Well-known merchants at BINGEN.

Scharzberger

Grosslage name of WILTINGEN and neighbours.

Scharzhofberger Saar w. ★★★★ 71 73 **75 76**

Superlative 30-acre SAAR v'yd.: austerely beautiful wines, the perfection of RIESLING Do not confuse with the last.

Schaumwein

Sparkling wine.

Schillerwein

Light red or rosé QbA from WÜRTTEMBERG.

Scheurebe

Fruity aromatic grape used in RHEINPFALZ.

Schlossabzug

Bottled at the Schloss (castle).

Schloss Böckelheim Nahe w.★★→★★★★ 71 *72 73* 74 **75 76**

Village with the best NAHE v'yds., incl. Kupfergrübe, Felsenberg. Firm yet delicate wine. Grosslage: Burgweg.

Schloss Böckelheim (Bereich)

District name for the whole s. NAHE.

Schloss Johannisberg

Famous RHEINGAU estate of 66 acres belonging to the Metternich family. Polished, elegant wine.

Schloss Reinhartshausen
　　Fine 99-acre estate in ERBACH, HATTENHEIM, etc.
Schloss Vollrads　Rhg. w. ★★★→★★★★ 71 72 73 **75 76**
　　Great estate at WINKEL, since 1300. 81 acres producing
　　classical RHEINGAU RIESLING.
Schmitt, Gustav Adolf
　　Fine old 124-acre family estate at NIERSTEIN.
Schmitt, Franz Karl
　　Even older 74-acre ditto.
Schönborn, Graf von
　　One of the biggest and best Rheingau estates, based at
　　HATTENHEIM.
Schoppenwein
　　Café wine: i.e. wine by the glass.

---

*If anything is stable in a changing world it seems to be the business of
making and selling refreshment. According to The Guinness Book of
the Business World seven of the twelve oldest companies on earth are
either brewers or wine-growers. The oldest company is an Assyrian
bank, Egibi and Son, founded in 700 BC. Then come two Bavarian
breweries dating from 1040 and 1119. Sixth and seventh come
Clerget-Buffet et Fils and Raoul Clerget et Fils, both wine-growers at
Beaune, in Burgundy, both founded in 1270. Tenth comes the
Burgerspital zum Heiligen Geist, Würzburg wine-growers, founded
in 1319.*

Schubert, von
　　Owner of MAXIMIN GRÜNHAUS.
Schweigen　Rhpf. w. ★→ ★★ 73 74 **75 76**
　　Southernmost Rheinpfalz village with big co-operative.
　　DEUTSCHES WEINTOR: Grosslage: Guttenberg.
Sekt
　　German (QbA) sparkling wine.
Serrig　M-S-R (Saar) w. ★★→★★★ 71 73 **75 76**
　　Village known for "steely" wine, excellent in hot years. Top
　　growers: VEREINIGTE HOSPITIEN and State Domain. Gross-
　　lage: Scharzberg.
Sichel H., Sohne
　　Famous wine-merchants of London and Mainz.
Silvaner
　　Common German white grape, best in FRANKEN.
Simmern, von
　　94-acre family estate at HATTENHEIM since 1464 and in ELT-
　　VILLE, RAUENTHAL, etc.
Sonnenuhr
　　"Sun-dial." Name of several famous v'yds., esp. one at
　　WEHLEN.
Spätburgunder
　　PINOT NOIR: the best red-wine grape in Germany.
Spätlese
　　"Late gathered." One better (stronger or sweeter) than
　　KABINETT.
Spindler
　　Fine 33-acre family estate at FORST, Rheinpfalz.
Staatsweingut (or Staatliche Weinbaudomäne)
　　The State wine estate or domain.
Steigerwald (Bereich)
　　District name for e. part of FRANKEN.
Steinberg　Rhg. w. ★★★→★★★★ 71 72 73 74 **75 76**
　　Famous 62-acre v'yd. at HATTENHEIM walled by Cistercians
　　700 yrs. ago. Now property of the State.

Steinwein

Wine from WÜRZBURG's best v'yd., Stein. Loosely used for all Franconian wine.

Stuttgart

Chief city of WÜRTTEMBERG, producer of some pleasant wines, not exported.

Südliche Weinstrasse (Bereich)

District name for the s. RHEINPFALZ.

Tafelwein

"Table wine." The vin ordinaire of Germany. Can be blended with other EEC wines. But Deutscher Tafelwein must come from Germany alone.

Thanisch, Dr.

32-acre BERNKASTEL family estate, incl. part of Doktor v'yd.

Traben-Trarbach M-M w. ★★ 73 75 76

Secondary wine-town, some good light wines. Top v'yds. incl. Schlossberg, Ungsberg. Grosslage: Schwarzlay.

Traisen Na. w. ★★★ 71 72 73 74 75 76

Small village incl. superlative Bastei v'yd., making wine of great concentration and class.

Traminer

See Gewürztraminer

Trier M-S-R w. ★★→★★★★

Important wine city of Roman origin, on the Mosel, adjacent to RUWER, now incl. AVELSBACH and EITELSBACH. Grosslage: Römerlay.

Trittenheim M-M w. ★★ →★★★ 71 73 75 76

Attractive light wines. Top v'yds.: Apotheke, Altärchen. Grosslage: Michelsberg.

Trocken

Dry. On labels Trocken *alone* means dry enough for diabetics. But see next entry.

Trockenbeerenauslese

The sweetest and most expensive category of wine, made from selected withered grapes. See also Edelfäule.

Trollinger

Common red grape of WÜRTTEMBERG: poor quality.

Urzig M-M w. ★★★ 71 73 75 76

Village famous for lively spicy wine. Top v'yd.: Würzgarten. Grosslage: Schwarzlay.

Vereinigte Hospitien

"United Hospitals." Ancient charity with large holdings in SERRIG, WILTINGEN, TRIER, PIESPORT, etc.

Verwaltung

Property.

Villa Sachsen

75-acre BINGEN estate belonging to ST. URSULA Weingut.

Wachenheim Rhpf. w. ★★★ →★★★★ 71 72 73 74 75 76

840 acres, incl. exceptionally fine Rieslings. V'yds. incl. Gerümpel, Böhlig, Rechbächel, etc. Top grower: Bürklin-Wolf. Grosslages: Schenkenbohl, Schnepfenflug, Mariengarten.

Waldrach M-S-R (Ruwer) w. ★★ 73 75 76

Some charming light wines. Grosslage: (Trierer) Römerlay.

Walluf Rhg. w. ★★ 73 75 76

Neighbour of ELTVILLE; formerly Nieder- and Ober-Walluf. Good but not top wines. Grosslage: Steinmacher.

Walporzheim-Ahrtal (Bereich)

District name for the whole AHR valley.

Wawern M-S-R (Saar) w. ★★→★★★ 71 73 75 76

Small village with fine Rieslings. Grosslage: Scharzberg.

Wegeler Erben

138-acre Rheingau estate owned by DEINHARD's. V'yds. in OESTRICH, MITTELHEIM, WINKEL, GEISENHEIM, RÜDESHEIM, etc.

Wehlen   M-M w. ★★★ → ★★★★ 71 72 73 75 76

Neighbour of BERNKASTEL with equally fine, somewhat richer, wine. Best v'yd.: Sonnenuhr. Top growers: Prüm family. Grosslage: Münzlay.

Weil, Dr.

45-acre private estate at KIEDRICH. Very fine wines.

Weingut

Wine estate.

Weinkellerei

Wine cellars or winery.

Weinstrasse

"Wine road." Scenic route through v'yds. Germany has several, the most famous in RHEINPFALZ.

Weintor

See Schweigen

Weissherbst

Rosé of QbA standard, speciality of BADEN and WÜRTTEMBERG.

Werner, Domdechant

Fine 32-acre family estate at HOCHHEIM.

Wiltingen   Saar w. ★★ → ★★★★ 71 73 75 76

The centre of the Saar. 330 acres. Beautiful subtle austere wine. Top v'yds. incl. SCHARZHOFBERG, Braune Kupp, Braunfels, Klosterberg. Grosslage (for the whole Saar): Scharzberg.

Winkel   Rhg. w. ★★★ → ★★★★ 71 72 73 74 75 76

Village famous for fragrant, elegant wine, incl. SCHLOSS VOLLRADS. Other v'yds. incl. Hasensprung, Jesuitengarten. Grosslage: Hönigberg.

Wintrich   M-M w. ★★ → ★★★ 71 73 75 76

Neighbour of PIESPORT; similar wines. Top v'yds.: Grosser Herrgott, Ohligsberg, Sonnenseite. Grosslage: Kurfürstlay.

Winzergenossenschaft

Wine-growers' co-operative, often making good and reasonably priced wine.

Winzerverein

The same as the last.

Wonnegau (Bereich)

District name for s. RHEINHESSEN.

Worms   Rhh. w. ★★

City with the famous LIEBFRAUENSTIFT v'yd.

Württemberg

Vast s. area with scattered v'yds. of secondary quality.

Würzburg   Frank. ★★ → ★★★★ 71 72 73 75 76

Great baroque city on the Main, centre of Franconian (FRANKEN) wine: fine, full-bodied and dry. Top v'yds.: Stein, Leiste, Schlossberg. No Grosslage. See also Maindreieck (Bereich).

Zell   M-S-R w. ★ → ★★ 73 75 76

Lower Mosel village famous for its Grosslage name Schwartze Katz ("Black Cat"). No fine wines.

Zell (Bereich)

District name for the whole lower Mosel from Zell to Koblenz.

Zeltingen-Rachtig   M-M w. ★★ → ★★★★ 71 73 75 76

Important Mosel village next to WEHLEN. Typically lively but full-bodied wine. Top v'yds.: Sonnenuhr, Schlossberg. Grosslage: Münzlay.

Switzerland

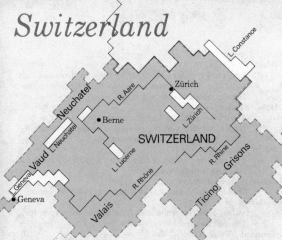

Switzerland has some of the world's most efficient and productive vineyards. Costs are high and nothing less is viable. All the most important are lined along the south-facing slopes of the upper Rhône valley and Lake Geneva, respectively the Valais and the Vaud. Wines are known both by place-names, grape-names, and legally controlled type-names. All three, with those of leading growers and merchants, appear in the following list. On the whole, D.Y.A.

Aigle   Vaud w. dr. ★★
> Principal town of CHABLAIS, between La. Geneva and the VALAIS. Dry whites of transitional style: at best strong and well balanced.

Amigne
> Traditional white grape of the VALAIS. Heavy but tasty wine, usually made dry.

Arvine
> Another old VALAIS white grape, similar to the last; perhaps better. Makes good dessert wine.

Auvernier   Neuchâtel r. p. w. dr. (sp.) ★★
> Village s. of NEUCHÂTEL known for PINOT NOIR, CHASSELAS and OEIL DE PERDRIX.

Blauburgunder
> One of the names given to the form of PINOT NOIR grown in German Switzerland.

Bonvin
> Old-established growers and merchants at SION.

Chablais   Vaud (r.) w. dr. ★★
> The district between Montreux on La. Geneva and Martigny where the Rhône leaves the VALAIS. Good DORIN wines. Best villages: AIGLE, YVORNE, Bex.

Chasselas
> The principal white grape of Switzerland, neutral in flavour but taking local character. Known as FENDANT in VALAIS, DORIN in VAUD and PERLAN round Geneva.

Clevner (or Klevner)
> Another name for BLAUBURGUNDER.

Cortaillod   Neuchâtel r. (p. w.) ★★
> Village near NEUCHÂTEL specializing in light PINOT NOIR reds.

Côte, La
> The n. shore of La. Geneva between Geneva and Lausanne. Pleasant DORIN and SALVAGNIN. Best villages incl. Féchy and Rolle.

Dézaley Vaud w. dr. ★★★

    Best-known village of LAVAUX, between Lausanne and Montreux. Steep s. slopes to the lake make fine fruity DORIN. Dézaley-Marsens is equally good.

Dôle Valais r. ★★

    Term for red VALAIS wine of PINOT NOIR or GAMAY or both grapes, reaching a statutory level of strength and quality. Often pleasing but never exciting.

Dorin Vaud w. dr. ★→★★

    The name for CHASSELAS wine in the VAUD, the equivalent of FENDANT from the VALAIS.

Epesses Vaud w. dr. ★★

    Well-known lakeside village of LAVAUX. Good dry DORIN.

Ermitage

    VALAIS name for white wine from MARSANNE grapes. Rich, concentrated and heavy; usually dry.

Fendant Valais w. dr. ★→★★★

    The name for CHASSELAS wine in the VALAIS, where it reaches its ripest and strongest. SION is the centre.

Glacier, vin du

    Almost legendary long-matured white stored at high altitudes. Virtually extinct today.

Goron Valais r. ★

    Red VALAIS wine that fails to reach the DÔLE standard.

Herrschaft Grisons r. (w. sw.) ★→★★★

    Small wine district near the border of Austria and Lichtenstein. Light PINOT NOIR reds and a few sweet whites, in tiny quantities.

Humagne

    Rare old VALAIS grape. Some red Humagne is sold: decent country wine. Apparently there was formerly white as well.

Johannisberg

    The Valais name for SYLVANER, which makes pleasant soft dry wine here.

Lavaux Vaud r. w. dr. ★→★★★

    The n. shore of La. Geneva between Lausanne and Montreux. The e. half of the VAUD. Best villages incl. DÉZALEY, EPESSES, Villette, Lutry, ST-SAPHORIN.

Légèrement doux

    Most Swiss wines are dry. Any with measurable sugar must be labelled thus or as "avec sucre residuel".

Malvoisie

    VALAIS name for PINOT GRIS.

Mandement Geneva r. (p.) w. dr. ★

    Wine district just w. of Geneva, centred on Satigny (see Vin-Union-Genève). Very light reds, chiefly GAMAY, and whites (PERLAN).

Marsanne

    The white grape of Hermitage on the French Rhône, used in the VALAIS to make ERMITAGE.

Merlot

    Bordeaux red grape (see Grapes for red wine) used to make the better wine of Italian Switzerland (TICINO). See also Viti.

Mont d'Or, Domaine du Valais w. dr. sw. ★★★★

    The best wine estate of Switzerland: 60 acres of steep hillside near SION. Good FENDANT, JOHANNISBERG, AMIGNE, etc., and Switzerland's only real Riesling. Very rich concentrated wines.

Neuchâtel Neuchâtel r. p. w. dr. sp. ★→★★★

    City of n.w. Switzerland and the wine from the n. shore of its lake. Pleasant light PINOT NOIR and attractive sometimes sparkling CHASSELAS.

Nostrano

Word meaning "ours" applied to the lesser red wine of the TICINO, made from a mixture of native and Italian grapes, in contrast to MERLOT from Bordeaux.

Oeil de Perdrix

Pale rosé of PINOT NOIR.

Orsat

Important and reliable wine firm at Martigny, VALAIS.

Perlan Geneva w. dr. ★

The MANDEMENT name for the ubiquitous CHASSELAS, here at its palest, driest and least impressive.

Premier Cru

Any wine from the maker's own estate can call itself this.

Provins

One of the best-known producers of VALAIS wine.

Rivaz Vaud r. w. dr. ★★

Well-known village of LAVAUX.

St-Saphorin Vaud w. dr. ★★

One of the principal villages of LAVAUX: wines drier and more austere than DÉZALEY or EPESSES.

Salvagnin Vaud r. ★→★★

Red VAUD wine of tested quality: the equivalent of DÔLE from the VALAIS.

Savagnin

Swiss name for the TRAMINER, called Païen in the VALAIS.

Schafiser Bern (r.) w. dr. ★→★★

The n. shore of La. Bienne (Bielersee) is well known for light CHASSELAS sold as either Schafiser or Twanner.

Sion Valais w. dr. ★→★★★

Centre of the VALAIS wine region, famous for its FENDANT.

Spätburgunder

PINOT NOIR; by far the commonest grape of German Switzerland, making very light wines.

Testuz

Well-known growers and merchants at Cully, LAVAUX.

Ticino

Italian-speaking s. Switzerland. See Merlot, Viti and Nostrano.

Twanner

See Schafiser

Valais

The Rhône valley between Brig and Martigny. Its n. side is an admirable dry sunny and sheltered v'yd., planted mainly, alas, to the second-rate CHASSELAS grape, which here makes its best wine.

Vaud

The region of La. Geneva. Its n. shore is Switzerland's biggest v'yd. and in places as good as any. DORIN and SALVAGNIN are the main wines.

Vétroz Valais (r.) w. dr. ★★

Village near SION in the best part of the VALAIS.

Vevey

Town near Montreux with a famous wine festival once every 30-odd years, 1977 included.

Vin-Union-Genève

Big growers' co-operative at Satigny in the MANDEMENT. Light reds and white PERLAN are Geneva's local wine.

Viti Ticino r. ★★

Legal designation of better-quality TICINO red, made of MERLOT and at least 12% alcohol.

Yvorne

Village near AIGLE with some of the best CHABLAIS v'yds.

Italy

Piemonte **Piem**
•Turin
Mila
Liguria **Lig**

Italy is the world's biggest wine producer with the biggest per capita consumption: 150 bottles a year. She is so at home with wine that she can seem alarmingly casual about it. A sense of humour is as important as a corkscrew to anyone who steps off the well-beaten track.

The chief clue to Italian wine is the DOC system, an approximate equivalent of France's Appellations Controlées, which has been taking shape since the 1960s. Most of Italy's worthwhile wines now have defined areas and standards under the new system. A few, like Chianti Classico, it must be said, had them long before. A few, however, have not—and DOCs have been granted to many areas of only local interest: so the mere existence of a DOC proves little. The entries in this book ignore a score of unimportant DOCs and include a dozen or so non-DOCs.

They also include a large number of grape-name entries. Italian wines are named in a variety of ways: some geographical like French wines, some historical, some folklorical, and many of the best from their grapes. These include old "native" grapes such as Barbera and Sangiovese and more and more imported "international" grapes from France and Germany. Many of the DOCs, particularly in the north-east, are area names applying to widely different wines from as many as a dozen different varieties. No overall comment on the quality of such a diversity is really possible.

Another rather disconcerting aspect of Italian wine is clear from the following pages: in many cases the same name applies to wine which can be red or white or in between, sweet or dry or in between, still or sparkling or in between. This must be taken into account when interpreting the necessarily cryptic grades of quality and vintage notes. Vintage notes are given when specific information has been available. You are unlikely to be faced with a wide choice in any case. Where there is no comment the best plan is to aim for the youngest available white wine and experiment with the oldest available red . . . within reason.

The map opposite is the key to the province-names used for locating each entry.

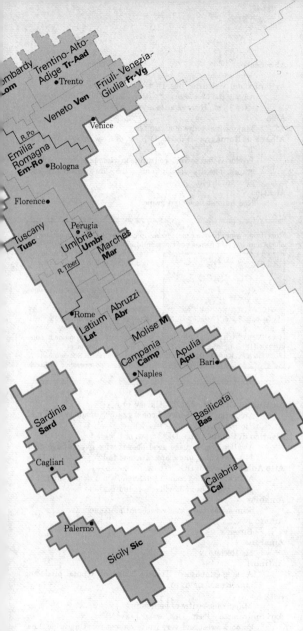

Lombardy **Lom**

Trentino-Alto-Adige **Tr-Aad**
•Trento

Friuli-Venezia-Giulia **Fr-Vg**

Veneto **Ven**

•Venice

R. Po

Emilia-Romagna **Em-Ro**
•Bologna

Florence•

Tuscany **Tusc**

Perugia•
Umbria **Umbr**

Marches **Mar**

R. Tiber

Abruzzi **Abr**

•Rome
Latium **Lat**

Molise **M**

Campania **Camp**

Apulia **Apu**

Bari•

•Naples

Sardinia **Sard**

Basilicata **Bas**

Cagliari

Calabria **Cal**

Palermo•

Sicily **Sic**

Abbreviations of regional names
shown in bold type are used in
the text.

Abboccato
    Semi-sweet.

Aglianico del Vulture   Bas. DOC r. (s/sw. sp.) ★★★ **70 71 73**
    Among the best wines of s. Italy. Ages well. Called Vecchio
    after 3 yrs., Riserva after 5 yrs.

Alba
    Major wine-centre of PIEMONTE.

Albana di Romagna   Em-Ro. DOC w. dr. s/sw. (sp.) ★★ **71 73 74
76**
    Produced for several centuries in Romagna from Albana
    grapes. The dry slightly tannic, the semi-sweet fruity with
    pleasant depth.

Aleatico
    Red muscat-flavoured grape.

Most Italian wines have a simple name, in contrast to the combination village and vineyard names of France and Germany.

> **SOAVE**
> **CLASSICO**
>
> VINO A DENOMINAZIONE DI
> ORIGINE CONTROLLATA
>
> IMBOTTIGLIATO DAL
> PRODUTTORE ALL ORIGINE
> CANTINA SOCIALE DI SOAVE

Soave is the name of this wine. It is qualified only by the word Classico, a legal term for the central (normally the best) part of many of the long-established wine regions. "Denominazione di Origine Controllata" is the official guarantee of authenticity. Imbottigliato . . . all origine means bottled by the producer. Cantina Sociale di Soave means the growers' co-operative of Soave.

Aleatico di Gradoli   Lat. DOC r. sw. or f. ★★
    Aromatic, fresh, fruity, alcohol 12–15%, made in the Pr. of
    Viterbo.

Aleatico di Puglia   Apu. DOC r. sw. or f. ★★
    Aleatico grapes make good dessert wine over a large area.
    14% alcohol or more, aromatic and full.

Alto Adige   Tr-AAd. DOC r. p. w. dr. sw. sp. ★★
    A DOC covering some 17 different wines named after their
    grape varieties in 33 villages round Bolzano.

Amabile
    Semi-sweet, but usually sweeter than ABBOCCATO.

Amaro
    Bitter.

Amarone
    See Recioto

Antinori
    A long-established Tuscan house of repute producing
    CHIANTI and ORVIETO.

Asti
    Major wine-centre of PIEMONTE.

Asti Spumante   Piem. DOC w. sp. ★★★ NV
    Famous sweet and very fruity muscat sparkling wine. Low
    in alcohol.

Barbacarlo (Oltrepo' Pavese)   Lomb. DOC r. dr. or sw. ★★ **70 71
73 76**
    Delicately flavoured with bitter after-taste, made in the
    Com. of Broni in the Pr. of Pavia.

Barbaresco   Piem. DOC r. dr. ★★★ **68 69 70 71** 74
    Neighbour of BAROLO from same grapes but lighter, ageing
    sooner. At best subtle and fine. At 3 yrs. becomes Riserva.

Barbera

Dark acidic Piemonte red grape, giving its name to:

Barbera d'Alba Piem. DOC r. dr. ⋆⋆ **71 73** 74

Round ALBA other grapes are added. Clean, tasty, fragrant red improves for 3-4 yrs.

Barbera d'Asti Piem. DOC r. dr. (s/sw.) ⋆⋆ **71 73** 74

The best of the Barberas; all Barbera grapes; dark, grapy and appetizing. Ages up to 7-8 yrs.

Barbera del Monferrato Piem. DOC r. dr. (s/sw.) ⋆ **71 73** 74

From a large area in the Pr. of Alessandria and ASTI. Pleasant, slightly fizzy, sometimes sweetish.

Bardolino Ven. DOC r. dr. (p.) ⋆⋆ D.Y.A.

Pale, light, slightly bitter red from e. shore of La. Garda. Sometimes quickly taken off the skins to make v. pale B. Chiaretto.

Barolo Piem. DOC r. dr. ⋆⋆⋆ **65 67** 70 71 74

Small area s. of Turin with one of the best Italian red wines, dark, rich, alcoholic (minimum 12°), dry but deep in flavour. From NEBBIOLO grapes. Ages for up to 15 yrs.

Bertani

Well-known producers of quality Veronese wines (VALPOLICELLA, SOAVE, etc.).

Bertolli, Francesco

Among the best-known producers of CHIANTI CLASSICO. Cellars at Castellina in Chianti, n. of Siena.

Bianco

White.

Bigi

Famous producers of ORVIETO and other wines of Umbria and Tuscany.

Boca Piem. DOC r. dr. ⋆⋆ **69 70** 71 74

From same grape as BAROLO in n. of PIEMONTE, Pr. of Novara.

Bolla

Famous Veronese firm producing VALPOLICELLA, SOAVE, etc.

Bonarda

Minor red grape widely grown in PIEMONTE and Lombardy.

Bonarda (Oltrepo' Pavese) Lomb. DOC r. dr. ⋆⋆ **71 73 74**

Soft, fresh, pleasant red from s. of Pavia.

Bosca

Wine-producers from PIEMONTE known for their ASTI SPUMANTE and Vermouths.

Botticino Lomb. DOC r. dr. ⋆ **70 72** 73 74

Strong, full-bodied red from Brescia.

Brachetto d'Acqui Piem. DOC r. sw. (sp.) ⋆ **71 74**

Sweet sparkling red with pleasant muscat aroma.

Brolio

The oldest (c. 1200) and most famous CHIANTI CLASSICO estate.

Brunello di Montalcino Tusc. DOC r. dr. ⋆⋆⋆⋆ **55 61 64** 66 67 70 73 75

Italy's most expensive wine. Strong, full-bodied, high-flavoured and long-lived. After 5 yrs. is called Riserva. Produced for over a century 15 miles s. of Siena.

Cabernet

Bordeaux grape much used in n.e. Italy. See place names, e.g.:

Cabernet di Pramaggiore Ven. DOC r. dr. ⋆⋆ **71** 73 75

Good, herb-scented, rather tannic, middle-weight red. Riserva after 3 yrs.

Calcinaia

First-class CHIANTI CLASSICO estate for centuries in the Caponi family.

Caldaro or Lago di Caldaro Tr-AAd. DOC r. dr. ★★ 72 73 74 75
> Light, soft, slightly bitter-almond red. Classico from a smaller area is better. From s. of Bolzano.

Calissano
> A long-established House of PIEMONTE producing ASTI SPUMANTE, Vermouths and red wines of that region.

Caluso Passito Piem. DOC w. sw. (f.) ★★ 64 70 71 74
> Made from selected Erbaluce grapes left to partly dry; delicate scent, velvety taste. From a large area in the Pr. of Turin and Vercelli.

Cannonau di Sardegna Sard. DOC r. dr. or s/sw. (f.) ★★ 68 70 72 73
> One of the good wines of the island capable of ageing.

Cantina
> 1. Cellar or winery. 2. Cantina Sociale = growers' co-op.

Capri
> Widely abused name of the famous island in the Bay of Naples. No guarantee of quality.

Carema Piem. DOC r. dr. ★★ 70 71 73 74
> Old speciality of Val d'Aosta. NEBBIOLO grapes fermented Beaujolais-style before crushing. (See France: Macération carbonique.)

Carmignano Tusc. DOC r. dr. ★★→★★★
> Section of CHIANTI using CABERNET to make good wine.

Casa fondata nel . . .
> Firm founded in . . .

Castel del Monte Apu. DOC r. p. w. dr. ★★ 68 69 73 74 75
> Dry, fresh, well-balanced southern wines. The red becomes Riserva after 3 yrs.

Cellatica Lomb. DOC r. dr. ★★ 72 73 75
> Light red with slightly bitter after-taste, from the Pr. of Brescia.

Chianti Tusc. DOC r. dr. 〔★★〕 70 71 74 75 76
> The lively local wine of Florence. Fresh but warmly fruity when young, usually sold in straw-covered flasks. Ages moderately. Montalbano, Rufina and Colli Fiorentini, Senesi, Aretini, Pisane are sub-districts.

Chianti Classico Tusc. DOC r. dr. 〔★★★〕 69 70 71 74 75
> Senior Chianti from the central area. Many estates make fine powerful scented wine. Riservas (after 3 yrs.) often have the bouquet of age in oak.

Cinque Terre Lig. DOC w. dr. or sw. or pa. ★★★
> Fragrant, fruity white made for centuries near La Spezia. The PASSITO is known as Sciacchetra.

Cinzano
> A Vermouth company also known for its ASTI SPUMANTE from PIEMONTE.

Ciro Cal. DOC r. (p. w.) dr. ★★ 70 71 73 74
> The wine of the ancient Olympic games. Very strong red, fruity white (to drink young).

Classico
> Term for wines from a restricted, usually central, area within the limits of a DOC. By implication, and often in practice, the best of the region.

Clastidio Lomb. r. (p.) w. dr. ★★ 70 71 73
> Pleasant, sour touch to the white. Full, slightly tannic to the red.

Collavini, Cantina
> High-quality producers of GRAVE DEL FRIULI wines: PINOT GRIGIO, RIESLING, MERLOT, PINOT NERO, etc.

Colli
> Means "hills" in many wine-names.

Colli Albani Lat. DOC w. dr. or s/sw. (sp.) ⋆⋆ **73 75**
Soft fruity wine of the Roman hills.

Colli Euganei Ven. DOC r. w. dr. or s/sw. (sp.) ⋆⋆ **72 73** 75
A DOC applicable to 3 wines produced s.w. of Padua. The red is scarcely memorable, the white soft and pleasant. The table wine of Venice.

Colli Orientali del Friuli Fr-VG. DOC r. w. dr. or sw. ⋆ **70 72 73 74 75**
12 different wines are produced under this DOC on the hills e. of Udine and named after their grapes.

Colli Goriziano Fr-VG. DOC r. w. dr. ⋆⋆ **71 72 74** 75
Ten different wines named after their grapes from a small area w. of Gorizia nr. the Jugoslav border.

Contratto
Piemonte firm known for BAROLO, ASTI SPUMANTE, etc.

Cora
A leading House producing ASTI SPUMANTE and Vermouth from PIEMONTE.

Cortese di Gavi Piem. DOC w. dr. (sp.) ⋆⋆ D.Y.A.
Delicate fresh white from between Alessandria and Genoa.

Cortese (Oltrepo' Pavese) Lomb. DOC w. dr. ⋆ D.Y.A.
The same from w. Lombardy.

Corvo Sic. r. w. dr. ⋆⋆
Popular Sicilian wines. Sound dry red, pleasant soft white.

Dolce
Sweet.

Dolceacqua
See Rossese di Dolceacqua

Dolcetto
Common red grape of PIEMONTE, giving its name to:

Dolcetto d'Acqui Piem. DOC r. dr. ⋆ D.Y.A.
Good standard table wine from s. of ASTI.

Dolcetto d'Alba Piem. DOC r. dr. ⋆⋆ **71** 74
Among the best Dolcetti, with a trace of bitter-almond.

Dolcetto d'Asti Piem. DOC r. dr. ⋆ D.Y.A.

Donnaz Vd'A. DOC dr. ⋆⋆
A mountain NEBBIOLO, fragrant, pale and faintly bitter. Aged for a statutory 3 yrs.

Donnici Cal. DOC r. (p.) dr. ⋆
Middle-weight southern red from Cosenza.

Elba Tusc. r. w. dr. (sp.) ⋆ **70 71 73**
The island's white is better: admirable with fish.

Enfer d'Arvier Vd'A. DOC r. dr. ⋆⋆
An Alpine speciality: pale, pleasantly bitter, light red.

Erbaluce di Caluso Piem. DOC w. dr. ⋆ **74 75 76**
Pleasant fresh hot-weather wine.

Est! Est!! Est!!! Lat. DOC w. dr. or s/sw. ⋆⋆ D.Y.A.
Famous soft fruity white from La. Bolsena, n. of Rome. The name is more remarkable than the wine.

Etna Sic. DOC r. p. w. dr. ⋆⋆ **67 68 70 73** 74 75
Wine from the volcanic slopes. The red is warm, full, balanced and ages very well; the white is delicate and distinctly grapy.

Falerio dei Colli Ascolani Mar. DOC w. dr. ⋆
Made in the Pr. of Ascoli Piceno, pleasant, fresh, fruity; a wine for the summer.

Falerno Camp. r. w. dr. ⋆
One of the best-known wines of ancient times, but nothing special today. Strong red, fruity white.

Fara Piem. DOC r. dr. ⋆⋆ **67 70 71 74**
Good NEBBIOLO wine from Novara, n. PIEMONTE. Fragrant; worth ageing. Small production.

Faro Sic. r. dr. ★★ **73 75**

Sound strong Sicilian red, made in sight of the Straits of Messina.

Fazi-Battaglia

Well-known producer of VERDICCHIO, etc.

Ferrari

Firm making Italy's best dry sparkling wine by the champagne method nr. Trento, Trentino-Alto Adige.

Fontana Candida

One of the best producers of FRASCATI.

Fontanafredda

Leading producer of Piemontese wines, incl. BAROLO.

Fracia Lomb. DOC r. dr. ★★ **70 71 73** 75

Good light but fragrant red from Valtellina.

Franciacorta Pinot Lomb. DOC w. dr. (sp.) ★★

Agreeable soft white made of PINOT BIANCO.

Franciacorta Rosso Lomb. DOC r. dr. ★★ **70 73 74** 75

Lightish red of mixed CABERNET and BARBERA from Brescia.

Frascati Lat. DOC w. dr. s/sw. sw. (sp.) ★★ **73** 75

Best-known wine of the Roman hills: soft, ripe, golden, tasting of whole grapes. The sweet is known as Cannellino.

Frecciarossa Lomb. r. w. dr. ★★ **69 70 71 73** 75

Sound wines produced nr. Casteggio in the Oltrepo' Pavese; the white is better known.

Freisa d'Asti Piem. DOC r. s/sw. or sw. (sp.) ★★ **70 71** 73 74

Sweet, often sparkling red, said to taste of raspberries and roses.

Gambellara Ven. DOC w. dr. or s/sw. (sp.) ★ **72** 75

Neighbour of SOAVE. Dry wine similar. Sweet (known as RECIOTO DI GAMBELLARA) agreeably fruity.

Gancia

Famous Vermouth House from PIEMONTE, also produces ASTI SPUMANTE.

Gattinara Piem. DOC r. dr. ★★★ **68 69 70** 74

Excellent big-scale BAROLO-type red from n. PIEMONTE. Made from NEBBIOLO, locally known as Spanna.

Ghemme Piem. DOC r. dr. ★★ **70 71** 73 74

Neighbour of GATTINARA, a shade less full and fine.

Gradi

Degrees (of alcohol) i.e. percent by volume.

Grave del Friuli Fr-VG. DOC r. w. dr. ★★ **71 72 73** 75

A DOC covering 7 different wines named after their grapes, from near the Jugoslav border.

Greco di Tufo Camp. DOC w. dr. s/sw. ★★ **73 74 75**

One of the best whites of the south, fruity and slightly bitter.

Grignolino d'Asti Piem. DOC r. dr. ★ **71 73 74**

Pleasant lively standard wine of PIEMONTE.

Grumello Lomb. DOC r. dr. ★★ **70 71** 73 75

NEBBIOLO wine from Valtellina, can be soft, delicate and fine.

Gutturnio dei Colli Piacentini Em-Ro. DOC r. dr. (s/sw.) ★★ **64 70** 71 74

Full-bodied wine of character from the hills of Piacenza. Named after a large Roman drinking cup.

Inferno Lomb. DOC r. dr. ★★ **68 70** 73 75

Similar to GRUMELLO and like it classified as VALTELLINA Superiore.

Ischia Camp. DOC (r.) w. dr. ★ **70 71 75**

The wine of the island off Naples. The slightly sharp white is best.

Isonzo Fr-VG. DOC r. w. dr. ★

DOC covering 10 varietal wines in the extreme n.e.

Kalterersee
German name for LAGO DI CALDARO.

Lacrima Cristi del Vesuvio Camp. r. p. w. (f.) dr. (sw.) ★ **70 71 73** 74
Famous but frankly ordinary wines in great variety from the slopes of Mount Vesuvius.

Lago di Caldaro
See Caldaro

Lagrein del Trentino Tr-AAd. DOC r. dr. ★★ **71** 74 75
Lagrein is a Tyrolean grape with a bitter twist. Good fruity light wine.

Lamberti
Producers of SOAVE, VALPOLICELLA and BARDOLINO at Lazise on the e. shore of La. Garda.

Lambrusco di Sorbara Em-Ro. DOC r. dr. or s/sw. sp. ★★★ **73 74** 75
Bizarre but popular fizzy red from near Modena.

Lambrusco Grasparossa di Castelvetro Em-Ro. DOC r. dr. or s/sw. sp. ★★ **73 74** 75
Similar to above. Highly scented, pleasantly acidic; often drunk with rich food.

Lambrusco Salamino di Santa Croce Em-Ro. DOC r. dr. or s/sw. sp. ★ **71 75**
Similar to above. Fruity smell, high acidity and a thick "head".

Langhe
The hills of central PIEMONTE.

Latisana Fr-VG. DOC r. w. dr. ★★
DOC for 7 varietal wines from some 50 miles n.e. of Venice.

Locorotondo Apu. DOC w. dr. ★ D.Y.A.
A pleasantly fresh southern white.

Lugana Lomb. DOC w. dr. ★★★ **74 76**
One of the best white wines of s. La. Garda: fragrant and delicate.

Malvasia
Important white or red grape for luscious wines, incl. Madeira's Malmsey. Used all over Italy.

Malvasia di Bosa Sard. DOC w. dr. sw. or f. ★★
A wine of character. Strong and aromatic with a slightly bitter after-taste. A liquoroso (fortified) version is best.

Malvasia di Cagliari Sard. DOC w. dr. s/sw. or sw. (f. dr. s.) ★★
Interesting strong Sardinian wine, fragrant and slightly bitter.

Malvasia di Casorzo d'Asti Piem. DOC r. p. sw. sp. ★★ **68 71**
Fragrant grapy sweet red, sometimes sparkling.

Malvasia di Castelnuovo Don Bosco Piem. DOC r. sw. (sp.) ★★
Peculiar method of interrupted fermentation gives very sweet aromatic red.

Malvasia delle Lipari Sic. DOC w. sw. (pa. f.) ★★★ **70 73**
Among the very best Malvasias, aromatic and rich, produced on the Lipari or Aeolian Islands n. of Sicily.

Malvasia di Nus Vd'A. w. dr. ★★★
Rare Alpine white, with a deep bouquet of honey. Small production and high reputation. Can age remarkably well.

Mamertino Sic. w. s/sw. ★★ **70 73 74 75**
Made near Messina since Roman times. Sweet-scented, rich in glycerine. Mentioned several times by Caesar in the *De Bello Gallico*.

Manduria (Primitivo di) Apu. DOC r. s/sw. (f. dr. or sw.) ★★
Heady red, naturally strong but often fortified. From nr. Taranto.

Mantonico Cal. w. sw. f. ★★

Fruity deep amber dessert wine from Reggio Calabria. Can age remarkably well. Named from the Greek for "prophetic".

Marino Lat. DOC w. dr. or s/sw. ★★ **73 75**

A neighbour of FRASCATI with similar wine.

Marsala Sic. DOC br. dr. s/sw. or sw. f. ★★★ NV

Dark sherry-type wine invented by the Woodhouse Brothers from Liverpool in 1773; excellent aperitif or for dessert. The dry ("virgin") made by the solera system.

Marsala Speciali

These are Marsalas with added flavours of egg, almond, strawberry, etc.

Martinafranca Apu. DOC w. dr. ★ D.Y.A.

Agreeable but rather neutral southern white.

Martini & Rossi

Well known vermouth House also famous for its fine wine museum in Pessione, PIEMONTE.

Marzemino (del Trentino) Tr-AAd. DOC r. dr. ★ **71 74 75**

Pleasant local red of Trento. Fruity fragrance; slightly bitter taste.

Masi, Cantina

Well-known specialist producers of VALPOLICELLA, RECIOTO, SOAVE, etc., incl. fine red Campo Fiorin.

Mastroberardino

Leading wine-producer of Campania, incl. TAURASI and LACRIMA CRISTI DEL VESUVIO.

Meleto

Another CHIANTI CLASSICO estate of Barone Ricasoli, proprietor of the famous BROLIO.

Melini

Long-established and important producers of CHIANTI CLASSICO at Pontassieve. Inventors of the standard *fiasco*, or litre flask.

Melissa Cal. r. dr. ★★ **71 74** 75

Mostly made from Gaglioppo grapes in the Pr. of Catanzaro. Delicate, balanced, ages rather well.

Meranese di Collina Tr-AAd. DOC r. dr. ★ **71 74 75**

Light red of Merano, known in German as Meraner.

Merlot

Adaptable red Bordeaux grape widely grown in n.e. Italy and elsewhere.

Merlot (del Trentino) Tr-AAd. DOC r. dr. ★ **71 74 75**

Full flavour, slightly grassy scent, improves for 2–3 yrs.

Merlot di Aprilia Lat. DOC r. dr. ★ **71 75**

Harsh at first, softer after 2–3 yrs.

Merlot Colli Berici Ven. DOC r. dr. ★ D.Y.A.

Pleasantly light and soft.

Merlot Colli Orientali del Friuli Fr-VG. DOC r. dr. ★

Pleasant herby character, best at 2–3 yrs.

Merlot Collio Goriziano Fr-VG. DOC r. dr. ★

Grassy scent, slightly bitter taste. Best at 2–3 yrs.

Merlot Grave del Friuli Fr-VG. DOC r. dr. ★

Pleasant light wine, best at 1–2 yrs.

Merlot del Piave Ven. DOC r. dr. ★★ 71 **72 75**

Sound tasty red, best at 2–3 yrs.

Merlot (Isonzo) Fr-VG. DOC r. dr. ★

A DOC in Gorizia. Dry, herby, agreeable wine.

Merlot de Pramaggiore Ven. DOC r. dr. ★★ **71** 74 75

A cut above other Merlots; improves in bottle. Riserva after 3 yrs.

Monica di Cagliari   Sard. DOC r. dr. or sw. (f. dr. or sw.) ★★
70 72 73
Strong spicy red, often fortified. Monica is a Sardinian grape.

Monica di Sardegna   Sard. DOC r. sw. ★ NV
Commoner form of above, not fortified.

Montecarlo   Tusc. DOC w. dr. ★★ D.Y.A.
One of Tuscany's best whites, smooth and delicate. From near Lucca.

Montecompatri-Colonna   Lat. DOC w. dr. or s/sw.★
A neighbour of FRASCATI. Similar wine.

Montepaldi
Well-known producers and merchants of CHIANTI CLASSICO at San Casciano Val di Pesa. Owned by the Corsini family.

Montepulciano d'Abruzzo   Abr&M. DOC r. p. dr. ★★★
68 73 74 75
One of Italy's best reds, from the Adriatic coast round Pescara. Lightish, soft, slightly tannic, reminiscent of MARSALA when aged. The best come from Francavilla al Mare, Sulmona and Pratola Peligna.

Monterosso (Val d'Arda)   Em-Ro. DOC w. dr. or sw. (sp.) ★
D.Y.A.
Agreeable and fresh minor white from Piacenza.

Moscato
Fruitily fragrant grape grown all over Italy.

Moscato d'Asti   Piem. DOC w. sw. sp. ★ NV
Low-strength sweet fruity sparkler made in bulk. ASTI SPUMANTE is the superior version.

Moscato dei Colli Euganei   Ven. DOC w. sw. (sp.) ★★ **71 72 73**
Golden wine, fruity and smooth, from nr. Padua.

Moscato Naturale d'Asti   Piem. DOC w. sw. ★ D.Y.A.
The light and fruity base wine for Moscato d'Asti.

Moscato di Noto   Sic. DOC w. s/sw. or sw. or sp. or f. ★ NV
Light sweet still and sparkling versions, or strong Liquoroso. Noto is nr. Siracuse.

Moscato (Oltrepo' Pavese)   Lomb. DOC w. sw. (sp.) ★★ **73 74**
Lomb. DOC w. sw. (sp.)   **73 74**
The Lombardy equivalent of Moscato d'Asti.

Moscato di Pantelleria   Sic. DOC w. sw. (sp.) (f. pa.) ★★★
Italy's best muscat, from the island of Pantelleria close to the Tunisian coast; rich, fruity and aromatic. Ages well.

Moscato di Siracusa   Sic. DOC w. sw. ★★ NV
Strong amber dessert wine from Siracuse. Can be outstandingly good.

Moscato di Sorso Sennori   Sard. DOC w. sw. (f.) ★
Strong golden dessert wine from Sassari, n. Sardinia.

Moscato di Trani   Apu. DOC w. sw. or f. ★ **68 70** 74
Another strong golden dessert wine, sometimes fortified, with "bouquet of faded roses".

Moscato (Trentino)   Tr-AAd. DOC w. sw.★
Typical muscat; high strength for the n.

Nasco di Cagliari   Sard. DOC w. dr. or sw. (f. dr. or sw.) ★ **72 73 74**
Sardinian speciality, delicate bouquet, light bitter taste, high alcoholic content.

Nebbiolo
The best red grape of PIEMONTE and Lombardy.

Nebbiolo d'Alba   Piem. DOC r. dr. s/sw. (sp.) ★★ **71 74**
Like light-weight BAROLO; often good. Barolo that fails to reach the statutory 12° alcohol is sold under this name. Some prefer it so.

Negri, Nino
Famous house of VALTELLINA known for its excellent reds.

Nipozzano, Castello di

The most important CHIANTI producer outside the Classico zone, to the n. near Florence.

Nuraghe Majore   Sard. w. dr.⋆⋆ D.Y.A.

North Sardinian white: delicate, fresh, among the best wines of the island.

Nuragus di Cagliari   Sard. DOC w. dr. ⋆ 72 73 74

Lively Sardinian white, not too strong.

Oliena   Sard. r. dr. ⋆⋆

Interesting strong fragrant red; a touch bitter.

Oltrepo' Pavese   Lomb. DOC r. w. dr. sw. sp. ⋆→⋆⋆

DOC applicable to 7 wines produced in the Pr. of Pavia, named after their grapes.

Orvieto   Umb. DOC w. dr. or s/sw. ⋆⋆→⋆⋆⋆ 73 74 75

The classical Umbrian golden-white, smooth and substantial. O. Classico is superior.

Ostuni   Apu. DOC w. dr. ⋆⋆

Rather delicate, dry, balanced; produced in the Pr. of Brindisi.

Parrina   Tusc. r. w. dr.⋆⋆ D.Y.A.

Light red and fresh appetizing white from n. Tuscany.

Passito

Strong sweet wine from grapes dried either in the sun or indoors.

Per' e' Palummo   Camp. r. dr.⋆⋆

Excellent red produced on the island of Ischia; delicate, slightly grassy, a bit tannic, balanced.

Piave   DOC r. w. dr.⋆⋆ 71 74 75

DOC covering 4 wines, 2 red and 2 white, named after their grapes.

Picolit (Colli Orientali del Friuli)   Fr-VG. DOC w. s/sw. or sw. ⋆⋆⋆⋆ 62 64 69 71

Known as Italy's Château d'Yquem. Delicate bouquet, well balanced, high alcoholic content. Ages very well.

Piemonte

The most important Italian region for quality wine. Turin is the capital, Asti the wine-centre. See Barolo, Barbera, Grignolino, Moscato, etc.

Pinot Bianco

Good rather neutral grape popular in n.e., good for sparkling wine.

Pinot Bianco (dei Colli Berici)   Ven. DOC w. dr.⋆⋆

Straight satisfying dry white.

Pinot Bianco (Colli Orientali del Friuli)   Fr-VG. DOC w. dr. ⋆⋆ 74 75

Good white; smooth rather than showy.

Pinot Bianco (Collio Goriziano)   Fr-VG. DOC w. dr. ⋆⋆ 73 74

Similar to the above.

Pinot Bianco (Grave del Friuli)   Fr-VG. DOC w. dr. ⋆⋆

Same again.

Pinot Grigio

Tasty, low-acid white grape popular in n.e.

Pinot Grigio (Collio Goriziano)   Fr-VG. DOC w. dr.⋆⋆ 73 74

Fruity, soft, agreeable dry white.

Pinot Grigio (Grave del Friuli)   Fr-VG. DOC w. dr. ⋆⋆ 73 75

Hardly distinguishable from the above.

Pinot Grigio (Oltrepo' Pavese)   Lomb. DOC w. dr. (sp.) ⋆⋆ 71 73 74

Lombardy's P.G. is considered best.

Pinot Nero Trentino   Tr-AAd. DOC r. dr. ⋆⋆ 71 73 75

Pinot Nero (Noir) gives lively burgundy-scented light wine in much of n.e. Italy, incl. Trentino.

Pio Cesare
>   A producer of quality red wines of PIEMONTE, incl. outstanding BAROLO.

Primitivo di Apulia   Apu. r. dr. ⭐⭐
>   One of the best southern reds. Fruity when young, soft and full-flavoured with age. Primitivo is the grape. (See also Manduria.)

Prosecco di Conegliano   Ven. DOC w. dr. or s/sw. (sp.) ⭐⭐⭐ **71 75**
>   Popular sparkling wine of the n.e. Slight fruity bouquet, the dry pleasantly bitter, the sw. fruity; the best are known as Superiore di Cartizze. Best producer: Carpene-Malvolti.

Raboso del Piave   Ven. r. dr. ⭐⭐ **67 69 71 73**
>   Powerful but sharp country red; needs age.

Ramandolo
>   See Verduzzo Colli Orientali del Friuli

Italian bottle shapes

1. Orvieto 2. Chianti 3. Verdicchio 4. Barolo

Ravello   Camp. r. p. w. dr. ⭐⭐
>   Among the best wines of Campania: full dry red, fresh clean white. Caruso is a good brand.

Recioto
>   Wine made of half-dried grapes. Speciality of Veneto.

Recioto di Gambellara   Ven. DOC w. s/sw. sp. ⭐
>   Sweetish golden wine, often half-sparkling.

Recioto di Soave   Ven. DOC w. s/sw. (sp.) ⭐⭐
>   Soave made from selected half-dried grapes; sweet, fruity, fresh, slightly almondy: high alcohol.

Recioto della Valpolicella   Ven. DOC r. s/sw. sp. ⭐⭐ **69 71 73**
>   Strong rather sweet red, sometimes sparkling. Popular in Verona.

Recioto Amarone della Valpolicella   Ven. DOC r. dr. ⭐⭐⭐⭐ **64 66 68 71** 74
>   Dry version of the above; strong concentrated flavour, rather bitter. Impressive and expensive.

Refosco (Colli Orientali del Friuli)   Fr-VG. DOC r. dr. ⭐⭐ **70 71 73**
>   Full-bodied dry red; Riserva after 2 yrs. Refosco is a grape of little character.

Refosco (Grave del Friuli)   Fr-VG. DOC r. dr. ⭐⭐
>   Similar to above but slightly lighter.

Ribolla (Colli Orientali del Friuli)   Fr-VG. DOC w. dr. ⭐ D.Y.A.
>   Clean and fruity n.e. white.

Ricasoli
>   Famous Tuscan family whose CHIANTI is named after their BROLIO estate and castle.

Riesling
>   Normally refers to Italian (R. Italico). German Riesling, uncommon, is R. Renano.

Riesling Italico (Collio Goriziano)   Fr-VG. DOC w. dr. ⭐⭐ **73 74 75**
>   Pleasantly fruity, fairly full-bodied n.e. white.

Riesling (Oltrepo' Pavese)   Lomb. DOC w. dr. (sp.) ★★
>   The Lombardy version, quite light and fresh. Occasionally
>   sparkling. Keeps well.

Riesling (Trentino)   Tr-AAd. DOC w. dr. ★★ D.Y.A.
>   Delicate, slightly acid, very fruity.

Riserva
>   Wine aged for a statutory period in barrels.

Riviera Rosso Stravecchio   Apu. r. dr. ★★ **60 67 70**
>   Good dry full-bodied red from Castel del Monte. Ages well.

Riviera del Garda Chiaretto   Ven. DOC p. dr. ★★ D.Y.A.
>   Charming cherry-pink, fresh and slightly bitter, from s.w.
>   Garda.

Riviera del Garda Rosso   Ven. DOC r. dr.★★ **70 71 73** 75
>   Red version of the above; ages surprisingly well.

Rosato
>   Rosé.

Rosato del Salento   Apu. DOC p. dr. ★ D.Y.A.
>   Strong but refreshing southern rosé from round Brindisi.

Rossese di Doleacqua   Lig. DOC r. dr. ★★ **70 73** 75
>   Well-known fragrant light red of the Riviera with typical
>   touch of bitterness. Superiore is stronger.

Rosso
>   Red.

Rosso delle Colline Lucchesi   Tusc. DOC r. dr.★★ **70 72 75**
>   Produced round Lucca but not greatly different from
>   CHIANTI.

Rosso Conero   Mar. DOC r. dr. ★★ **72 73 74** 75
>   Substantial CHIANTI-style wine from the Adriatic coast.

Rosso Piceno   Mar. DOC r. dr. ★ **70 73** 75
>   Unremarkable Adriatic red.

Rubesco
>   See Torgiano

Rubino di Cantavenna   Piem. DOC r. dr. ★★
>   Lively red, principally BARBERA, from a well-known
>   co-operative s.e. of Turin.

Rufina
>   A sub-region of CHIANTI.

Ruffino
>   Well-known CHIANTI merchants.

Runchet (Valtellina)   Lomb. DOC r. dr. ★★
>   Small production, soft bouquet, slightly tannic, drink
>   relatively young.

Sangiovese
>   Principal red grape of CHIANTI, used alone for:

Sangiovese d'Aprilia   Lat. DOC p. dr. ★ **71 74**
>   Strong dry rosé from s. of Rome.

Sangiovese di Romagna   Em-Ro. DOC r. dr.★★ **70 71** 75
>   Pleasant standard red; gains character with a little age.

Sangue di Giuda (Oltrepo' Pavese)   Lomb. DOC r. dr. ★★
>   "Judas' blood": Strong rather tannic red of w. Lombardy.

San Severo   Apu. DOC r. p. w. dr. ★ **71 73 74** 75
>   Sound neutral southern wine; not particularly strong.

Santa Maddalena   Tr-AAd. DOC r. dr. ★★ **71 73 75**
>   Perhaps the best Tyrolean red. Round and warm, slightly
>   almondy. From Bolzano.

Sassella (Valtellina)   Lomb. DOC r. dr.★★★ **69 70 71 73** 75
>   Considerable NEBBIOLO wine, tough when young. Known
>   since Roman times, mentioned by Leonardo da Vinci.

Sauvignon
>   The Sauvignon Blanc: excellent white grape used in n.e.

Sauvignon (Colli Berici)   Ven. DOC w. dr.★★ D.Y.A.
>   Delicate, slightly aromatic, fresh white from near Vicenza.

Sauvignon (Colli Orientali del Friuli)   Fr-VG. DOC w. dr. ★★
71 72 73
> Full, smooth, freshly aromatic n.e. white.

Sauvignon (Collio Goriziano)   Fr-VG. DOC w. dr. ★★ **72 73 74**
> Very similar to the last; slightly higher alcohol.

Savuto   Cal. DOC r. p. dr. ★★
> The ancient Savuto produced in the Pr. of Cosenza and
> Catanzaro. Big juicy wine.

Sciacchetra
> See Cinque Terre

Secco
> Dry.

Sella & Mosca
> Major Sardinian growers and merchants at Alghero.

Sforzato (Valtellina)   Lomb. DOC r. dr. ★★★ **64 67 68 70** 71 75
> Valtellina equivalent of RECIOTO AMARONE made with
> partly dried grapes. Velvety, strong, ages remarkably well.
> Also called Sfursat.

Sizzano   Piem. DOC r. dr. ★★ **70 71 74**
> Attractive full-bodied red produced at Sizzano in the Pr. of
> Novara, mostly from NEBBIOLO.

Soave   Ven. DOC w. dr. ★★★ **74 75**
> Famous, if not very characterful, Veronese white. Fresh
> with attractive texture. Classico is more restricted and
> better. Drink young.

Solopaca   Camp. DOC r. w. dr. ★
> Comes from nr. Benevento, rather sharp when young, the
> white soft and fruity.

Sorni   Tr-AAd. r. w. dr. ★★ **74 75**
> Made in the Pr. of Trento. Light, fresh and soft. Drink young.

Spanna
> See Gattinara

Spumante
> Sparkling.

Squinzano   Apu. r. p. dr. ★
> Strong southern red from Lecce.

Stravecchio
> Very old.

Sylvaner
> German white grape used successfully in ALTO ADIGE and
> elsewhere.

Sylvaner (Alto Adige)   Tr-AAd. DOC w. dr. ★★ **73 74** 75
> Pleasant grapy well-balanced white.

Sylvaner (Terlano)   Tr-AAd. DOC w. dr. ★★ **73 74** 75
> Attractive lively and delicate wines.

Sylvaner (Valle Isarco)   Tr-AAd. DOC w. dr. ★★
> Similar to the last.

Taurasi   Camp. DOC r. dr. ★★ **68 70 71 73** 75
> The best Campanian red, from Avellino. Bouquet of cherries,
> harsh when young, improves with age. Riserva after 4 yrs.

Terlano   Tr-AAd. DOC w. dr. ★★ **73 74** 75
> A DOC applicable to 6 white wines from the Pr. of Bolzano,
> named after their grapes. Terlaner in German.

Termeno   Tr-AAd. r. w. dr. ★★
> Village nr. Bolzano. Tramin in German, reputedly the
> origin of the TRAMINER. Its red is light and slightly bitter.

Teroldego Rotaliano   Tr-AAd. DOC r. dr. ★★ **69 71 73** 75
> The attractive local red of Trento. Blackberry-scented,
> slight bitter after-taste, ages moderately.

Tocai
> North-east Italian white grape; no relation of Hungarian
> or Alsace Tokay.

Tocai di Lison   Ven. DOC w. dr.★★ 74 76
> From Treviso, delicate smoky/fruity scent, fruity taste.
> Classico is better.

Tocai (Colli Berici)   Ven. DOC w. dr. ★
> Less character than the last.

Tocai (Grave del Friuli)   Fr-VG. DOC w. dr. ★★
> Similar to TOCAI DI LISON, generally rather milder.

Tocai di S. Martino della Battaglia   Lomb. DOC. w. dr. ★★
D.Y.A.
> Small production s. of La. Garda. Light, slightly bitter.

Torbato   Sard. w. dr. (pa.) ★★
> Good n. Sardinian table wine, also PASSITO of high quality.

Torgiano, Rubesco di   Umb. DOC r. w. dr. ★★★ 70 71 73 75
> Excellent red from near Perugia comparable with CHIANTI
> CLASSICO. Small production. White also good, but not as
> outstanding as the red.

---

*A new top category, DOCG, Denominazione Controllata e Garantita,
is to be added to the Italian wine classification in due course. It will be
awarded only to certain wines from top-quality zones-within-zones
which have been bottled and sealed with a government seal by the
producer, or someone who takes full responsibility for the contents. So
far no wine has been classified as DOCG. Barolo will probably be
the first.*

Traminer Aromatico (Trentino)   Tr-AAd. DOC w. dr. ★★
D.Y.A.
> Delicate, aromatic, rather soft Traminer.

Trebbiano
> The principal white grape of Tuscany and most of central
> Italy. Ugni Blanc in French.

Trebbiano d'Abruzzo   Abr&M. DOC w. dr. ★ D.Y.A.
> Gentle, rather neutral, slightly tannic. From round Pescara.

Trebbiano d'Aprilia   Lat. DOC w. dr. ★ D.Y.A.
> Heady, mild-flavoured, rather yellow. From s. of Rome.

Trebbiano di Romagna   Em-Ro. DOC w. dr. or s/sw. (sp.) ★ 71
74 75
> Clean, pleasant white from near Bologna.

Trentino   Tr-AAd. DOC r. w. dr. or sw. ★→★★
> DOC applicable to 10 wines named after their grapes.

Umani-Ronchi
> A firm producing VERDICCHIO and ROSSO CONERO from nr.
> Ancona.

Uzzano
> Fine old estate at Greve. First-class CHIANTI CLASSICO.

Valcalepio   Lomb. DOC r. w. dr. ★ 70 74
> From nr. Bergamo. Pleasant red; lightly scented, fresh
> white.

Valdadige   Tr-AAd. DOC r. w. dr. or s/sw. ★
> Name for the ordinary table wines of the Adige valley—
> in German Etschtal.

Valgella (Valtellina)   Lomb. DOC r. dr. ★★ 69 73
> One of the VALTELLINA NEBBIOLOS: good dry red growing
> nutty with age. Riserva at 4 yrs.

Valle Isarco   Tr-AAd. DOC w. dr. ★→★★
> A DOC applicable to 5 varietal wines made n.e. of Bolzano.

Valpolicella   Ven. DOC r. dr.★★★ 71 73 74
> Attractive light red from nr. Verona. Delicate nutty scent,
> slightly bitter taste. Classico more restricted; Superiore has
> 12% alcohol and 1 yr. of age.

Valtellina   Lomb. DOC r. dr. ★★ → ★★★

A DOC applicable to wines made principally from Chiavennasca (NEBBIOLO) grapes, in the Pr. of Sondrio, n. Lombardy. V. Superiore is better.

Velletri   Lat. DOC r. w. dr. or s/sw. ★★

Agreeable Roman dry red and smooth white. Drink young.

Vendemmia

Vintage.

Venegazzu'   Fr-VG. r. dr. ★★

Little-known red produced nr. Treviso. Rich bouquet, soft, warm taste, 13.5% alcohol, ages well.

Verdicchio dei Castelli di Jesi   Mar. DOC w. dr. (sp.) ★★★ D.Y.A.

Ancient, famous and very pleasant fresh pale white from nr. Ancona. Goes back to the Etruscans. Classico is more restricted.

Verdicchio di Matelica   Mar. DOC w. dr. (sp.) ★★

Similar to the last, though less well known.

Verdiso

Native white grape of n.e., used for PROSECCO.

Verduzzo (Colli Orientali del Friuli)   Fr-VG. DOC w. dr. s/sw. sw. ★★

Full-bodied white from a native grape. The sweet is called Ramandolo.

Verduzzo (Del Piave)   Ven. DOC w. dr. ★★

Similar to the last but dry.

Vermentino   Lig. w. dr. ★★ D.Y.A.

The best dry white of the Riviera: good clean seafood wine made at Pietra Ligure and San Remo.

Vermentino di Gallura   Sard. DOC w. dr. ★★

Soft, dry, rather strong white from n. Sardinia.

Vernaccia di Oristano   Sard. DOC w. dr. (f.) ★★★ 72 74 75

Sardinian speciality, like light sherry, a touch bitter, full-bodied and interesting. Superiore with 15.5% alcohol and 3 yrs. of age.

Vernaccia di San Gimignano   Tosc. DOC w. dr. (f.) ★★ 73 74 75

Distinctive strong high-flavoured wine from nr. Siena. Michelangelo's favourite.

Vernaccia di Serrapetrona   Mar. DOC r. dr. s/sw. sw. sp. ★★

Comes from the Pr. of Macerata; aromatic bouquet, pleasantly bitter after-taste.

Vignamaggio

Historic and beautiful CHIANTI CLASSICO estate.

Villa Terciona

Important CHIANTI CLASSICO estate.

Vino da arrosto

"Wine for roast meat", i.e. good dry red.

Vino da pasto

Table wine: i.e. nothing special.

Vino Nobile di Montepulciano   Tusc. DOC r. dr. ★★★ 67 70 73 75

Impressive traditional Tuscan red with bouquet and style. Aged for 3 yrs. Riserva; for 4 yrs. Riserva Speciale.

Vinsanto

Term for certain strong sweet wines esp. in Tuscany: usually PASSITI.

Vinsanto di Gambellara   Ven. DOC w. sw. ★★

Powerful, velvety, golden: made between Vicenza and Verona.

Vinsanto Toscano   Tusc. w. s/sw. ★★

Made in the Pr. of Siena. Aromatic bouquet, rich and smooth. Aged in very small barrels known as Carratelli.

Zagarolo   Lat. DOC w. dr. or s/sw. ★★

Neighbour of FRASCATI, similar wine.

Spain & Portugal

The very finest wines of Spain and Portugal are respectively sherry and port and madeira, which have a section to themselves on pages 139 to 143.

Spain's table wines divide naturally into those from the Mediterranean climate of the centre, south and east and those from the Atlantic climate of the north and west. The former are strong and with rare exceptions dull. The latter include the very good wines of Rioja, certainly the most important quality table-wine region of the peninsula.

Rainy north-west Spain and northern Portugal make their very similar "green" wines. Central Portugal has an excellent climate for wines like full-bodied Bordeaux.

The Portuguese system of controlled appellation is old and unrealistic today: it includes areas of dwindling interest and excludes several good new areas. The Spanish system is new (since 1971) and for the moment over-optimistic, delimiting some areas of purely local interest.

The listing here includes the best and most interesting types and regions of each country, whether legally delimited or not. Geographical references (see map) are to the traditional division of Spain into the old kingdoms, and the major provinces of Portugal.

Spain

Aguardiente
Colloquially, the pungent spirit made like the French *marc* by distilling grape skins and pips.

Albariño del Palacio   Gal. w. dr.★★
Flowery "green wine" from FEFIÑANES near Cambados, made with the Albariño grape, the best of the region.

Alella   Cat. r. (p.) w. dr. or sw. ★★
Small demarcated region just n. of Barcelona. Makes pleasantly fresh and fruity wines in limited amounts. (See Marfil.)

Alicante   Lev. r. (w.) ★
Demarcated region. Its wines tend to be "earthy", high in alcohol and heavy.

Almansa   Lev. r. ★
Demarcated region w. of ALICANTE, producing heavy wines high in alcohol.

Aloque   N.Cas. r. ★
A light (though not in alcohol) variety of VALDEPEÑAS, made by fermenting together red and white grapes.

Almendralejo   Ext. r. w. ★
Commercial wine centre of the Extremadura. Much of its produce is distilled to make the spirit for fortifying sherry.

Ampurdan
See Perelada

Año
4° Año (or Años) means 4 years old when bottled.

Benicarlo   Lev. r. ★
Town on the Mediterranean. Its strong red wines were formerly used for adding colour and body to Bordeaux.

Blanco
White.

Bodega
1. a wineshop; 2. a concern occupied in the making, blending and/or shipping of wine.

The following additional abbreviations are used in the Spanish section (see p. 98):
R'a.A. Rioja Alta
R'a.Al. Rioja Alavesa
Res. Reserva

Abbreviations of regional names shown in bold type are used in the text.

Bodegas Bilbainas R'a.A. r. (p.) w. dr. sw. or sp. res. ★★ → ★★★
Large bodega in HARO, making a wide range of reliable wines, including "Royal Carlton" by the champagne method.

Campanas, Las Nav. r. (w.) ★★
Small wine area near Pamplona. Clarete Campanas is a sturdy red. Mature 5° año Castillo de Tiebas is like a heavy Rioja Reserva.

Cañamero Ext. w. ★
Remote village near Guadalupe whose wines grow FLOR and acquire a sherry-like taste.

Caralt, Cavas Conde de Cat. sp. ★★★
Good sparkling wines from SAN SADURNÍ DE NOYA, made by the champagne method.

Cariñena Ara. r. (p. w.) ★
Demarcated region and large-scale supplier of strong wine for everyday drinking.

Carlos Primero And. Brandy ★★★
Spanish favourite among the more expensive and delicate brandies.

Castillo Ygay
See Marques de Murrieta

Cenicero
Wine township in the RIOJA ALTA.

Cepa
Wine or grape variety.

Chacoli Gui. (r.) w. ★
Alarmingly sharp "GREEN WINE" from the Basque coast, containing only 8% to 9% alcohol.

Cheste Lev. r. w. ★
Demarcated region inland of VALENCIA. Blackstrap wines with 13% to 15% alcohol.

Clarete
Light red wine (occasionally dark rosé).

Codorniu, S.A.   Cat. sp. $\boxed{\star\star\star}$

> Best known of the firms in SAN SADURNÍ DE NOYA making good sparkling wines by the champagne method. Ask for the *bruto* (extra dry).

Compañía Vinícola del Norte de España (C.V.N.E.)   R'a.A. r. w. dr. or sw. res. $\boxed{\star\to\star\star\star}$

> Good red wines from HARO: 3° año is currently the best young red Rioja. MONOPOLE is a good dry white.

Cosecha

> Crop or vintage.

Consejo Regulador

> Official organization for the defence, control and promotion of a DENOMINACIÓN DE ORIGEN.

Criado y embottellado por . . .

> Grown and bottled by . . .

Denominación de origen

> Officially regulated wine region. (See Introduction p. 94.)

Dulce

> Sweet.

Elaborado y añejado por . . .

> Made and aged by . . .

Espumoso

> Sparkling.

Fefiñanes Palacio   Gal. w. res. ★★★

> Best of the ALBARIÑO wines, though hardly "green", since it is aged for 2-6 yrs.

Ferrer, José L.   Mallorca r. res. ★★

> His wines, made in Binisalem, are the only ones of any distinction from Mallorca.

Flor

> A wine-yeast peculiar to sherry and certain other wines that oxidize slowly and tastily under its influence.

Franco–Españolas, Bodegas   R'a.A. r. w. dr. or sw. res. ★→★★★

> Reliable wines from LOGROÑO. The sweet white Diamante is a favourite in Spain.

Fuenmayor

> Wine township in the RIOJA ALTA.

Fundador   And. Brandy ★★

> One of the drier of the large-selling Spanish brandies.

Green Wines

> See under Portugal

Haro

> The wine centre of the RIOJA ALTA.

Huelva   And. r. w. br. ★→★★

> Demarcated region w. of Cadiz. The best of its wine is not on sale, since it goes to JEREZ for blending.

Jerez de la Frontera

> The city of sherry. (See page 141.)

Jumilla   Lev. r. ★

> Demarcated region in the mountains behind ALICANTE. Its full-bodied wines may approach 18% alcohol.

La Rioja Alta, S.A.   R'a.A. r. (p.) w. dr. or sw. res. $\boxed{\star\star}\to\star\star\star$

> Well-known RIOJA bodega in HARO. Excellent wines, especially the red 6° año Viña Arana and 8° año Reserva.

Lepanto   And. Brandy $\boxed{\star\star\star}$

> Delicate and expensive, perhaps the best of Spanish brandies.

Logroño

> Principal town of the RIOJA region.

López de Heredia, S.A.   R'a.A. r. (p.) w. dr. or sw. res. ★★→ $\boxed{\star\star\star}$

> Old-established bodega in HARO with typical and good dry red Viña Tondonia of 6° año or more. Old Tondonia whites are also impressive.

Málaga And. br. sw. ★★→★★★

Demarcated region around the city of Málaga. At their best, its dessert wines yield nothing to tawny port.

Mallorca

No wine of interest except from José FERRER.

Mancha/Manchuela N.Cas. r. w. ★

Large demarcated regions n. and n.e. of VALDEPEÑAS, but wines without the light and fresh flavour of the latter.

Marqués de Riscal, S.A. R'a.Al. r. (p. and w.) res. ★★→⟦★★★⟧

The best bodega of the RIOJA ALAVESA. Its red wines are relatively light and dry.

Marqués de Murrieta, S.A. R'a.A. r. w. dr. ★★★→⟦★★★★⟧

Highly reputed bodega near LOGROÑO. Makes the 4° año Etiqueta Blanca, the superb red Castillo Ygay and a dry fruity white.

Masía Bach Cat. r. p. w. dr. or sw. ⟦★★⟧

Extrísimo Bach from SAN SADURNÍ DE NOYA, flowery and refined, is one of the best sweet white wines of Spain.

Marfil Cat. r. (p.) w. ★★

Brand name of Alella Vinícola (Bodegas Cooperativas) best known of the producers in ALELLA. Means "ivory".

Medellín Ext. r. (p.) w. ★

The Castillo de Medellín from this town near Mérida is of better quality than the local plonk.

Méntrida N.Cas. r. w. ★

Demarcated region w. of Madrid, supplying everyday wine to the capital.

Monopole

See Compañía Vinícola del Norte de España

Montanchez Ext. r. g. ★

Village near Mérida, interesting because its red wines grow FLOR yeast like FINO sherry.

Monterrey Gal. r. ★

Demarcated region near the n. border of Portugal, making wines like those of VÉRIN.

Montilla–Moriles And. g. ⟦★★★⟧

Demarcated region near Cordoba. Its crisp, sherry-like FINO and AMONTILLADO contain 14% to 17.5% natural alcohol and remain unfortified and singularly toothsome.

Navarra Nav. r. (w.) ★→★★

Demarcated region, but little better than sturdy wine for everyday drinking.

Palacio, Bodegas R'a.Al. r. w. dr. or sw. res. ⟦★★⟧ → ★★★

Well-known bodega at Laguardia. Its velvety red Glorioso is excellent value.

Panades Cat. r. w. dr. sp. ★→⟦★★★⟧

Demarcated region including Vilafranca del Panadés, SAN SADURNÍ DE NOYA and SITGES. See also Torres.

Paternina, S.A. R'a.A. r. (p.) w. dr. or sw. res. ★→★★★

Bodega at Ollauri and a household name, though its big-selling 3° año Banda Azul has recently been disappointing.

Pazo Gal. r. p. w. dr. ★

Brand name of the co-operative at RIBEIRO, making "GREEN WINES". The rasping red is the local favourite. The pleasant faintly fizzy white is safer.

Peñafiel O.Cas. r. ★

Sturdy red wine from the village of the same name on the R. Duero near Valladolid.

Perelada Cat. (r. p.) w. sp. ★★

In the demarcated region of AMPURDAN on the Costa Brava. Best known for a sparkling wine made by the tank or *cuve close* system.

Priorato Cat. r. (w.) ⭐

Demarcated region, an enclave in that of TARRAGONA, known for its strong dark full-bodied red wine, often used for blending. Lighter Priorato is good carafe wine in Barcelona restaurants.

Queimada

Rib-warming Galician drink for the winter, made by spicing and burning AGUARDIENTE.

Reserva

Good-quality wine matured for long periods in cask.

Ribeiro Gal. r. (p.) w. dr. ⭐→⭐⭐

Demarcated region on the n. border of Portugal—the heart of the "GREEN WINE" country.

Rioja O.Cas.

This upland region along the R. Ebro in the n. of Spain produces most of the country's best table wines in some 50 BODEGAS DE EXPORTACION. It is sub-divided into:

Rioja Alavesa

North of the R. Ebro, the R'a.Al. produces fine red wines, mostly the lighter CLARETES.

Rioja Alta

South of the R. Ebro and w. of LOGROÑO, the R'a.A. grows fine red and white wines and also makes some rosé.

Rioja Baja

Stretching e. from LOGROÑO, the Rioja Baja makes coarser red wines, high in alcohol and often used for blending.

Rioja Santiago, S.A. R'a.A. r. w. dr. or sw. p. res. ⭐→⭐⭐⭐

Bodega at HARO with well-known wines. The flavour sometimes suffers from pasteurization, but the red RESERVAS can be first-rate. Makes the biggest-selling bottled SANGRÍA.

Rosado

Rosé.

Rueda O.Cas. w. ⭐→⭐⭐

Village-name given to the golden FLOR-growing wines with sherry-like taste and up to 17% alcohol, grown w. of Valladolid.

Salvatierra de Barros Ext. r. ⭐

Village near Zafra. Peasant-made wines with a certain extra something.

Sangre de Toro

1. Red wine from TORO. 2. Brand name for a soft, rich-flavoured red wine from TORRES, S.A.

Sangría

Cold wine cup made by adding ice, citrus fruit, fizzy lemonade and brandy to red wine.

Sanlucar de Barrameda

Centre of the Manzanilla district. (See Sherry page 142.)

San Sadurní de Noya Cat. sp. ⭐⭐→⭐⭐⭐

Town s. of Barcelona, hollow with cellars where dozens of firms produce sparkling wine by the champagne method. Standards are high, even if the ultimate finesse is lacking.

Sarría, Señorio de Nav. r. (p.) w. dr. ⭐⭐→⭐⭐⭐

The model winery of H. Beaumont y Cia. near Pamplona produces wines up to RIOJA standards.

Scholtz, Hermanos, S.A. And. br. ⭐⭐⭐

Makers of some of the best MÁLAGA, notably Solera Scholtz 1885.

Seco

Dry.

Sitges Cat. w. sw. ⭐⭐

Coastal resort s. of Barcelona noted for sweet dessert wines made from Sumoll and Malvasia grapes.

Soberano And. Brandy ★★
> One of the drier of the popular Spanish brandies.

Tarragona Cat. r. w. dr. or sw. br. ★
> 1. The demarcated region produces little wine of note.
> 2. The town makes vermouth and blends and exports cheap wine in bulk.

Terry And. Brandy ★
> Highly caramelized brandy—definitely for those with a sweet tooth.

Tierra del Vino O.Cas. w. ★→★★
> Area w. of Valladolid including the wine villages of La Nava and RUEDA.

Tinto
> Red.

Toro O.Cas. r. ★
> Town from which the strong red SANGRE DE TORO takes its name.

Torres, S.A. Cat. r. w. dr. ★★ →★★★
> Distinguished family firm making the best wines of PANADÉS, esp. the dry white Viña Sol and red Gran Coronas Reserva.

Utiel-Requeña Lev. r. (w.) ★
> Demarcated region w. of Valencia. The CLARETES from the mountainous hinterland are best.

Valbuena O.Cas. r. ★★★
> Made with the same grapes as VEGA SICILIA but sold as 3° año or 5° año.

Valdeorras Gal. r. w. dr. ★→ ★★
> Demarcated region e. of Orense, making dry and refreshing wines, some slightly fizzy.

Valdepeñas N.Cas. r. (w.) ★→★★
> Demarcated region near the border of Andalucia. The supplier of most of the carafe wine to Madrid. Its wines, though high in alcohol, are surprisingly light in flavour.

Valencia Lev. r. w. ★
> Demarcated region producing earthy high-strength wine.

Vega Sicilia O.Cas. r. res. **41 48 53 59 61** ★★★★
> One of the very best Spanish wines, full-bodied, fruity, and almost impossible to find. Containing up to 16% alcohol.

Vendimia
> Vintage.

Vérin Gal. r. ★
> Town near n. border of Portugal. Its wines are the strongest from Galicia, without a bubble, and up to 14% alcohol.

Viña
> Vineyard.

Vino blanco
> White wine.
> **comun/corriente** Ordinary wine.
> **clarete** Light red wine.
> **dulce** Sweet wine.
> **espumoso** Sparkling wine.
> **generoso** Aperitif or dessert wine rich in alcohol.
> **rancio** Maderized (brown) white wine.
> **rosado** Rosé wine.
> **seco** Dry wine.
> **tinto** Red wine.
> **verde** See Green wine under Portugal

Xampán
> "Champagne": i.e. Spanish sparkling wine.

Yecla Lev. r. ★
> Demarcated region w. of Alicante. Heavy-weight champion of Spanish reds with more alcohol than a FINO sherry.

Portugal

For Port and Madeira see pages 139 to 143.

Adega
> A cellar or winery.

Aguardente
> The Portuguese word for brandy, made by a multiplicity of firms. Safest to ask for one from a port concern.

Algarve   Alg. r. w. ⋆
> Lagoa is the wine centre of the holiday area. It is nothing to write home about.

Amarante
> Sub-region in the VINHOS VERDES area. Rather heavier and stronger wines than those from farther n.

Aveleda   Douro w. dr. ⋆⋆
> A first-class "GREEN WINE" made on the Aveleda estate of the Guedes family, proprietors of SOGRAPE. Sold dry in Portugal but sweetened for export.

Bagaceira
> A potent spirit made like the Spanish *aguardiente*. One of the best is CEPA VELHA from MONÇÃO.

Basto
> A sub-region of the VINHOS VERDES area on the R. Tamega, producing more astringent red wine than white.

Braga
> Sub-region of the VINHOS VERDES area, good for both red and white.

Bairrada   Bei. Lit. r. and sp. ⋆⋆
> Undemarcated region supplying much of Oporto's (often good) carafe wine. Also makes good-quality sparkling wines by the champagne method.

Borba   Alen. r. ⋆
> Small enclave near Evora, making the only wine of any class from Alentejo (s. of the R. Tagus).

Bual
> A type of sweet dessert MADEIRA; less sweet and more smoky than MALMSEY.

Buçaco   B'a.Al. r. (w.) ⋆⋆⋆
> The speciality of the luxury Buçaco hotel near Coimbra, not seen elsewhere.

Bucelas   Est'a. w. dr. ⋆⋆⋆
> Tiny demarcated region just n. of Lisbon. João Camilo Alves Lda. and Caves Velhas make delicate, perfumed wines with 11% to 12% alcohol.

Carcavelos   Est'a. br. sw. ⋆⋆⋆
> Minute demarcated region w. of Lisbon. Its excellent sweet wines average 19% alcohol and are drunk cold as an aperitif or with dessert.

Cartaxo   Rib. r. w. ⋆
> Brand name of adequate carafe wine from the Ribatejo n. of Lisbon, popular in the capital.

Casal Mendes   M'o. w. dr. ⋆⋆
> The "GREEN WINE" from Caves Aliança.

Casaleiro
> Trade mark of Caves Dom Teodosio—João T. Barbosa, who make a variety of reliable wines: DÃO, VINHOS VERDES, etc.

Casal Garcia   Douro w. dr. ⋆⋆
> One of the biggest-selling "GREEN WINES" in Portugal, made by SOGRAPE.

Cepa Velha   M'o. (r.) w. dr. ⋆⋆⋆
> Brand name of Vinhos de Monçao, Lda. Their Alvarinho, from the grape of that name, is the best of all "GREEN WINES".

Clarete
> Light red wine.

Colares Est'a. r. ★★★

Small demarcated region on the coast w. of Lisbon. Its classical dark red wines, rich in tannin, are from vines which survived the phylloxera epidemic. Drink the oldest available.

Dão B'a.Al. r. w. ★→ ★★

Demarcated region round Viseu on the R. Mondego. Produces some of Portugal's best table wines: solid reds of some subtlety with age: substantial dry whites. All are sold under brand names.

Douro

The n. river whose valley produces port and more than adequate (though undemarcated) table wines.

White table wines have recently come into fashion as an aperitif, an end-of-the-day or any-time drink, taking the place of hard liquor in many households. German wines are riding high on the new wave, but in almost all countries the shift of emphasis from red wine to white is noticeable. Whoever coined the phrase "the thinking man's martini" summed up the arguments for wine: it provides refreshment and stimulus without stopping you thinking.

Evel Trás-os-M. r. ★

Reliable middle-weight red made near VILA REAL by Real Companhia Vinícola do Norte de Portugal.

Faisca Est'a. p. ★

Big-selling sweet carbonated rosé from J. M. da Fonseca.

Ferreirinha Trás-os-M. r. res. ★★★★

One of Portugal's best wines, made in very limited quantity by the port firm of Ferreira. Fruity and fine with deep bouquet.

Gaeiras Est'a. r. ★★

Dry, full-bodied and well-balanced red made in the neighbourhood of Óbidos.

Gatão M'o. w. dr. ★★

Reliable "GREEN WINE" from the firm of Borges & Irmão.

Grão Vasco B'a.A. r. w. res. ★★

One of the best brands of DÃO, blended and matured at Viseu by SOGRAPE.

Green Wine (Vinho verde)

Wine made from barely ripe grapes and undergoing a special secondary fermentation, which leaves it with a slight sparkle. Ready for drinking in the spring after the harvest. It may be white or red.

Lagoa.

See Algarve

Lagosta M'o. w. dr. ★★

Well-known "GREEN WINE" from the Real Companhia Vinícola do Norte de Portugal.

Lancers Est'a. p. ★

Sweet carbonated rosé extensively shipped to the USA by J. M. da Fonseca.

Lima

Sub-region in the n. of the VINHOS VERDES area making mainly harsh red wines.

Madeira Island br. dr./sw. ★★→★★★★

Producer of the famous aperitif and dessert wines. See Bual, Malmsey, Sercial, Verdelho and pages 139 to 143.

Malmsey

The sweetest and most unctuous dessert madeira.

Mateus Rosé Trás-os-M. p. ★

World's biggest-selling medium-sweet carbonated rosé, made by SOGRAPE at VILLA REAL.

Monção
>   Sub-region of the VINHOS VERDES area on the R. Minho, producing the best of the "GREEN WINES" from the ALVARINHO grape.

Moscatel de Setubal Est'a. br. ★★★
>   Small demarcated region s. of the R. Tagus, where J. M. da Fonseca make an aromatic dessert muscat, 6 and 25 years old.

Palmela Est'a. r. ★★
>   Reliable CLARETES made by J. M. da Fonseca at Azeitão, s. of Lisbon.

Penafiel
>   Sub-region in the s. of the VINHOS VERDES area.

Perequita Est'a. r. ★★
>   One of Portugal's more robust reds, made by J. M. da Fonseca at Azeitão s. of Lisbon from a grape of that name.

Pinhel B'a.Al. r. ★
>   Undemarcated region e. of the DÃO, making similar wine.

Quinta de S. Claudio M'o. w. dr. ★★★
>   Estate at Esposende and maker of the best "GREEN WINE" outside MONÇÃO.

Quinta do Corval Trás-os-M. r. ★★
>   Estate near Pinhão making good light CLARETES.

Raposeira B'a.Al. sp. ★★
>   One of the best-known Portuguese sparkling wines, made by the champagne method at Lamego. Ask for the *bruto* (extra dry).

Ribeiros D'o. w. dr. ★★
>   "GREEN WINE" from the firm of Ribeiro & Irmão.

Sercial
>   The driest of madeiras, drunk as an aperitif. Made from a grape thought to have originated from the Riesling.

Serradayres Est'a. r. (w.) ★★
>   Blended table wines from Carvalho, Ribeiro & Ferreira, Lda. Sound and very drinkable.

Setubal
>   See Moscatel

Sogrape
>   Sociedad Comercial dos Vinhos de Mesa de Portugal. Largest wine concern in the country, making VINHOS VERDES, DÃO, MATEUS ROSÉ, VILA REAL red, etc.

Terras Altas B'a.Al. r. w. res. ★★
>   Good DÃO wines made by J. M. da Fonseca.

Verdelho
>   A semi-sweet madeira, drunk either at the beginning of a meal or with Madeira cake.

Vila Real Trás-os-M. r. ★→★★
>   Town in the upper DOURO now making some good undemarcated red table wine.

Vinho branco White wine.
>   **consumo** Ordinary wine.
>   **doce** Sweet wine.
>   **espumante** Sparkling wine.
>   **generoso** Aperitif or dessert wine rich in alcohol.
>   **maduro** A normal, mature table wine—as opposed to a VINHO VERDE.
>   **rosado** Rosé wine.
>   **seco** Dry wine.
>   **tinto** Red wine.
>   **verde** See under Green Wines

Vinhos Verdes M'o. and D'o. r. ★ w. dr. ★→★★★
>   Demarcated region between R. Douro and n. frontier with Spain, producing "GREEN WINES".

North Africa & Asia

Algeria

The massive v'yds. of Algeria have dwindled in the last ten years from 860,000 acres to under 600,000. Red wines of some quality are made in the coastal hills of Tlemcen, Mascara, Haut-Dahra, Zaccar and Ain-Bessem. Most goes for blending today. The Soviet Union is the biggest buyer.

Iran

One of the first of all wine countries, after a long period of abstention, is making wine again in considerable quantities and of fair quality.

Israel

Israeli wine, since the industry was re-established by a Rothschild in the 1880s, has been primarily of Kosher interest until recently, when CABERNET, SAUVIGNON BLANC, SEMILLON and GRENACHE of fair quality have been introduced. Carmel is the principal brand.

Lebanon

The small Lebanese wine industry, based on Ksara, has made red wine of real vigour and quality.

Morocco

Morocco today makes North Africa's best wine from v'yds. along the Atlantic coast and round Meknes. In ten years the v'yds. have declined from 190,000 to 170,000 acres. Sidi Larbi and Dar Bel Amri are the best reds; Gris de Boulaoune a very dry pale rosé.

Tunisia

Tunisia now has 90,000 acres compared with 120,000 ten years ago. Her speciality is sweet muscat, but reasonable reds come from Carthage, Grombalia and Cap Bon.

Turkey

Most of Turkey's huge v'yds. produce table grapes. But her wines, from Thrace, Anatolia and the Aegean, are remarkably good. Trakya (Thrace) white and Buzbag red are the well-known standards of the State wineries. Doluca and Kavaklidere are private firms of good quality. Villa Doluca red is remarkable: dry, full-bodied, deep-flavoured and vigorous.

USSR

With over 3 million acres of v'yds. the USSR is the world's fourth-biggest wine-producer—but almost entirely for home consumption. The Ukraine (incl. the Crimea) is the biggest v'yd. republic, followed by Moldavia, the Russian Republic and Georgia. The Soviet consumer has a sweet tooth, for both table and dessert wines. Of the latter the best come from the Crimea (esp. Massandra). Moldavia and the Ukraine use the same grapes as Romania, plus Cabernet, Riesling, Pinot Gris, etc. The Russian Republic makes the best Rieslings (esp. Arbau, Beshtau, Anapa) and sweet sparkling Tsimlanskoye "Champanski". Georgia uses mainly traditional grapes (esp. white Tsinandali and red Mukuzani) for good table wines.

Soviet wines are classified as ordinary (unmatured), "named" (matured in cask or vat) or "kollektsionye" (which are matured both in cask and bottle).

Japan

Japan has a small wine industry in Yamanashi Prefecture, w. of Tokyo. Standard wines are mainly blended with imports from Argentina, E. Europe, etc. Premium wines of Semillon, Cabernet and the local white grape, Koshu, are light but can be good, though expensive. Remarkable sweet wines with noble rot have been made. Main producers: Suntory, Mercian, Mann's.

Central & South-east Europe

Langenlois
Wachau Weinviertel
Vienna

AUSTRIA
Burgenland
Sopron Somló
Mátraalya
Budapest ●
HUNGARY
Styria
Lutomer
Balaton

Ljubljana ●
Slovenia
Slavonia
Zagreb ●
Vilányi-Pécs
Croatia
Vojvodina

Bosnia-
Herzegovina
JUGOSLAVIA
Dalmatia
Sarajevo ●

Montenegro

ALBAN

Corfu

Cep

The huge range of wines from the countries covered by this map offers some of the best value for money in the world today. Quality is moderate to high, tending to improve, and reliability on the whole is excellent.

The references are arranged country by country, with all geographical references back to the map on this page.

Labelling in all the countries involved except Greece is based on the German, now international, pattern of place-name plus grape-variety. The main grape-varieties are therefore included alongside areas and other terms in the alphabetic listings. Quality ratings in this section are given where there is enough information to warrant it.

Austria

Austria is new to the international wine trade—her domestic market has hitherto absorbed her whole crop—and consequently is still undervalued. Most of her practices and terms are similar to the German; the basic difference is a higher alcoholic degree in almost all her wine. New legislation is in force to control names and qualities. The Austrian Wine Quality Seal (Weingutesiegel or WGS), in the form of a red, white and gold disc on the bottle, means the wine has met fixed standards, been officially tested and approved.

Recent vintages:

1976	Big; good average quality.
1975	Big, high quality, alcoholic. Some wines lack acid.
1974	Small, light wines, the best delicate.
1973	Excellent quality.

Apetlon Burgenland w. s./sw. or sw. ★→ ★★

Village of the SEEWINKEL making tasty whites on sandy soil, incl. very good sweet wines.

Ausbruch

Means "syrupy"; specifically used for very sweet wines between Beerenauslese and Trockenbeerenauslese (see Germany) in richness.

Baden Vienna (r.) w. dr. or sw. ★→★★★

Town and area s. of VIENNA incl. GUMPOLDSKIRCHEN. Good lively high-flavoured wines, best from ROTGIPFLER and ZIERFÄNDLER grapes.

Blaufränkisch

The GAMAY grape.

Bouvier

Native Austrian grape giving soft but aromatic wine.

Burgenland Burgenland r. w. dr. sw. ★→ ★★★★

Region on the Hungarian border with ideal conditions for sweet wines. "Noble rot" occurs regularly and Ausleses are abundant. (See Rust, etc.)

Dürnstein w. dr. sw. ★★→★★★

Wine centre of the WACHAU with a famous ruined castle and important Winzergenossenschaft (co-op.). Some of Austria's best whites, esp. Rheinriesling and GRÜNER VELTLINER.

Eisenstadt Burgenland (r.) w. dr. or sw. ★★→★★★★

Town in BURGENLAND and historic seat of the ESTERHAZY family and their splendid cellars.

Esterhazy

Quasi-royal family whose AUSBRUCH and other BURGENLAND wines are of superlative quality.

Grinzing Vienna w. ★★ D.Y.A.

Suburb of VIENNA with delicious lively HEURIGE wines.

Grüner Veltliner

Austria's most characteristic white grape (26% of her white v'yds.) making short-lived but marvellously spicy and flowery, racy and vital wine.

Gumpoldskirchen Vienna (r.) w. dr. or sw. ★★→★★★

Pretty resort s. of VIENNA with wines of great character.

Heiligenkreuz, Stift

Cistercian Monestary at THALLERN making some of Austria's best wine, particularly from a fine steep v'yd.: Wiege.

Heurige

Means both new wine and the tavern where it is drunk.

Kahlenberg Vienna w. ★★ D.Y.A.

Village and v'yd. hill n. of VIENNA, famous for HEURIGEN.

Kamp Langenlois (r.) w. dr. or sw. ★→★★

Tributary of the Danube (Donau) giving its name to wines from its valley, n. and e. of the WACHAU, incl. pleasant Veltliner (see Grüner Veltliner) and RIESLING.

Klöch Steiermark (r.) p. w. ★→★★

Capital of Styria, the s.e. province. No famous wines, but agreeable ones, esp. Traminer.

Klosterneuburg

Famous monastery, now a wine college and research station with magnificent cellars, just n. of VIENNA.

Krems Danube. w. ★ → ★★★

Town and district just e. of the WACHAU with good GRÜNER VELTLINER and Rheinriesling (see Riesling).

Langenlois Langenlois r. w. ★→★★

Chief town of the KAMP valley with many modest and some good wines, esp. peppery GRÜNER VELTLINER and Rheinriesling (see Riesling). Reds less interesting.

Lenz Moser

Austria's best known and most progressive grower, invented a high vine system and makes good to excellent wine at Röhrendorf near KREMS, APETLON, MAILBERG and elsewhere.

Mailberg Weinviertel w. ★★

Town of the WEINVIERTEL known for lively light wine, esp. LENZ MOSER's Malteser.

Morandell, Alois

Big-scale Viennese wine-merchant.

Mörbisch Burgenland r. w. dr. or sw. ★→★★★

Leading wine-village of BURGENLAND. Good sweet wines. Reds and dry whites not inspiring.

Müller-Thurgau

9% of all Austria's white grapes are Müller-Thurgau.

Muskat-Ottonel

The strain of muscat grape grown in e. Europe, incl. Austria.

Niederösterreich

Lower Austria: i.e. all the n.e. corner of the country.

Neuburger

Popular white grape: pleasant wine in KREMS/LANGENLOIS but soft and coarse in BURGENLAND.

Neusiedlersee

Shallow lake in sandy country on the Hungarian border, creating autumn mists and giving character to the sweet wines of BURGENLAND.

Nussdorf Vienna w. ★★

Suburb of VIENNA with well-known HEURIGEN.

Oggau Burgenland (r.) w. sw. ★★→★★★

One of the wine-centres of BURGENLAND, famous for Beerenausleses (see Germany) and AUSBRUCH.

Portugieser

With BLAUFRÄNKISCH, one of the two main red-wine grapes of Austria, giving dark but rather characterless wine.

Retz Weinviertel (r.) w. ★

Leading wine-centre of the WEINVIERTEL, known for pleasant GRÜNER VELTLINER, etc.

Ried

Vineyard: when named it is usually a good one.

Riesling

German Riesling is always called Rheinriesling. Riesling is Wälschriesling.

Rotgipfler

Good and high-flavoured grape peculiar to BADEN and GUMPOLDSKIRCHEN. Used with ZIERFÄNDLER to make lively whites. Very heavy/sweet on its own.

Ruländer
>   The PINOT GRIS grape.

Rust Burgenland (r.) w. dr. or sw. ★→★★★
>   Most famous wine centre of BURGENLAND, long and justly
>   famous for its AUSBRUCH, often made of mixed grape varieties.

St. Laurent
>   Traditional Austrian red grape, faintly muscat-flavoured.

Schilcher
>   Pleasant sharp rosé, speciality of STYRIA.

Schloss Grafenegg
>   Famous property of the Metternich family near KREMS.
>   Good standard white and excellent Auslesen.

Schluck
>   Name for the common white wine of the WACHAU, good when
>   drunk very young.

Seewinkel
>   "Sea corner": the sandy district around the NEUSIEDLERSEE.

Sievering Vienna w. ★★
>   Suburb of VIENNA with notable HEURIGEN.

Spätrot
>   Another name for ZIERFÄNDLER.

Spitzenwein
>   Top wines—as opposed to TISCHWEIN: ordinary "dish
>   wines".

Steiermark
>   Province in the s.e., not remarkable for wine but well-
>   supplied with it.

Stift
>   The word for a monastery. Monasteries have been, and still
>   are, very important in Austria's wine-making, combining
>   tradition and high standards with modern resources.

Styria
>   English name for STEIERMARK.

Thallern Vienna (r.) w. dr. or sw. ★★ →★★★
>   Village near GUMPOLDSKIRCHEN and trade-name of wines
>   from Stift HEILIGENKREUZ.

Tischwein
>   Everyday wine, as opposed to SPITZENWEIN.

Traiskirchen Vienna (r.) w. ★★
>   Village near GUMPOLDSKIRCHEN with similar wine.

Veltliner
>   See Grüner Veltliner

Vienna
>   See Wien

Vöslau Baden r. (w.) ★
>   Spa town s. of BADEN (and VIENNA) known for its reds
>   made of PORTUGIESER and BLAUFRÄNKISCH: sound and
>   refreshing but no more.

Wachau
>   District on the n. bank of the Danube round DÜRNSTEIN
>   with cliff-like slopes giving some of Austria's best whites,
>   esp. Rheinriesling (see Riesling) and GRÜNER VELTLINER.

Weinviertel
>   "The wine quarter": name given to the huge and productive
>   district between VIENNA and the Czech border. Mainly
>   light white wines.

Wien (Vienna)
>   The Capital city, with 1,800 acres of v'yds. in its suburbs
>   to supply its cafés and HEURIGEN.

Zierfändler
>   White grape of high flavour peculiar to the BADEN area. Used
>   with ROTGIPFLER.

Hungary

Aszu

> Word meaning "syrupy" applied to very sweet wines, esp. Tokay (TOKAJI), where the "aszu" is late-picked and "nobly rotten" as in Sauternes. (See p. 52.)

Badacsony   Balaton w. dr. sw. `★★→★★★`

> 1,400 ft. hill on the n. shore of La. BALATON whose basalt soil gives rich high-flavoured wines, among Hungary's best.

Balatonfüred   Balaton (r.) w. dr. sw. ★★

> Town on the n. shore of La. BALATON e. of BADACSONY. Good but softer, less fiery wines.

Balaton   Balaton r. w. dr. sw. `★` → ★★★

> Hungary's inland sea and Europe's largest lake. Many wines take its name and most are good. The ending "i" (e.g. Balatoni, Egri) is the equivalent of -er in German names, or in Londoner.

Bársonyos–Császár

> Wine-district of n. Hungary. MÓR is its best-known centre.

Bikavér

> "Bull's Blood"—or words to that effect. The historic name of the best-selling red wine of EGER: full-bodied and well-balanced, improving considerably with age.

Csopak

> Village next to BALATONFÜRED, with similar wines.

Debrö   Mátraalya w. sw. ★★★

> Important centre of the MÁTRAALYA famous for its pale, aromatic and sweet HÁRSLEVELÜ.

Eger   Mátraalya r. w. dr. sw. ★→ `★★`

> Best-known MÁTRAALYA wine-centre: fine baroque city of cellars full of BIKAVÉR. Also delicate white LEANYKA and dark sweetish MERLOT, known as MÉDOC NOIR.

Eszencia

> The fabulous quintessence of Tokay (TOKAJI): intensely sweet grape-juice of very low, if any, alcoholic strength, reputed to have miraculous properties. Now almost unobtainable.

Ezerjó

> The grape grown at MÓR to make one of Hungary's best dry white wines: distinguished, fragrant and fine.

Furmint

> The classic grape of Tokay (TOKAJI), with great flavour and fire, also grown for table wine on La. BALATON with excellent results.

Hajós   Mecsek r. `★`

> Town in s. Hungary becoming known as a centre for good CABERNET SAUVIGNON reds.

Hárslevelü

> The "lime-leaved" grape used at DEBRÖ to make good gently sweet wine.

Kadarka

> The commonest red grape of Hungary, grown in vast quantities for everyday wine on the plains in the s.; also used at EGER; capable of ample flavour and interesting maturity.

Kékfrankos

> Hungarian for GAMAY, literally "blue French". Makes good light red at SOPRON on the Austrian border.

Kéknelyü

> High-flavoured white grape making the best and "stiffest" wine of Mt. BADACSONY: fiery and spicy stuff.

Leanyka

> East-European white grape better known in Romania but making admirable pale soft wine at EGER.

Mátraalya
> Wine-district in the foothills of the Matra range in n. Hungary, incl. DEBRÖ and EGER.

Mecsek
> District in s. Hungary known for the good reds of VILÁNY and whites of PÉCS.

Médoc Noir
> Hungarian name for MERLOT, used to make sweet red at EGER.

Monimpex
> The Hungarian state export monopoly, with great cellars at Budafok, near Budapest.

Mór North Hungary w. dr. ★★★
> Town in n. Hungary famous for its fresh dry EZERJÓ.

Muskotály
> Hungarian muscat, used to add aroma to Tokay (TOKAJI) and occasionally alone at EGER, where its wine is long-lived and worth tasting.

Nágyburgundi
> Literally "black burgundy"—the PINOT NOIR makes admirable wine in s. Hungary, esp. round VILÁNY.

Olasz Riesling
> The Hungarian name for the Italian, or Wälsch riesling.

Pécs Mecsek (r.) w. dr. ★★
> Town in the Mecsek hills known in the West for its agreeable well-balanced (if rather sweet) Riesling.

Puttonyos
> The measure of sweetness in Tokay (TOKAJI). A 7-gal. container from which ASZU is added to SZAMORODNI. One "putt" makes it sweetish; 5 (the maximum) very sweet indeed.

Siller
> Pale red or rosé. Usually made from KADARKA grapes.

Somló North Hungary w. dr. ★★★
> Isolated small v'yd. district n. of BALATON making intense white wines of high repute from FURMINT and RIESLING.

Sopron Burgenland r. ★★
> Little Hungarian enclave in Burgenland s. of the Neusiedlersee (see Austria) specializing in KÉKFRANKOS (Gamay) red.

Szamorodni
> Word meaning "as it comes": i.e. fully fermented (therefore dry) wine from all the grapes not specially selected. Used to describe the unsweetened form of Tokay (TOKAJI).

Szürkebarát
> Literally means "grey friar": Hungarian for PINOT GRIS, which makes rich heavy wine in the BALATON v'yds.

Szekszárdi Vörös Mecsek r. ★★
> The red (KADARKA) wine of Szekszárd in south-central Hungary. Dark strong wine which needs age.

Tokaji (Tokay) Tokaji w. dr. sw. ★★ → ★★★★
> Hungary's famous strong sweet wine, comparable to an oxidized Sauternes, from hills on the Russian border in the n.e. See Aszu, Eszencia, Furmint, Puttonyos, Szamorodni.

Tramini
> The TRAMINER grape; little grown in Hungary.

Vilány Mecsek r. p. (w.) ★★
> Southernmost city of Hungary and well-known centre of red wine production. Vilányi Burgundi is largely PINOT NOIR—and very good.

Wälschriesling
> Austrian name sometimes used for Olasz (Italian) Riesling.

Zöldszilváni
> "Green Sylvaner"—i.e. Sylvaner. Grown round La. BALATON.

Romania

Alba Iulia

Town in the TIRNĂVE area in Transylvania, known for off-dry whites blended from Italian Riesling, FETEASCĂ and MUSCAT OTTONEL.

Aligoté

The junior white burgundy grape makes pleasantly fresh white wine in Romania.

Babeaşcă

Traditional red grape of the FOCSANI area: agreeably sharp wine tasting slightly of cloves.

Banat

The plain on the border with Serbia. Workaday Riesling and light red CADARCA.

Cabernet

Increasingly grown in Romania, particularly at DEALUL MARE, to make dark intense wines often too sweet for French-trained palates.

Cadarca

Romanian spelling of the Hungarian Kadarka.

Chardonnay

The great white burgundy grape is used at MURFATLAR to make honey-sweet dessert wine.

Cotesti

Part of the FOCSANI area making reds of PINOT NOIR, MERLOT, etc., and dry whites said to resemble Alsace wines.

Cotnari

Romania's most famous historical wine: light dessert wine from MOLDAVIA. Like very delicate Tokay.

Dealul Mare

Important up-to-date vineyard area in the s.e. Carpathian foothills, specializing in red wines from CABERNET, MERLOT, PINOT NOIR, etc.

Dobruja

Black Sea region round the port of Constanta. MURFATLAR is the main v'yd. area.

Drăgăşani

Region on the river Olt s. of the Carpathians, growing both traditional and "modern" grapes. Good MUSCAT-OTTONEL.

Fetească

Romanian white grape of mild character, the same as Hungary's Leanyka (and some say Switzerland's Chasselas).

Focsani

Important eastern wine region including those of COTESTI, ODOBESTI and NICORESTI.

Grasă

A form of the Hungarian Furmint grape grown in Romania and used in, among other wines, COTNARI.

Moldavia

The n.e. province, now largely within the USSR.

Murfatlar

Big modern v'yds. near the Black Sea specializing in sweet wines, incl. very sweet CHARDONNAY.

Muskat-Ottonel

The e. European muscat, at its best in Romania.

Nicoresti

Eastern area of FOCSANI best known for its red BABEAŞCĂ.

Odobesti

The central part of FOCSANI; mainly white wines of FETEASCĂ, RIESLING, etc.

Perla

The speciality of TÎRNĂVE: a pleasant blended semi-sweet white of RIESLING, FETEASCĂ and MUSCAT OTTONEL.

Pitesti

    Principal town of the Arges region s. of the Carpathians.
Traditionally whites from FETEASCĂ, TĂMIÎOASĂ, RIESLING.

Riesling

    I.e. Italian Riesling. Very widely planted. No exceptional
wines.

Sadova

    Town in the SEGARCEA area exporting an unexciting sweetish
rosé.

Segarcea

    Southern wine area near the Danube. Exports rather sweet
CABERNET.

Tămiîoasă

    A traditional white-wine grape variety of no very distinct
character.

Tîrnăve

    Important Transylvanian wine region, known for its PERLA
and MUSCAT OTTONEL.

Valea Călugărească

    "The Valley of the Monks", part of the DEALUL MARE v'yd.
with a well-known research station. CABERNET, MERLOT and
PINOT NOIR are made into heavy sweet wines.

Jugoslavia

Amselfelder

    German marketing name for the red Burgundac (Spät-
burgunder or PINOT NOIR) wine of KOSOVO.

Banat

    North-eastern area, partly in Romania, with up-to-date
wineries making adequate RIESLING.

Beli Pinot

    The PINOT BLANC, a popular grape in SLOVENIA.

Bijelo

    White.

Blatina

    The red grape and wine of MOSTAR. Not in the same class as
the white ZILAVKA.

Bogdanuşa

    Local white grape of the Dalmatian islands, esp. Hvar and
Brac. Pleasant fresh faintly fragrant wine.

Burgundac Bijeli

    The CHARDONNAY, grown a little in SLAVONIA and VOJVODINA.

Cabernet

    See Grapes for red wine. Now introduced in many places,
without notable success so far.

Crno

    Black—i.e. red wine.

Ćviček

    Traditional pale red or dark rosé of SLOVENIA.

Dalmaciajavino

    Important co-operative based at Split and selling a full range
of coastal and island wines.

Dalmatia

    The middle coast of Jugoslavia from Rijeka to Dubrovnik.
Has a remarkable variety of wines of character.

Dingac

    Heavy sweetish red from the local PLAVAC grape, speciality
of the mid-Dalmatian coast.

Fruska Gora
> Hills in VOJVODINA, on the Danube n.w. of Belgrade, with a growing modern v'yd. and a wide range of wines, incl. good Traminer and Sauvignon Blanc.

Graševina
> Slovenian for Italian Riesling (also called Wälschriesling, LASKI RIZLING, etc.). The normal Riesling of Jugoslavia.

Grk
> Strong almost sherry-like white from the Grk grape. Speciality of the island of Korcula.

Istria
> Peninsula in the n. Adriatic, Porec its centre, with a variety of pleasant wines, the MERLOT as good as any.

Jerusalem
> Jugoslavia's most famous v'yd., at LJUTOMER.

Kadarka
> The major red grape of Hungary, widely grown in SERBIA.

Kosovo
> Region in the s., between SERBIA and Macedonia, with modern v'yds. The source of AMSELFELDER.

Laski Rizling
> Yet another name for Italian Riesling.

Ljutomer (or Lutomer)-Ormoz
> Jugoslavia's best known and probably best wine district, in n.e. SLOVENIA, famous for its RIESLING: full-flavoured, full-strength and at its best rich and satisfying wine.

Malvasia
> White grape giving luscious heavy wine, used in w. SLOVENIA.

Marastina
> Strong dry white of the Dalmatian islands.

Maribor
> Important wine-centre of n. SLOVENIA. White wines incl. SIPON, Ruländer, etc., as well as RIESLING and Austrian BOUVIER (see Austria).

Merlot
> The Bordeaux red grape, grown in SLOVENIA and ISTRIA with reasonable results.

Mostar
> Islamic-looking little city inland from DALMATIA, making admirable dry white from the ZILAVKA grape. Also BLATINA.

Muskat-Ottonel
> The East European muscat, grown in VOJVODINA.

Navip
> The big growers' co-operative of SERBIA, with its headquarters at Belgrade.

Opol
> Pleasantly light pale red made of PLAVAĆ grapes round Split and Sibenik in DALMATIA.

Plavać Mali
> Native red grape of SLOVENIA and DALMATIA: makes DINGAC, POSTUP, OPOL, etc.

Plavina
> Light red of the DALMATIAN coast round Zadar.

Plovdina
> Native red grape of Macedonia in the s., giving mild wine. Grown and generally blended with PROKUPAC.

Posip
> Pleasant, not-too-heavy white wine of the Dalmatian islands, notably Korcula.

Postup
> Sweet and heavy DALMATIAN red from the Peljesac peninsula near Korcula. Highly esteemed locally.

Portugizac

Austria's Portugieser: plain red wine.

Prokupac

Principal native red grape of s. SERBIA and Macedonia: 85% of the production. Makes good dark rosé (RUZICA) and full-bodied red of character. Some of the best comes from ZUPA. PLOVDINA is often added for smoothness.

Prosek

The dessert wine of DALMATIA, of stupefying natural strength and very variable quality. The best is excellent, but hard to find.

Radgonska Ranina

Ranina is Austria's BOUVIER grape (see Austria). Radgona is near Maribor. The wine is sweet and carries the trade name TIGROVO MLJEKO (Tiger's Milk).

Rajnski Rizling

The Rhine Riesling, rare in Jugoslavia but grown a little in LJUTOMER-ORMOZ.

Refosco

Italian grape grown in e. SLOVENIA and ISTRIA under the name TERAN.

Renski Rizling

Alternative spelling for Rhine Riesling.

Riesling

Without qualification means Italian Riesling.

Ruzica

Rosé, usually from PROKUPAC. Darker than most; and better.

Serbia

The e. state of Jugoslavia, with nearly half the country's v'yds., stretching from VOJVODINA to Macedonia.

Sipon

Jugoslav name for the FURMINT grape of Hungary, also grown in SLOVENIA.

Slavonia

Northern Croatia, on the Hungarian border between SLOVENIA and SERBIA. A big producer of standard wines, mainly white.

Slovenia

The n.w. state, incl. Jugoslavia's most European-style v'yds. and wines: LJUTOMER, etc.

Teran

Stout dark red of ISTRIA. See REFOSCO.

Tigrovo Mljeko

See Radgonska Ranina

Tocai

The PINOT GRIS, making rather heavy white wine in SLOVENIA, as in n.e. Italy.

Traminac

The TRAMINER. Grown in SLOVENIA and VOJVODINA. Particularly successful in the latter.

Vojvodina

An autonomous province of n. SERBIA with substantial, growing and improving v'yds. Wide range of grapes, both European and Balkan.

Zilavka

The white wine of MOSTAR in Hercegovina. One of Jugoslavia's best: dry, pungent and memorably fruity, with a faint flavour of apricots.

Zupa

Central SERBIAN district giving its name to above-average red and rosé (or dark and light red) of PROKUPAC and PLOVDINA: respectively Zupsko Crno and Zupsko Ruzica.

Bulgaria

Cabernet
> The Bordeaux grape is highly successful in n. Bulgaria. Excellent dark, vigorous, fruity and well-balanced wine.

Chardonnay
> The white burgundy grape is scarcely less successful. Very dry but full and deep-flavoured wine.

Dimiat
> The common native white grape, grown in the e. towards the coast. Agreeable dry white without memorable character.

Euxinograd
> Brand of blended white wine produced for export.

Fetiaska
> The same grape as Romania's Fetească and Hungary's Leanyka. Rather neutral but pleasant pale wine, best a trifle sweet, sold as Donau Perle.

Gamza
> The common red grape, Hungary's Kadarka: gives fairly light but "stiff" and worthwhile wine.

Hemus
> A pale medium to sweet muscat from KARLOVO.

Iskra
> The national brand of sparkling wine, normally sweet but of fair quality.

Karlovo
> Town in central Bulgaria famous for the "Valley of Roses" and its very pleasant white MISKET.

Mavrud
> Darkly plummy red from s. Bulgaria. Improves with age.

Melnik
> City of the extreme s.e. Such concentrated MAVRUD that the locals say it can be carried in a handkerchief.

Misket
> Bulgaria's muscat: locally popular flavour in sweet whites.

Pamid
> The light, quite soft, everyday red of s. and central Bulgaria.

Rcatzitelli
> One of Russia's favourite white grapes for strong sweet wine. Grown in n.e. Bulgaria.

Riesling
> Normally refers to Italian Riesling, though some Rhine Riesling is grown. In the brand known as Rosenthaler Riesling (for export to Germany) the two are apparently blended.

Saperavi
> Russian red grape, presumably used for export to Russia: the biggest export market.

Sonnenküste
> Brand of medium-sweet white sold in Germany.

Sungurlare
> Eastern town giving its name to a sweet MISKET, similar to that of KARLOVO.

Sylvaner
> Some pleasant dry SYLVANER is exported as "Klosterkeller".

Tamianka
> Sweet white; sweeter than HEMUS.

Tirnovo
> Strong sweet red wine.

Trakia
> Dry or medium-dry white.

Vinimpex
> The "State Commercial Enterprise for Export and Import of Wines and Spirits".

Greece

Achaia–Clauss

The best-known Greek wine-merchant, with cellars at Patras, n. PELOPONNESE.

Attica

Region round Athens, the chief source of RETSINA.

Cambas, Andrew

Important Athenian wine-growers and merchants.

Castel Danielis

One of the best brands of dry red wine, from ACHAIA-CLAUSS.

Corfu

Adriatic island with wines scarcely worthy of it. Ropa is the traditional red.

Crete

Island with the name for some of Greece's better wine, esp. MAVRO ROMEIKO.

Demestica

A reliable standard brand of dry red and white from ACHAIA-CLAUSS.

Hymettus

Standard brand of dry white without resin.

Kokkineli

The rosé version of RETSINA: very like the white. Drink very cold.

Lindos

Name for the higher quality of RHODES wine, whether from Lindos itself or not. Acceptable; no more.

Malvasia

The famous grape is said to originate from Monemvasia in the s. PELOPONNESE.

Mavro

"Black"—the word for dark red wine.

Mavrodaphne

Literally "black laurel": dark sweet concentrated red; a speciality of the Patras region, n. PELOPONNESE.

Mavro Romeiko

The best red wine of Crete, reputedly among the best of Greece: dry and full-bodied.

Mavroudi

The red wine of Delphi and the n. shore of the Gulf of Corinth: dark and plummy.

Naoussa

Above-average strong dry red from Macedonia in the n.

Nemea

Town in the e. PELOPONNESE famous for its lion (a victim of Hercules) and its fittingly forceful MAVRO.

Peloponnese

The s. landmass of mainland Greece, with a third of the whole country's v'yds.

Pendeli

Reliable brand of dry red from ATTICA, grown and bottled by Andrew CAMBAS.

Retsina

White wine with pine resin added, tasting of turpentine and oddly appropriate with Greek food. The speciality of ATTICA. Drink it very cold.

Rhodes

Easternmost Greek island. Its sweet MALVASIAS are its best wines. LINDOS is the brand name for tolerable table wines.

Rombola

The dry white of Cephalonia; island off the Gulf of Corinth.

Ropa

See Corfu

Samos

Island off the Turkish coast with a reputation for its sweet pale-golden muscat. The normal commercial quality is nothing much.

Santorin

Island north of Crete, making sweet Vinsanto from sun-dried grapes, and dry white Thira.

Verdea

The dry white of Zakinthos, the island just w. of the PELO-PONNESE.

Cyprus

Afames

Village at the foot of Mt. Olympus, giving its name to one of the better red (MAVRON) wines.

Aphrodite

Full-bodied medium-dry white, named after the Greek goddess of love.

Arsinöe

Dry white wine, named after an unfortunate female whom Aphrodite turned to stone.

Bellapais

Rather fizzy medium-sweet white named after the famous abbey near Kyrenia.

Christoforou

Family-directed wine firm at LIMASSOL.

Commandaria

Good-quality brown dessert wine made since ancient times and named after a crusading order of knights. The best is superb, of incredible sweetness. Normal qualities are much used as Communion wine.

Haggipavlu

Well-known wine-merchant at LIMASSOL.

Keo

One of the biggest firms in the wine trade at LIMASSOL.

Kokkineli

Rosé: the name is related to "cochineal".

Limassol

" The Bordeaux of Cyprus". The wine-port in the s.

Mavron

The black grape of Cyprus (and Greece) and its dark wine.

Mosaic

The brand-name of KEO's Cyprus sherries.

Othello

Perhaps the best dry red: solid, satisfying wine.

Pitsilia

Region s. of Mt. Olympus producing the best white and COMMANDARIA wines.

Rosella

Brand of strong medium-sweet rosé.

St Panteleimon

Brand of strong sweet white.

Sherry

Cyprus makes a full range of sherry-style wines, the best (particularly the dry) of very good quality.

SODAP

Major wine firm at LIMASSOL.

Xynisteri

The native white grape of Cyprus.

117

California

California has been making wine for 150 years, but her modern wine industry has grown from scratch in scarcely more than 25. Today it leads the world in good-quality cheap wines and startles it with a handful of luxury wines of brilliant quality. In the last five years the industry has expanded and altered at a frenzied pace, which is reflected in the entries that follow: nearly 30 of them state "new winery . . .". Quality ratings must therefore be tentative.

Grape-varieties (combined with brand-names) are the key to California wine. Since grapes in California play many new roles they are separately listed on the next two pages. For recent vintages see p. 127.

The areas referred to in the winery entries (and shown on the map) are listed below.

Vineyard areas

Central Coast
> A long sweep of coast with scattered wine activity, from San Francisco Bay s. to San Luis Obispo.

Central Coast/Santa Barbara
> Some of the newest planting in the state is round the Santa Maria river n. of Santa Barbara, where coastal fog gives particularly cool conditions.

Central Coast/Santa Cruz
> Wineries are scattered round the Santa Cruz mountains s. of San Francisco Bay, from Paul Masson at Saratoga down to the HECKER PASS.

Central Coast/Hecker Pass
> Pass through the Santa Cruz Mts. s. of San Francisco Bay with a cluster of small old-style wineries.

Central Coast/Salinas
> The main concentration of new planting in the Central Coast: the Salinas valley runs inland s.e. from Monterey.

Livermore
> Valley e. of San Francisco Bay long famous for white wines but now largely built over.

California grape varieties

CALIFORNIA

Lodi

San Joaquin

San Joaquin R.

San Luis Obispo

Santa Barbara

● Los Angeles

Southern California

● San Diego

Lodi

Town and district at the n. end of the San Joaquin Valley, its hot climate modified by a westerly air-stream.

Mendocino

Northernmost coastal wine country; a varied climate, much of it hotter than Sonoma and Napa farther s.

Napa

The Napa Valley, n. of San Francisco Bay, well-established as the top-quality wine area.

Rancho California

Very new small area in s. California, 25 miles inland halfway between San Diego and Riverside.

San Joaquin Valley

The great central valley of California, fertile and hot; the source of most of the jug wines and dessert wines in the State.

Sonoma and Sonoma/Russian River (R.R.)

County n. of San Francisco Bay, between Napa and the sea. Most v'yds. are in the n. round the Russian River. A few, historically important, are in the Valley of the Moon in the s.

Sonoma/Alexander Valley

New quality area in Sonoma county, between the Russian River and the n. end of the Napa Valley.

California: grape varieties

Barbera
> Darkly plummy variety from Piemonte (see Italy). Gives full-blooded and astringent wine in cool areas, good but softer wine in hot ones.

Cabernet Sauvignon
> The best red-wine grape in California with a wide range of styles from delicately woody to overpoweringly fruity. The classic Napa grape.

Carignane
> Common bulk-producing red grape rarely used as a "varietal", but occasionally with some success.

Charbono
> Rare red grape of Italian origin and no distinction, like eviscerated Barbera.

Chardonnay
> The best white-wine grape—indeed the best wine-grape—in California. Styles of making vary from merely clean and grapy to rich, concentrated and complex like the best white burgundies.

Chenin Blanc
> A work-horse white grape with a surprising turn of speed when made dry and in limited, concentrated quantities. But usually made soft and sweet.

Emerald Riesling
> A Californian original in the German manner. Clean, flowery/fruity and a touch tart.

Flora
> Another California-bred white grape. Mildly flowery; best made sweet.

Folle Blanche
> Acidic white with good performance but little used.

French Colombard
> Another high-acid white coming into favour for clean semi-dry wines made more German-style than French.

Gamay (or Napa Gamay)
> The red grape of Beaujolais. Agreeable but never remarkable in California.

Gamay Beaujolais
> Not the red grape of Beaujolais, but a selection of Pinot Noir good for light summer wines.

Gewürztraminer
> Generally softer and less aromatically thrilling in California than in France, but at best one of the real successes.

Green Hungarian
> A minority interest: rather tasteless white, but capable of liveliness.

Grenache
> The most successful grape for rosé in California; generally, alas, made sweet.

Grey Riesling
> Not a Riesling but a minor French grape used for full-bodied but scarcely notable white.

Grignolino
> Distinctive highly seasoned grape good for young reds and rosés.

Johannisberg Riesling
> Real Rhine Riesling (also known as White Riesling). Often rather strong and bland in California, but at its best (and in Auslese-style wines) gloriously complex and satisfying.

Merlot
> The St-Emilion grape is oddly rare in California. Very good heavy reds have been made.

Muscat

Light sweet pale gold muscat is one of California's prettiest treats.

Petite Syrah

The name of the Rhône's and Australia's great red grape has been wrongly applied to a poor one. Generally used in Burgundy blends. But the real one is present in small quantities, and has great promise.

Pinot Blanc

Has been ousted by the better Chardonnay.

Pinot Noir

Has yet to reach consummation in California. Most wine with the name is disappointing; a minute proportion thrilling.

Pinot St George

Only used by one winery—The Christian Brothers—to make a thoroughly agreeable sturdy red.

Riesling

See Johannisberg Riesling. Also Sylvaner

Ruby Cabernet

A California-bred cross between Carignane and Cabernet Sauvignon with enough of the character of the latter to be interesting. Good in hot conditions.

Sauvignon Blanc

Excellent white grape used either Sancerre style (fresh, aromatic, effervescent) or Graves style (fat, chewable). The former usually called Fumé Blanc.

Semillon

High-flavoured whites from the cooler areas; bland ones from hotter places. The most memorable are sweet.

Sylvaner

Is often labelled Riesling, but has none of its finesse or balance. Often decent semi-dry wine.

Zinfandel

California's own red grape, open to many interpretations from light-weight fruity to galumphing. Capable of ageing to great quality.

Recent Vintages

The Californian climate is far from being as consistent as its reputation. Although on the whole grapes ripen regularly, they are subject to severe spring frosts in many areas, sometimes a wet harvest-time, and such occasional calamities as the two-year drought of 1975–7.

Wines from the San Joaquin Valley tend to be most consistent year by year. The vintage date on these, where there is one, is more important for telling the age of the wine than its character.

Vineyards in the Central Coast are mainly so new that no pattern of vintage qualities has yet emerged.

The Napa Valley is the one area where comment can be made on the last ten vintages of the top varietal wines: Cabernet Sauvignon and Chardonnay.

	Chardonnay	Cabernet Sauvignon
1966	Now mature: solid, not great.	Huge and uniformly very good.
1967	Weak.	Weak.
1968	Well-balanced: now ageing.	Fine, well balanced, for keeping.
1969	Weak.	Good, not great.
1970	Good all round: not great: mature.	Best ever.
1971	Good balance: long lived.	Average.
1972	The best wines of a cool year.	Uneven: rain: many poor wines.
1973	Good.	Big and good.
1974	Very good.	Difficult: the best excellent.
1975	Good.	Good.
1976	Difficult: variable.	Small crop but splendid.

Wineries

Almaden   Central Coast. Full range ⋆→ ⎡⋆⋆⎤
> Big winery famous for pioneer varietal labelling and pioneer planting in the Central Coast. Now owned by National Distillers. Reliable popular wines tend to sweetness.

Ambassador
> Brand name of PERELLI-MINETTI.

Assumption Abbey
> Brand name of BROOKSIDE.

Barengo   Lodi. Table and dessert ⋆→⋆⋆
> Small firm making wines of character, especially ZINFANDEL and RUBY CABERNET.

Bear Mountain   San Joaquin. Table and dessert ⎡⋆⎤
> Growers' co-operative near Bakersfield. Uses the M. Lamont label for well-made varietals, incl. a good FRENCH COLOMBARD.

Beaulieu   Napa. Table and sp. ⋆⋆→⋆⋆⋆⋆
> Rightly famous medium-size growers and makers of esp. CABERNET and CHARDONNAY. Top wine: De Latour Private Reserve Cabernet. Now owned by Heublein Corp.

Beringer   Napa. Table and dessert ⎡⋆⋆⎤ → ⋆⋆⋆
> Century-old winery recently modernized by Nestlé Co. Increasingly interesting wines incl. Auslese types.

Brookside   S. California. Table and dessert ⋆→⋆⋆
> Traditional dessert wine firm also making table varietals from RANCHO CALIFORNIA under the Assumption Abbey label.

Buena Vista   Sonoma. Table ⋆⋆
> Historic pioneer winery with chequered recent record. Wines include old-style ZINFANDEL from its reputed original v'yd.

Burgess Cellars   Napa. Table ⋆⋆
> Small hillside winery, originally called Souverain, making sound traditional-style wine.

B.V.
> Abbreviation of BEAULIEU VINEYARDS used on their labels.

California Growers   San Joaquin. Table and dessert ⋆
> Co-operative known for sherry and brandy, now also varietal table wines, some labelled Setrakian.

California Wine Association
> See Perelli-Minetti

Callaway   S. California. Table ⋆⋆
> Small new winery in new territory at RANCHO CALIFORNIA. Early reds are strong, dark, conservative.

Cambiaso   Sonoma R-R. Table ⋆
> Recently rebuilt old country winery.

Camus   Napa. Table ⎡⋆⋆⋆⎤
> New small winery at Rutherford with Fumé-style SAUVIGNON, Spätlese-style RIESLING and 1974 CABERNET all notable.

Carneros Creek   Napa. Table ⋆⋆
> The first winery in the cool Carneros area between Napa and San Francisco Bay. Specialities will be PINOT NOIR and CHARDONNAY.

Chalone   Central Coast/Salinas. Table ⎡⋆⋆⋆⋆⎤
> Unique small hilltop v'yd. and winery at the Pinnacles. French-style CHARDONNAY and PINOT NOIR of superb quality, good FRENCH COLOMBARD.

Chappellet   Napa. Table ⋆⋆⋆⋆
> Small modern luxury winery and hillside v'yd. Good CABERNET SAUVIGNON and RIESLING, very good dry CHENIN BLANC.

Château Montelena   Napa. Table ⋆⋆→⋆⋆⋆
> New small winery making good distinctive RIESLING, CHARDONNAY, ZINFANDEL and CABERNET SAUVIGNON.

Château St Jean   Sonoma. Table ⋆⋆⋆
> New small winery specializing in richly flavoured whites, incl. CHARDONNAY and PINOT BLANC.

Christian Brothers   Napa and San Joaquin. Full range `★★→★★★`
The biggest Napa winery, run by a religious order, specializing in consistent undated blends, incl. excellent CABERNET SAUVIGNON, useful PINOT ST GEORGE, sweet white Ch. La Salle and very good brandy. Best wines labelled Brother Timothy Selection.

Clos du Val   Napa. Table ★★
New small French-owned winery making strong rustic ZINFANDEL and fine delicate CABERNET SAUVIGNON.

Concannon   Livermore. Table ★★→★★★
Substantial family winery famous for SAUVIGNON BLANC and SEMILLON, but with reds of equal quality.

Cresta Blanca   Mendocino and San Joaquin. Table and dessert ★★
Old name from Livermore revived on the n. coast by new owners, GUILD co-op. Husky ZINFANDEL and PETITE SYRAH. Mild whites.

Cuvaison   Napa. Table ★★
Small winery with expert new direction. Too soon to say more.

David Bruce   Central Coast. Table ★★★★
Small luxury winery with heavy-weight old-style wines.

Domaine Chandon   Napa. sp. ★★★
Californian outpost of Moët & Chandon Champagne. Launched 1976.

Dry Creek   Sonoma. Table ★★★
New small winery with high ideals, making old-fashioned dry wines, esp. CHARDONNAY and CHENIN BLANC.

East-Side   San Joaquin. Table and dessert ★
Progressive growers' co-operative best known for its Royal Host label. Good RUBY CABERNET, EMERALD RIESLING, ZINFANDEL.

Eleven Cellars
Brand name of PERELLI-MINETTI.

Fetzer   Mendocino. Table ★★
Ten-year-old small winery with interesting but inconsistent wines, incl. CABERNET SAUVIGNON, SAUVIGNON BLANC, ZINFANDEL, SEMILLON.

Ficklin   San Joaquin. Dessert (and table) ★★★
Family firm making California's best "port" and minute quantities of table wine.

Firestone   Central Coast/Santa Barbara. Table ★★
Ambitious new (1975) winery in a new area n. of Santa Barbara. Cool conditions are producing interesting wines, incl. PINOT NOIR and RIESLING.

Franciscan Vineyard   Napa. ★★
New small-to-medium winery run by an ex-Christian Brother. Good ZINFANDEL and dry White RIESLING.

Franzia   San Joaquin. Full range ★→★★
Large old family winery now owned by Coca Cola. Various labels, but all say "made and bottled in Ripon". Noteworthy Burgundy and ZINFANDEL.

Freemark Abbey   Napa. Table ★★★
Small connoisseur's winery with high reputation for CABERNET SAUVIGNON, CHARDONNAY, PINOT NOIR and RIESLING.

Gallo, E. & J.   San Joaquin. Full range ★→ `★★`
The world's biggest winery, pioneer in both quantity and quality. Family owned. Hearty Burgundy and Chablis Blanc set national standards. Varietals incl. good FRENCH COLOMBARD, RUBY CABERNET, BARBERA.

Geyser Peak   Sonoma. Table ★★
Old winery recently revived and expanded by Schlitz Brewery. More steady than inspired.

Giumarra San Joaquin. Table ⋆

Recent installation making sound RUBY CABERNET and PETITE SYRAH from family v'yds. in hottest part of valley.

Grand Cru Sonoma. Table ⋆⋆

New small winery making good GEWÜRZ and light-weight ZINFANDEL.

Guild San Joaquin. Table and dessert ⋆

Big growers' co-operative famous for Vino da Tavola semi-sweet red. New line of varietals with Winemasters label incl. good ZINFANDEL.

Gundlach-Bundschu Sonoma. Table ⋆⋆

Very old small family winery revived by the new generation. So far good whites: SYLVANER, CHARDONNAY, ZINFANDEL and CABERNET look promising.

Hacienda Sonoma. Table ⋆⋆

New small winery specializing in high-quality CHARDONNAY.

Hanzell Sonoma. Table ⋆⋆⋆

Small winery which revolutionized Californian CHARDONNAYS in the '50s under its founder, now in (very) new hands.

Hecker Pass

See Central Coast Districts

Heitz Napa. Table (and dessert) ⋆⋆⋆⋆

In many eyes the first name in California. An inspired individual wine-maker who has set standards for the whole industry. His CABERNETS (esp. "Martha's Vineyard") are dark, deep and emphatic, his best CHARDONNAYS peers of Montrachet.

Hoffmann Mtn. Ranch Cen. Coast San Luis Obispo. Table ⋆⋆⋆

New mid-sized winery in new area near Paso Robles. CHARDONNAY and PINOT NOIR are promising.

Inglenook Napa and San Joaquin. Table and dessert ⋆ → ⋆⋆⋆

One of the great old Napa wineries recently much changed by new owners: Heublein Corp. Special Cask CABERNET SAUVIGNON remains best wine. Other varieties sound. Inglenook Vintage is a second label, Inglenook Navalle a third and the best value: good cheap RUBY, ZINFANDEL and FRENCH COLOMBARD.

Italian Swiss Colony San Joaquin and Sonoma. Full range ⋆ → ⋆⋆

Honourable old name from Sonoma transferred to San Joaquin by new owners: Heublein Corp. Adequate standards; one wine of note: Tipo Chianti. Lejon is a second label.

Korbel Sonoma. Sp. and table ⋆⋆⋆

Distinguished sparkling wine specialists. "Natural" and "Brut" are among California's best "champagnes".

Kornell Napa. Sp. ⋆⋆⋆

Fine sparkling wine house making excellent full-flavoured dry wines: Brut and Sehr Trocken.

Krug, Charles Napa. Table and dessert ⋆⋆ → ⋆⋆⋆

Important old winery with reliable range, incl. good CABERNET SAUVIGNON, CHARDONNAY, sweet CHENIN BLANC and very sweet Moscato di Canelli. C.K. is the jug-wine brand.

Lamont, M.

Brand name of BEAR MOUNTAIN.

Lejon

Brand name of ITALIAN SWISS COLONY.

Los Hermanos

Second label of BERINGER.

Martini, Louis Napa. Table and dessert ⋆⋆ → ⋆⋆⋆

Large but individual winery with very high standards, from jug wines (called "Mountain") up. CABERNET SAUVIGNON one of California's best. BARBERA, PINOT NOIR, ZINFANDEL, GEWÜRZ, FOLLE BLANCHE and Moscati Amabile are all fine.

Martini & Prati Sonoma. Table ★★
Important winery selling mainly in bulk to others, but using the name Fountaingrove for a small quantity of good CABERNET SAUVIGNON.

Masson, Paul Central Coast. Full range ★→★★
Big, lively and reliable middle-quality winery with good-value varietals, incl. Emerald Dry (EM. RIES.) Rubion (RUBY), CHARDONNAY, ZINFANDEL, good cheap sparkling and very good Souzão port-type.

Mayacamas Napa. Table ★★★
First-rate very small v'yd. and winery offering CABERNET SAUVIGNON, CHARDONNAY, ZINFANDEL (sometimes).

Mirassou Central Coast. Full range ★★→★★★
Dynamic mid-sized growers and makers, the fifth generation of the family. Pioneers in SALINAS v'yds. Notable ZINFANDEL, GAMAY BEAUJOLAIS, PETITE SYRAH, GEWÜRZ and sparkling.

Mondavi, Robert Napa. Table ★★★
Ten-year-old winery with a brilliant record of innovation in styles, equipment and technique. Wines of grace and character incl. CABERNET SAUVIGNON, SAUVIGNON BLANC (sold as Fumé Blanc), CHARDONNAY, PINOT NOIR.

Monterey Peninsula Central Coast/Salinas. Table ★★★
Very small new winery near Carmel making chunky chewable ZINFANDEL from SALINAS grapes.

Monterey Vineyard Central Coast/Salinas. Table ★★★
The first big modern winery of SALINAS, opened 1974. Superb direction has already produced first-class ZINFANDEL, GEWÜRZ and SYLVANER and fruity feather-weight GAMAY BEAUJOLAIS.

Monteviña San Joaquin. Table ★★
Pioneer small winery in new area: the Shenandoah valley, Amador County, in the Sierra foothills. ZINFANDEL and Nebbiolo are the great hopes.

Mount Veeder Napa. Table ★★
Ambitious little new winery. High prices but early signs of quality.

Nichelini Napa. Table ★★
Small old-style family winery selling sound varietals at the cellar door.

Novitiate of Los Gatos Central Coast. Dessert and table ★★
Jesuit-run altar-wine-orientated unrevolutionary winery with some adequate varietals, inadequately distributed.

Papagni, Angelo San Joaquin. Table and sp. ★★→★★★
Grower of an old family with a technically outstanding modern winery at Madera. Dry coastal-style varietals include excellent ZINFANDEL, good Alicante Bouschet, light "Moscato d'Angelo".

Parducci Mendocino. Table ★★
Well-established mid-sized winery with v'yds. in several locations. Good sturdy reds: CABERNET SAUVIGNON, PETITE SYRAH, ZINFANDEL, Burgundy. Also pleasant FRENCH COLOMBARD.

Pedroncelli Sonoma R-R. Table ★★
Second-generation family business with recent reputation for well-above-average ZINFANDEL, PINOT NOIR and CHARDONNAY in a ripe rural style.

Perelli-Minetti San Joaquin. Table and dessert ★
Big firm with chequered history as California Wine Association, now in family hands. Two principal labels: Ambassador and Eleven Cellars.

Phelps, Joseph   Napa. Table ★★★ → ★★★★
Very new very de luxe small winery and v'yd. First RIESLING, PINOT NOIR, (PETITE) SYRAH all extremely promising.

Ray, Martin   Central Coast S. CRUZ. Table ★★★★
Eccentric small winery famous for high prices and unpredictable wines, occasionally very good.

Ridge   Central Coast S. CRUZ. Table ★★★★
Small winery of high repute among connoisseurs for powerful concentrated reds needing long maturing in bottle. Notable CABERNET SAUVIGNON and very strong ZINFANDEL.

Royal Host
Brand name for EAST-SIDE winery.

Rutherford Hill   Napa. Table ★★
Change of ownership and name (in 1976) for Souverain of Rutherford, an ambitious new winery yet to establish a reputation.

San Martin   Central Coast. Table and dessert ★★
Newly restructured old company using SALINAS and Amador County (SAN JOAQUIN) grapes to make clean, correct varietals of increasing quality.

Schramsberg   Napa. Sp. ★★★★
A dedicated specialist using historic old cellars to make California's best "champagne".

Sebastiani   Sonoma. Table ★★
Substantial and distinguished old family firm with robust appetizing wines, esp. BARBERA, GAMAY BEAUJOLAIS, PINOT NOIR.

Setrakian
See California Growers

Simi   Alexander Valley. Table ★★★
Restored old winery with expert direction. Several notable wines, incl. racy GEWÜRZ, gentle ZINFANDEL, delicate CABERNET SAUVIGNON.

Sonoma Vineyards   Sonoma R-R. Table and sp. ★★★
Quick-growing business, formerly called Windsor Vineyards, well-regarded for varietals, esp. RIESLING and CHARDONNAY. Range includes single-v'yd. wines.

Souverain   Alexander Valley. Table ★★
Luxurious new mid-sized winery with highly competent wines, esp. whites, if no great ones.

Spring Mountain   Napa. Table ★★★
Recently renovated small 19th-century property with new small winery already noted for good CHARDONNAY and SAUVIGNON BLANC.

Stag's Leap   Napa. Table ★★★
New small v'yd. and cellar with high standards. Fruity CABERNET SAUVIGNON, fresh GAMAY, soft Riesling.

Sterling   Napa. Table ★★★
Spectacular new mid-sized winery with high ambitions and already startling achievements. Rich heavy SAUVIGNON BLANC and CHARDONNAY; fruity CABERNET and MERLOT.

Stonegate   Napa. Table ★★
New small privately owned winery and v'yd. making CHENIN BLANC, SAUVIGNON BLANC, CHARDONNAY, PINOT NOIR.

Stony Hill   Napa. Table ★★★★
Many of California's very best whites have come from this minute winery over 25 years. Alas, Fred McCrea died in 1977. His CHARDONNAY, GEWÜRZ and RIESLING are all delicate and fine.

Sutter Home   Napa. Table ★★
Small winery revived, specializing in ZINFANDEL from Amador County grapes: excellent heavy-weight.

Swan, J.   Sonoma. Table ★★
> New one-man winery with a name for rich ZINFANDEL.

Trefethen   Napa. Table ★★★
> Small family-owned winery in Napa's finest old wooden building. Good Riesling and CHARDONNAY.

Trentadue   Sonoma R-R. Table ★★
> Small v'yd. and smaller winery making sound big-flavoured wines, incl. some from unorthodox varieties.

Turgeon & Lohr   Central Coast. Table ★★
> Small winery in San Jose with its own v'yds. in SALINAS. Looks promising.

Veedercrest   Napa. Table ★★
> Still nascent small winery with promise of talent.

Villa Armando   Livermore/San Joaquin. Table ★
> Specialist in the American-Italian market for coarse sweet table wines.

Villa Mount Eden   Napa. ★★★
> Small Oakville estate with excellent dry CHENIN BLANC, good CHARDONNAY, and CABERNET '74 outstanding.

Weibel   Central Coast. Table and sp. ★
> Veteran mid-sized winery apparently without high ambitions.

Wente   Livermore and Central Coast. Table ★★→★★★
> Important and historic specialists in Bordeaux-style whites. Fourth-generation Wentes are as dynamic as ever. CHARDONNAY, SAUVIGNON BLANC and RIESLING are all standards. PINOT NOIR is also good.

Winemasters
> Brand name of GUILD.

Z-D Wines   Sonoma. Table ★★★
> Very small winery with a name for powerful PINOT NOIR and CHARDONNAY.

New York

New York State and its neighbours Ohio and Ontario make their own style of wine from grapes of native American ancestry, rather than the European vines of California. American grapes have a flavour known as "foxy"; a taste acquired by many easterners. Fashion is slowly moving in favour of hybrids between these and European grapes with less, or no, foxiness. The entries below include both wineries and grape varieties.

Aurora
> One of the best white French-American hybrid grapes, the most widely planted in New York. Formerly known as Seibel 5279. Good for sparkling wine.

Baco Noir
> One of the better red French-American hybrid grapes. High acidity but good clean dark wine.

Benmarl
> Highly regarded and expanding v'yd. and winery at Marlboro on the Hudson River. Wines are mainly from French-American hybrids, but European vines have also made good wine.

Boordy Vineyards

The winery which pioneered French-American hybrid grapes in the USA. Started by Philip Wagner in Maryland in the '50s, now also established in the FINGER LAKES and Washington State.

Brights

Canada's biggest winery, in Ontario, formerly grew American vines exclusively, now tending towards French-American hybrids and experiments with European vines. Their CHELOIS and BACO NOIR are pleasant reds, respectively lighter and more full-bodied.

Bully Hill

New (since 1970) FINGER LAKES winery using both American and hybrid grapes to make varietal wines.

Château Gai

Canadian (Ontario) winery making European and hybrid wines, incl. successful GAMAY and PINOT NOIR.

Catawba

One of the first American wine-grapes, still the second most widely grown. Pale red and foxy flavoured. Used for sweet and sparkling wines.

Chautauqua

The biggest grape-growing district in the e., along the s. shore of La. Erie from New York to Ohio.

Chelois

Popular red French-American hybrid grape, formerly called Seibel 10878. Makes dry red wine with some richness, slightly foxy.

Concord

The archetypal American grape, dark red, strongly foxy, making good grape jelly but dreadful wine. By far the most widely planted in New York (23,000 acres).

Delaware

Old American white-wine grape making pleasant, only slightly foxy dry wines. Used in "Champagne" and for still wine.

De Chaunac

A good red French-American hybrid grape, popular in Canada as well as New York. Full-bodied dark wine.

Duchess

Old American white grape making clean and neutral wine, but can be difficult to grow.

Elvira

Another old American white grape now being gradually abandoned. Foxy wine.

Finger Lakes

Century-old wine district in upper New York State, best-known for its sparkling "Champagne". The centre is Hammondsport.

Fournier, Charles

The top quality of "Champagne" made by the GOLD SEAL company, named for a former distinguished and pioneering wine-maker.

Frank, Dr. Konstantin

A controversial figure in the FINGER LAKES: the protagonist of European vinifera vines. See Vinifera Wines.

Gold Seal

One of New York's biggest wineries, makers of Charles FOURNIER "Champagne" and the HENRI MARCHANT range. Known for high quality and readiness to experiment with new ideas.

Great Western

The brand name of the PLEASANT VALLEY WINE CO's "Champagne", one of New York's best wines.

Henri Marchant

Brand name of GOLD SEAL's standard range of mainly traditional American-grape wines.

High Tor

Well-known small winery on the Hudson River only 28 miles from Manhattan. Wines are entirely from French-American hybrids.

Inniskillin

Small new Canadian winery at Niagara making European and hybrid wines, incl. good MARÉCHAL FOCH.

Isabella

Old American Concord-style red grape making strongly foxy wine.

Lake Country

Brand name of TAYLOR's denoting the Finger Lakes origin of their wines.

Phylloxera is an insect that lives on the roots of the vine. Its arrival in Europe from North America in the 1860s was an international catastrophe. It destroyed almost every vineyard on the continent before it was discovered that the native American vine is immune to its attacks. The remedy was (and still is) to graft European vines on to American rootstocks. Virtually all Europe's vineyards are so grafted today. Whether their produce is just as good as the wine of pre-phylloxera days is a favourite to date among old school wine-lovers.

Maréchal Foch

Promising red French hybrid between PINOT NOIR and GAMAY. Makes good burgundy-style wine in Ontario.

Moore's Diamond

Old American white grape still grown in New York.

Niagara

Old American white grape used for sweet wine. Very foxy.

Pleasant Valley Wine Co.

Winery at Hammondsport, FINGER LAKES, owned by TAYLORS, producing GREAT WESTERN wines.

Seibel

One of the most famous French grape hybridists, responsible for many successful French-American crosses originally known by numbers, since christened with such names as AURORA, DE CHAUNAC, CHELOIS.

Seyve-Villard

Another well-known French hybridist. His best-known cross, no. 5276, is known as Seyval Blanc.

Taylor's

The biggest wine-company of the Eastern States, based at Hammondsport in the FINGER LAKES. Brands incl. GREAT WESTERN and LAKE COUNTRY. Most wines are from native American grapes.

Vinifera Wines

Small but influential winery of Dr Frank, pioneer in growing European vines, incl. RIESLING, CHARDONNAY and PINOT NOIR, in the FINGER LAKES area. Some excellent wines.

Widmers

Major FINGER LAKES winery selling native American varietal wines: DELAWARE, NIAGARA, etc.

Australia

Clare/Watervale
S.A.
Barossa
Langhorne Creek
Adelaide
Southern Vales
Coonawarra
Murray Valley
Murray R.
Riverina
N.S.W.
N.E. VIC
Canber
CENTRAL VIC.
Melbourne

The secret of how good Australian wine is today is only slowly filtering through to the outside world for the simple reason that Australians are taking full advantage of it themselves.

It is only ten years since modern wine technology revolutionized Australia's 150-year-old industry. Already the results are as impressive as California's. Australia's best reds are to be counted among the best wines in the world today.

Two grapes have dominated table-wine making in Australia from the start: the Shiraz (also known as the Hermitage) for red, and the Semillon (usually called "Riesling") for white. Australia developed her own styles with these two thick-set burly wines, which aged remarkably well and became subtle and thoroughly rewarding drinks.

Most of her wine-makers have departed from this old style since technology gave them the means to do so. The Cabernet Sauvignon has gained on Shiraz, either blended or on its own. Real Riesling (and recently Chardonnay) are edging Semillon aside. New technology, new vines and new vineyards are changing the scene rapidly. But there is no fear of the wine-makers losing sight of the sort of great wine Australia can make, and every probability that they will improve on it.

Australia's wine labels are among the world's most communicative. Since Australians started to take their own wine seriously they have become longer and longer winded, with information about grapes, soil, sunshine, fermenting periods and temperatures, wine-makers' biographies and serving hints. Little of this is pure salesmanship. It is intended to be, and really is, helpful. Bin-numbers mean something. They need to be noted and remembered. Prizes in shows (which are highly competitive) mean a great deal. In a country without any sort of established grades of quality the buyer needs all the help he can get.

N.B. "Value" boxes have been omitted from this section for the present as information is inconclusive.

Wine areas

The vintages mentioned here are those rated as good or excellent for the reds of the areas in question in an authoritative chart published by the Rothbury Estate Society.

Adelaide 66 67 70 71 72 73 75 76
> The capital of South Australia had the state's first v'yds. A few are still making wine.

Barossa 66 68 72 73 75 76
> Australia's biggest high-quality area, of German origin, specializing in white (esp. Riesling) and good dessert wines.

Clare-Watervale 66 68 70 71 72 75 76 .
> Small warm-climate area 90 miles n. of Adelaide best known for white wines, though mainly planted with Shiraz.

Central Victoria 66 68 71 73 74 76
> Scattered v'yds. remaining from vast pre-phylloxera plantings include GT. WESTERN and CH. TAHBILK.

Coonawarra 66 68 70 71 72 73 74 75 76
> Southernmost v'yd. of South Australia, long famous for well-balanced reds, recently successful with Riesling.

Hunter Valley 66 67 70 72 73 74 75 76
> The great name in N.S.W. Broad deep Shiraz reds and Semillon ("Riesling") whites with a style of their own. Recent expansion at Mudgee, Wybong, etc., to the w.

Langhorne Creek 66 67 70 73 75 76
> Small irrigated area specializing in full-flavoured reds.

N.E. Victoria 66 70 71 72 73 75 76
> Historic area incl. Rutherglen, Corowa, Wangaratta. Heavy reds and magnificent sweet dessert wines.

McLaren Vale and S. Adelaide
> See Southern Vales

Murray Valley N.V.
> Important scattered v'yds. irrigated from the Murray river, incl. Renmark, Berri, Loxton, Waikerie. Largely sherry, brandy, "jug" and dessert wines.

Riverina N.V.
> Fruit- and vine-growing district irrigated from the Murrumbidgee river. Mainly jug wines, but good light "varietals".

Southern Vales 66 67 70 71 72 73 75 76
> General name for several small pockets of wine-growing s. of Adelaide. Fine full-blooded reds.

Swan Valley
> The main v'yd. of Western Australia, on the n. outskirts of Perth. Hot climate makes strong low-acid wines.

Wineries

All Saints N.E. Vic. Full range ★→★★★
> Big old family-run winery in dessert-wine country. Sturdy reds. Sweet brown muscat is exceptional.

Angove's S.A. Table and dessert ★★
> Family business in Adelaide and Renmark in the Murray Valley. Sound traditional wines, incl. "Bookmark Riesling".

Bailey's N.E. Vic. Table and dessert ★★
> Small family concern making rich old-fashioned reds of great character, and admirable dessert muscat.

Best's Central Vic. Full range ★→★★
> Conservative old family winery at Great Western with good strong old-style claret, hock, etc.

Bleasdale Langhorne Creek, S.A. Full range ★→★★
> Small family business making above-average reds of Cabernet and Shiraz.

Brand Coonawarra, S.A. Table ★★

Recently opened little winery. Outstandingly fine and stylish Cabernet and Shiraz with more flavour than strength.

Buring, Leo Barossa, S.A. Full range ★→★★★

"Château Leonay", old white-wine specialists, now owned by LINDEMAN. Very good "Reserve Bin" Rhine Riesling.

Burgoyne

A well-known name in the traditional "Australian Burgundy" market. Now owned by EMU.

Château Tahbilk Central Vic. Table ★★→★★★

Family-owned wine-estate making Cabernet, Shiraz, Rhine Riesling and Marsanne. "Special Bins" are outstanding.

Château Yaldara Barossa, S.A. Full range ★

A showpiece of Barossa, popular with tourists. Sparkling wines are a speciality.

d'Arenberg McLaren Vale, S.A. Table and dessert ★→★★★

Small-scale old-style family outfit s. of Adelaide. Strapping rustic reds; Cabernet, Shiraz and Burgundy. Unusual soft white of Palomino.

Drayton Hunter Valley, N.S.W. Table ★★

Traditional Hunter wines, Hermitage red and Semillon white, from the old Bellevue estate.

Elliott Hunter Valley, N.S.W. Table ★★

Long-established grower. "Tallawanta" reds and "Belford" whites are in the bosomy, deep-flavoured Hunter style.

Emu S.A. Table and dessert ★

Bulk shippers of high-strength wine to Britain and Canada.

Gramp Barossa, S.A. Full range ★→★★★

Great pioneering family company, now owned by Reckitt & Colman. Range includes sweet fizzy "Barossa Pearl", good standard Cabernet, etc., and some of Australia's best Rhine Riesling: Steingarten. Typed labels on special wines.

Hamilton's S. Adelaide and Barossa, S.A. Full range ★★

Big family business making popular rather light and "modern" wines, e.g. Ewell Moselle and Springton Riesling.

Hardy's Southern Vales, S.A., Barossa, Hunter Valley, etc. Full range ★→★★★

Famous wide-spread family-run company using and blending wines from several areas, incl. a classic Cabernet, reliable light St. Thomas Burgundy and good Old Castle Riesling.

Henschke Barossa, S.A. Table ★★

Family business known for white wines, esp. Rhine Riesling.

Houghton Swan Valley, W.A. Table and dessert ★★

The one famous winery of W. Australia. Now belongs to EMU. Soft, ripe "White Burgundy" is the top wine.

Hungerford Hill Hunter Valley, N.S.W. Table ★★→★★★

Big new winery with over 1,000 acres and modern ideas. REYNELLA is in the same hands.

Kaiserstuhl Barossa, S.A. Full range ★→★★★

The Barossa growers' co-operative. A fine modern winery with high standards. "Individual v'yd." Rieslings are excellent. So is "Special Reserve" Cabernet.

Lake's Folly Hunter Valley, N.S.W. Table ★★★

The work of an inspired surgeon from Sydney. A new style for the Hunter Valley: Cabernet and new barrels to make rich complex California-style reds.

Lindeman Orig. Hunter Valley, now everywhere. Full range ★→★★★

One of the oldest firms, now a giant owned by Phillip Morris Corp. Hunter wines (Ben Ean and Sunshine) still famous. Owns BURINGS in Barossa and Rouge Homme in Coonawarra. Dessert-wine v'yds. at Corowa, N. Victoria. Many inter-state blends. Pioneers in modernizing wine styles.

McWilliams Hunter Valley and Riverina, N.S.W. Full range ★→★★★
Famous and first-rate Hunter wine-makers at Mount Pleasant and Lovedale (Hermitage and Semillon). Pioneers in Riverina with lighter wines, incl. sweet white "Lexia".

Mildara Murray Valley, S.A. Full range ★★→★★★
Sherry and brandy specialists at Mildura on the Murray river also making fine Cabernet and Riesling at Coonawarra.

Morris N.E. Vic. Table and dessert ★★→★★★
Old winery at Rutherglen making Australia's best brown "liqueur" muscat. Now owned by Reckitt & Colman.

Orlando See Gramps

Penfold's Orig. Adelaide, now everywhere. Full range ★→★★★★
Ubiquitous and excellent company: in Barossa, Hunter Valley, Riverina, Coonawarra, etc. Grange Hermitage is ★★★★, St. Henri Claret not far behind. Bin-numbered wines are usually outstanding. "Grandfather Port" is remarkable. Many inter-state blends.

Quelltaler Clare-Watervale, S.A. Full range ★★
Old winery n. of Adelaide known for good "Granfiesta" sherry and full dry "hock".

Redman Coonawarra, S.A. Table ★★★
Small new winery making only Coonawarra claret of Shiraz and Cabernet.

Reynella Southern Vales, S.A. Full range ★→★★★
Red-wine specialists s. of Adelaide. Highly esteemed rich Cabernet and "Vintage Reserve" claret.

Rothbury Estate Hunter Valley, N.S.W. Table ★★★
Important new syndicate-owned wine estate concentrating on traditional Hunter wines: "Hermitage" and "Riesling".

Ryecroft McLaren Vale, S.A. Table ★★
Specialists in typical sturdy Cabernet and Shiraz.

Saltram Barossa, S.A. Full range ★★
One of the smaller wineries making a notable Cabernet, "Mamre Brook" and good "Selected Vintage" claret and Rhine Riesling.

Seaview Southern Vales, S.A. Table and dessert ★★
Old-established winery now owned by Allied Breweries. Good reputation for Cabernet and Rhine Riesling.

Seppelt Barossa, S.A. Central Vic. and elsewhere. Full range ★→★★★
Far-flung producers of Australia's best "champagne" (Gt. Western Brut), good dessert wines (from Rutherglen, the Murray Valley, Barossa) and the excellent Chalambar, Moyston and Rhymney brands from Gt. Western in Victoria.

Smith's Yalumba Barossa, S.A. Full range ★→★★★
Big old family firm. Best wines incl. Rhine Riesling from Pewsey Vale above Barossa, good "Galway Vintage" claret, "Galway Pipe" port and Chiquita sherry.

Stonyfell Adelaide, S.A. Full range ★→★★★
Long-established company best known for "Metala" Cabernet Shiraz from Langhorne Creek, typical of the intense and rich-flavoured S.A. reds.

Tolley, Scott & Tolley Barossa, S.A. Full range ★→★★
Old company famous for brandy, has recently made some remarkable Cabernet and Rhine Riesling.

Tulloch Hunter Valley, N.S.W. Table ★★
An old name at Pokolbin, with good dry reds and "Riesling".

Tyrell Hunter Valley, N.S.W. Table ★★→★★★
Up-to-date old family business at "Ashman's". Some of the best traditional Hunter wines, Hermitage and Riesling, are distinguished by Vat Numbers.

South Africa

South Africa has made excellent sherry and port for many years, but has taken table wine seriously only in the last decade. Since 1972 a new system of Wines of Origin and registered "estates" has started a new era of competitive modern wine-making. The following list includes areas of origin, wineries, grape varieties and other label terms. Star-ratings have been omitted for the present until more information is available.

Alphen
> Estate originally at Constantia, owned by the famous Cloete family (see Groot Constantia), now at Somerset West with a new winery. Expert direction should make good wines.

Allesverloren
> Estate in MALMESBURY with over 325 acres of v'yds., formerly well known for "port", now specializing in red wines made with modern technology. Distributed by BERGKELDER.

Alto
> STELLENBOSCH estate of about 200 acres best known for massive-bodied CABERNET and a good blend: Alto Rouge. Distributed by BERGKELDER.

Backsberg
> Name formerly associated with commercial blends, now a 400-acre estate at PAARL with good varietal reds.

Bergkelder
> Big wine concern at STELLENBOSCH, member of the OUDE MEESTER group, making and distributing many brands and estate wines, incl. FLEUR DU CAP, ALTO, HAZENDAL, etc.

Bertrams
> Major wine company owned by Gilbeys with a wide range of well-made varietals.

Boberg
> Controlled area of origin consisting of the regions of PAARL and TULBAGH, applying only to their fortified or dessert wines.

Bukettraube
> New German white-wine grapes with acidity and aroma, popular in S. Africa for blending.

Cabernet
> The great Bordeaux grape, very successful in S. Africa, particularly in the STELLENBOSCH area. Gives very sturdy wines for long ageing.

Cavendish Cape
> Best-quality range of sherries from the K.W.V. Remarkably good wines.

Château Libertas
> Also known as Oude Libertas. A standard good-quality blended red from the STELLENBOSCH FARMERS' WINERY.

Cinsaut
> Bulk-producing French red grape formerly known as Hermitage in S. Africa. Chiefly blended with CABERNET, but can make good wine on its own.

Colombard
> The "FRENCH COLOMBARD" of California. Prized in S. Africa for its high acidity and fruity flavour.

Constantia
> Once the world's most famous muscat wine, from the Cape. Now the southernmost area of origin ("Constantia and Durbanville"). See also Groot Constantia.

Delheim
> Winery at Driesprong in the best and highest area of STELLENBOSCH, known for delicate STEEN whites. Driesprong is the estate label.

Drostdy
> Well-known growers' co-operative in TULBAGH.

Estate wine
> A strictly controlled term applying only to wines made of grapes grown on the same property. Some 40 estates are registered as qualifying for the description.

Fleur du Cap
> Popular and well-made range of wines from the BERGKELDER, Stellenbosch. Particularly good SHIRAZ.

Gewürztraminer
> The famous spicy grape of Alsace, successfully grown in the TULBAGH area.

La Gratitude
> Well-known brand of dry white from the STELLENBOSCH FARMERS' WINERY.

Groot Constantia
> Historic estate, now government-owned, near Cape Town. Source of superlative muscat wine in the early 19th century. Now making CABERNET, PINOT NOIR, PINOTAGE and SHIRAZ reds, the Shiraz apparently being best.

Grünberger
> A good brand of dry STEEN white from the BERGKELDER, though flagrantly dressed up as a German Franconian "Steinwein".

Hazendal
> Family estate in w. STELLENBOSCH making STEEN, CINSAUT and PINOTAGE, all marketed by the BERGKELDER.

Johann Graue
> Name of the founder of NEDERBURG, now the estate name for what were formerly called Nederburg Estate wines. The property, just n. of PAARL, makes some of S. Africa's best RIESLING, STEEN and CABERNET.

Kanon Kop
> Estate in n. STELLENBOSCH, specializing in high-quality and particularly full-bodied CABERNET and PINOTAGE.

Klein Karoo
> The easternmost S. African wine region, warm and dry, specializing in dessert and distilling wine.

K.W.V.
> The Kooperativ Wijnbouwers Vereeniging, S. Africa's national wine co-operative, originally organized by the State to absorb embarrassing surpluses, now at vast and splendidly equipped premises in PAARL making a range of good wines, particularly sherries.

Landgoed
> South African for Estate; a word which appears on all estate-wine labels and official seals.

Lanzerac
> Brand name of a range of low-price wines from the STELLENBOSCH FARMERS' WINERY. Lanzerac Stein is lively and semi-sweet, RIESLING dry, PINOTAGE light red and CABERNET relatively heavy.

Malmesbury
> Wine region on the w. coast n. of Cape Town, specializing in dry whites and distilling wine.

Monis
> Well-known wine concern of PAARL now merged with the STELLENBOSCH FARMERS' WINERY.

Montagne
> Relatively new but successful estate of 300+ acres near STELLENBOSCH. Wines incl. CABERNET, STEEN (sold as "Chenin Blanc"), RIESLING, and a dry rosé.

Montpellier

Famous pioneering TULBAGH estate with 350 acres of v'yds. specializing in white wine. Produced the first two whites to be officially designated SUPERIOR (RIESLING and GEWÜRZ-TRAMINER), also French CHENIN BLANC and a small quantity of excellent méthode champenoise sparkling wine.

Muratie

Ancient estate in n. STELLENBOSCH, best known for its Pinot Noir. 160 acres of v'yds. also grow CABERNET, RIESLING, STEEN and CINSAUT.

Nederburg

The most famous wine farm in modern S. Africa, now operated by the STELLENBOSCH FARMERS' WINERY. Pioneer in modern cellar practice, popularized both CABERNET and the idea of estate wines, although no longer technically an estate itself (see Johann Graue). Recent innovations have included an Auslese-type RIESLING: Nederburg Edelkeur.

Olifantsrivier

The northernmost Demarcated wine region of the Cape with a warm dry climate. Mainly distilling wine.

Paarl

South Africa's wine capital, 50 miles n.e. of Cape Town, and the surrounding region, among the best in the country, particularly for white wine and sherry. Most of its wine is made by co-operatives.

Paarlsack

Well-known range of sherries made at PAARL by the K.W.V.

Pinotage

South African red grape, a cross between PINOT NOIR and CINSAUT, useful for high yields, hardiness and good quality.

Piquetberg

Small demarcated region on the w. coast with Porterville for its centre. A warm dry climate gives mainly dessert and distilling wine.

Riesling

South African Riesling makes some of the country's better white wines, but is not the same as Rhine Riesling, which has only recently been planted in any quantity in S. Africa.

Robertson

Small demarcated region e. of the Cape and inland. Mainly dessert wines (notably MUSCAT), but red and white table wines are on the increase.

Roodeberg

High-quality brand of blended red wine from the K.W.V. Has good colour, body and flavour and ages well in bottle.

Rustenburg

Effectively, if not officially, an estate red wine from just n.e. of STELLENBOSCH. Rustenburg and SCHOONGEZICHT are managed together and the name Rustenburg used for the red of CABERNET and CINSAUT, one of S. Africa's best.

Schoongezicht

Partner of RUSTENBURG, one of S. Africa's most beautiful old farms and producer of agreeable white wine from STEEN, RIESLING and Clairette Blanche.

Shiraz

The red Rhône grape, recently gaining in popularity in S. Africa for rich deep-coloured wine.

Simonsvlei

One of S. Africa's best-known co-operative cellars, just outside PAARL. A frequent prize-winner with both whites and reds.

Steen (or Stein)

South Africa's commonest white grape, said to be a clone of the CHENIN BLANC. It gives strong, tasty and lively wine, sweet or dry, normally better than S. African RIESLING.

Stellenbosch

Town and demarcated region 30 miles e. of Cape Town, extending to the Ocean at False Bay. Most of the best estates, esp. for red wine, are in the mountain foothills of the region.

Stellenbosch Farmers' Winery

South Africa's biggest winery (after the K.W.V.) with several ranges of wines, incl. NEDERBURG, ZONNEBLOEM, LANZERAC, and the popular TASSENBERG.

Superior

An official designation of quality for WINES OF ORIGIN. The wine must meet standards set by the Wine & Spirit Board.

Swellendam

Demarcated region of the s.e., with Bonnievale as its centre. Dessert, distilling and light table wines.

Tassenberg

Popular and good-value red table wine known to thousands as Oom Tassie.

Tawny

Used in the same sense as in Portugal for port-style wines aged in wood.

Theuniskraal

Well-known TULBAGH estate specializing in white wines, esp. RIESLING. Also STEEN, Semillon and GEWÜRZTRAMINER. Distributed by the BERGKELDER.

Tulbagh

Demarcated region n. of PAARL best known for the white wines of its three famous estates, MONTPELLIER, THEUNIS-KRAAL and TWEE JONGEGEZELLEN, and the dessert wines of its co-operative at Drostdy. See also Boberg.

Twee Jongegezellen

Estate at TULBAGH. One of the great pioneers which revolutionized S. African wine in the 1950s, still in the family of its 18th-century founder. White wine only, incl. RIESLING, STEEN and SEMILLON. Best wine: "T.J.39". The name means "two young friends".

Uitkyk

Old estate at STELLENBOSCH formerly famous for Cabernet red and Carlsheim white, recently recovering from a bad patch with good CABERNET, STEEN, etc. Now over 350 acres. Distribution by BERGKELDER.

Van Riebeck

Co-operative at Riebeck Kasteel, MALMESBURY, known for pioneering work in white wine technology.

Vergenoede

Old family estate in s. STELLENBOSCH supplying high-quality sherry to the K.W.V. but recently offering prize-winning reds under an estate label.

Wine of Origin

The S. African equivalent of Appellation Controlée. The demarcated regions involved are all described on these pages.

Worcester

Demarcated wine region round the Breede and Hex river valleys, e. of PAARL. Many co-operative cellars make mainly dessert wines, brandy and dry whites.

Zonnebloem

Popular brand of CABERNET, RIESLING and STEEN from the STELLENBOSCH FARMERS' WINERY. The Cabernet is vintage-dated and ages well in bottle.

South America

The flourishing vineyards of Argentina (the world's fifth largest) and Chile are known to the world chiefly as a source of cheap wine of sometimes remarkable quality. But their main market is within South America. The following is a list of some of the chief exporters.

ARGENTINA

The following five major exporters are grouped together as Vinos Argentinos S.A. Exportadora:

Furlotti, Angel

Big bodega at Maipu, Mendoza. 2,500 acres making its best red wine from a blend of CABERNET, MERLOT and Lambrusco, white from PINOT BLANC and RIESLING.

Greco Hermanos

1,750-acre v'yds. at St. Martin, Mendoza, with Malbec, Lambrusco, BARBERA, SEMILLON, PALOMINO, etc. Range incl. El Greco "selection" and Oro del Rhin (PINOT BLANC).

Orfila, José

Long-established bodega at St. Martin, Mendoza. Top export wines are CABERNET and white Extra Dry (PINOT BLANC).

Peñaflor

Four bodegas and 3,000 acres in San Juan and Mendoza. Specialities: sherry and dessert wine, also red in cans. Tio Quinto is their popular medium sherry.

Toso, Pascual

Old Mendoza winery at San José, making one of Argentina's best reds, Cabernet Toso. Also RIESLING and sparkling wines.

CHILE

The principal bodegas exporting wine from Chile are:

Canepa, José

A modern establishment at Valparaiso handling wine from several areas. Very good French-style CABERNET from Lontüé, Talca, 100 miles south; dry SEMILLON, sweet Moscatel. Exports to Switzerland, Mexico, U.K., etc.

Concha y Toro

The biggest wine firm, with several bodegas and 2,500 acres in the Maipo valley. Remarkable dark and deep CABERNET, MERLOT, Verdot. Good SAUVIGNON BLANC. Wines go to Venezuela, Brazil, etc., Canada and Germany.

Cousiño Macul

Distinguished estate near Santiago. Very dry "green" SEMILLON and CHARDONNAY. Don Luis light red, Don Matias dark and tannic, tastes of oak and cheese. Colombia is a big market, also Benelux.

Santa Carolina

A bodega with pleasant widely available dry wines.

San Pedro

Brand name for Wagner Stein & Co., long-established at Lontüé, Talca. Range of good wines sold all over S. America, esp. Bordeaux-like CABERNET.

Santa Rita

Bodega in the Maipo valley s. of Santiago. Pleasant soft wines including the "120" brand.

Tocornal, José

Considerable exporter to Venezuela and Canada. His wines are unknown to me.

Undurraga

Famous family business; one of the first to export to the U.S.A. Wines in both old and modern styles: good clean SAUVIGNON BLANC and oaky yellow "Viejo Roble". "Gran Vino Tinto" is one of the best buys in Chile.

Sherry, Port & Madeira

The original, classical sherries of Spain, ports of Portugal and madeiras of Madeira are listed in the A–Z below. Their many imitators in South Africa, California, Australia, Cyprus, Argentina are not. References to them will be found under their respective countries.

The map on page 95 locates the port and sherry districts. Madeira is an island 400 miles out in the Atlantic from the coast of Morocco, a port of call for west-bound ships: hence its traditional market in North America.

In this section most of the entries are shippers' names followed by a brief account of their wines. The names of wine-types are included in the alphabetical listing.

Amontillado

In general use means medium sherry; technically means a wine which has been aged to become more powerful and pungent. A FINO can be amontillado.

Amoroso

A style of sweet sherry, not noticeably different from a sweet OLOROSO.

Barbeito

Shippers of good-quality Madeira, including the driest and best aperitif Madeira, "Island Dry".

Bertola

Sherry shippers, owned by the giant Rumasa group, best-known for their Bertola Cream Sherry.

Blandy

Old family firm of Madeira shippers at Funchal. Duke of Clarence Malmsey is their most famous wine.

Blazquez

Sherry bodega at JEREZ with outstanding FINO, "Carta Blanca", and "Carta Oro" amontillado "al natural" (unsweetened).

Brown sherry

British term for a style of dark sweet sherry, not normally of the best quality.

Bual

One of the grapes of Madeira, making a soft smoky sweet wine, not as sweet as Malmsey.

Caballero

Sherry shippers best known for Gran Señor Choice Old Cream. Their best FINO is Don Guisa.

Cockburn

British-owned port shippers with a range of good wines. Fine vintage port from very high v'yds. can look light when young, but has great lasting power. Vintages: **55 60** 63 67 70.

Cossart Gordon

Leading firm of Madeira shippers, best known for their "Good Company" range of wines.

Cream sherry

A style of fairly pale sweet sherry made by sweetening a blend of well-aged OLOROSOS.

Crofts

The second-oldest firm shipping vintage port: 300 years old in 1978. Bought early this century by Gilbey's. "Particular" is an excellent old tawny. Well-balanced vintage wines last as long as any. Vintages: **55 60** 63 66 70, and lighter vintage wines under the name of their Quinta da Roeda in several other years. Also now in the sherry business with Croft Original (pale cream), Croft Fino and Gilbey's sherries.

Crusted

Term for a vintage-style port, but blended from several vintages not one, bottled young and aged in bottle, so forming a "crust" in the bottle. Needs decanting.

Cuvillo

Sherry bodega at Puerto de Santa Maria best known for their Cream, dry Oloroso Sangre y Trabajadero and Fino "C".

Delaforce

Port shippers particularly well known in Germany. "His Eminence" is an excellent tawny. "Vintage character" is also good. Vintage wines are very fine, among the lighter kind: **55 58 60** 63 66 70.

Domecq

Giant family-owned sherry bodega at JEREZ. Double Century Amontillado is their biggest brand, La Ina their excellent FINO. Other famous wines: Celebration Cream and Rio Viejo (dry oloroso).

Dow

Old name used on the British market by the port shippers Silva & Cosens, well known for their rather light and relatively early maturing vintage wines, said to have a faint "cedarwood" character. Vintages: **55 57 58 60** 63 66 70.

Dry

As applied to sherry (as in "Dry Sack") often means medium-sweet.

Duff Gordon

Sherry shippers best known for their El Cid AMONTILLADO. Owned by the big Spanish firm Bodegas Osborne.

Findlater's

London wine merchant shipping his own very successful brand of medium sherry: Dry Fly.

Fino

Term for the lightest and finest of sherries, completely dry, very pale and with great delicacy. Fino should always be drunk cool and fresh: it deteriorates rapidly once opened. TIO PEPE is the classic example.

Flor

The characteristic natural yeast which gives FINO sherry its unique flavour.

Fonseca

British-owned port shipper of high reputation. Makes robust, deeply coloured vintage wine, sometimes said to have a slight "burnt" flavour. Vintages: **55 60** 63 66 70.

Garvey's

Famous old sherry shippers at JEREZ. Their finest wines are Fino San Patricio, Tio Guillermo Dry Amontillado and Ochavico Dry Oloroso. San Angelo Medium Amontillado is their most popular.

Gonzales Byass

Enormous concern shipping the world's most famous and one of the best of sherries: Tio Pepe. Other brands incl. La Concha Medium Amontillado, Gordo Dry Amontillado, Palacio Medium Sweet Oloroso, Romano Cream.

Graham

Port shippers famous for one of the richest and sweetest of vintage ports, largely from their own Quinta Malvedos, also excellent brands, incl. Emperor Tawny. Vintages: **55 58 60** 63 66 70 75.

Harvey's

World-famous Bristol shippers of Bristol Milk and Bristol Cream sweet sherries, also Bristol Fino and Bristol Dry, which is medium.

Henriques & Henriques

Well-known Madeira shippers of Funchal. Their range includes a good dry aperitif wine: Ribeiro Seco.

Jerez de la Frontera

Centre of the sherry industry, between Cadiz and Seville in s. Spain. The word sherry is a corruption of the name, pronounced in Spanish "Hereth".

Late-bottled vintage

Port of a single good vintage kept in wood for twice as long as Vintage port (about 5 years). Therefore lighter when bottled and ageing quicker.

Leacock

One of the oldest firms of Madeira shippers. Most famous wine is "Penny Black" Malmsey.

Lustau

The largest independent family-owned sherry bodega in JEREZ, making many wines for other shippers, but with a very good "Dry Lustau" range and "Emilio" Palo Cortado.

Lomelino, Tarquinio

Madeira shippers famous for their collection of antique wines. Their standard range is called Dom Henriques.

Macharnudo

One of the best parts of the sherry v'yds., n. of Jerez, famous for wines of the highest quality, both FINO and OLOROSO.

Malmsey

The sweetest form of Madeira; dark amber, rich and honeyed yet with Madeira's unique sharp tang.

Manzanilla

Sherry, normally FINO, which has acquired a peculiar bracing salty character from being kept in bodegas at Sanlucar de Barrameda, on the Guadalquivir estuary near JEREZ.

Offley Forester

Port shippers and owners of the famous Quinta Boa Vista. Their vintage wines tend to be round, "fat" and sweet, good for relatively early drinking. Vintages: **55 60 62** 63 66 67 70 72.

Oloroso

Style of sherry, heavier and less brilliant than FINO when young, but maturing to greater richness and roundness. Naturally dry, but generally sweetened for sale, as CREAM.

Palomino & Vergara

Sherry shippers of JEREZ, best known for Palomino Cream, Medium and Dry. Best FINO: Tio Mateo.

Palo Cortado

A style of sherry close to OLOROSO but with some of the character of a FINO. Dry but rich and soft. Not often seen.

Puerto de Santa Maria

The port and second city of the sherry area with a number of important bodegas.

P.X.

Short for Pedro Ximenez, the grape used in JEREZ for sweetening blends. P.X. wine alone is almost like treacle.

Rainwater

A fairly light, not very sweet blend of Madeira—in fact of VERDELHO wine—popular in the USA and Canada.

Real Tesoro, Marques de

Sherry shippers of SANLUCAR, specializing in MANZANILLA.

Rebello Valente

Name used for the vintage port of ROBERTSON. Their vintage wines are light but elegant and well-balanced, maturing rather early. Vintages: **55 60** 63 70.

La Riva

Distinguished firm of sherry shippers making one of the best FINOS, Tres Palmas, among many good wines.

Rivero

Considerable sherry concern best known for their CZ range of wines.

Robertson

Subsidiary of SANDEMAN'S, shipping REBELLO VALENTE vintage port and Gamebird Tawny and Ruby.

Ruby

The youngest (and cheapest) style of port: very sweet and red. The best are vigorous and full of flavour. Others can be merely strong and rather thin.

Ruiz Mateos

The sherry bodega which gave its name to the mammoth Rumasa group of bodegas, banks, etc. Its Don Zoilo sherries are some of the most expensive and best. Ruiz Hermanos is a cheaper range.

Rutherford & Miles

Madeira shippers with one of the best known of all Bual wines: Old Trinity House.

Quinta

Portuguese for "estate".

Quinta da Noval

Great Portuguese port house making splendidly dark, rich and full-bodied vintage port; a few pre-phylloxera vines still at the Quinta make a small quantity of "Nacional"—very dark, full and slow-maturing wine. Vintages: **55 58** 60 63 66 67 70 75.

Saccone & Speed

British sherry shippers owned by Courage's Brewery, make the popular Troubador range and a good Fino.

Sandeman

Giant of the port trade and a major figure in the sherry one. Still family controlled. "Partners" is their best-known tawny port; their vintage wines are robust—some of the old vintages were superlative [**55 58 60** 63 66 67 70 75]. Of the sherries, Medium Dry Amontillado is the best-seller, their Fino "Apitiv" is particularly good and Armada Cream and Dry Don Amontillado are both well known.

Sanlucar

Seaside sherry-town (see Manzanilla) 15 miles from JEREZ.

Sercial

Grape (reputedly a RIESLING) grown in Madeira to make the driest of the island's wines—a good aperitif.

Solera

System used in making both sherry and Madeira, also some port. It consists of topping up progressively more mature barrels with slightly younger wine of the same sort: the object to attain continuity in the final wine. Most commercial sherries are blends of several solera wines.

Tawny

A style of port aged for many years in wood (in contrast to vintage port, which is aged in bottle) until it becomes tawny in colour.

Taylor

One of the best port shippers, particularly for their full, rich, long-lived vintage wine and tawnies of stated age (40-year-old, 30-year-old, etc.). Their Quinta de Vargellas is said to give Taylor's its distinctive scent of violets. Vintages: **55** 60 63 70. Some lighter vintages are shipped with the Quinta name.

De Terry, Carlos y Javier

Family-owned bodega at PUERTO DE SANTA MARIA with a good range of sherries known as "501".

Tio Pepe

The most famous of FINO sherries (see Gonzales Byass).

Valdespino

Famous bodega at JEREZ, owner of the Inocente v'yd., making the excellent FINO of the same name. Tio Diego is their splendid dry AMONTILLADO, Matador the name of their popular range.

Varela

Sherry shippers, members of the Rumasa group, best-known for their Varela Cream.

Verdelho

Madeira grape making fairly dry wine without the distinction of SERCIAL. A pleasant aperitif.

Vintage Port

The best port of exceptional vintages is bottled after only 2 years in wood and matures very slowly, for up to 20 years or even more, in its bottle. It always leaves a heavy deposit and therefore needs decanting.

Vintage port is almost as much a ritual as a drink. It always needs to be decanted with great care (since the method of making it leaves a heavy deposit in the bottle). The simplest and surest way of doing this is by filtering it through clean muslin or a coffee filter-paper into either a decanter or a well-rinsed bottle. All except very old ports can safely be decanted the day before drinking. At table the decanter is traditionally passed from guest to guest clockwise.

Vintage port can be immensely long-lived. Particularly good vintages older than those mentioned in the text include 1950, 48, 45, 35, 34, 27, 20, 11, 08, 04.

Vintage character

Somewhat misleading term used for a good-quality full and meaty port like a first-class RUBY made by the solera system. Lacks the splendid "nose" of vintage port.

Warre

Probably the oldest of all port shippers. Makes fine long-maturing vintage wines and a good TAWNY, Warrior. Vintages: **55** 60 63 66 70

White Port

Port made of white grapes and therefore golden in colour. Formerly made sweet, now more often dry: a good aperitif but a heavy one.

Williams & Humbert

Famous and first-class sherry bodega now owned by the giant Rumasa group. Dry Sack (medium AMONTILLADO) is their best-selling wine. Pando is an excellent FINO. Canasta Cream and Walnut Brown are good in their class.

QUICK REFERENCE VINTAGE CHARTS FOR FRANCE AND GERMANY

These charts give a rough and generalized picture of the range of qualities made in the principal areas (since every year has its relative successes and failures) and a guide as to whether the wine is ready to drink or should be kept.

0   no good

10   the best

  ▮   drink now

  ✓   can be drunk with pleasure now, but the better wines will continue to improve

  ▬   needs keeping

Combinations of these symbols mean that these are wines in more than one of the categories.

FRANCE

	Red Bordeaux				White Bordeaux			
	Médoc/Graves		Pom/St-Em.		Sauternes & sw.		Graves & dr.	
76	?–8	▬	?–9	▬	2–5	✓	4–8	✓
75	8–10	▬	9–10	▬	9–10	▬	8–10	▮
74	4–6	✓	3–5	✓	0		6–7	▮
73	5–7	▮	5–7	▮	0		7–8	▮
72	2–5	▮	2–4	▮	2–4	▮	4–7	▮
71	5–8	✓	6–8	✓	8–9	▮	8–10	▮
70	9–10	✓	9–10	▮	9–10	▮	9–10	▮
69	1–4	▮	0–3	▮	6–8	▮	8–9	▮
68	0–2		0		0		0	
67	5–7	▮	6–8	▮	7–10	▮	8–10	▮
66	7–9	▮	8–9	▮	4–7	▮	7–8	▮
65	0–2		0					
64	2–7	▮	5–9	▮				
63	0		0					
62	4–8	▮	3–6	▮				
61	10	✓	10	✓				

	Red Burgundy		White Burgundy					
	Côte d'Or (Beaune, Pommard, Nuits, Chambertin, etc.)		Côte d'Or (Montrachet, Meursault, etc.)		Chablis		Alsace	
76	9–10	▬	7–9	▬	8–9	▬	10	
75	0–5	✓	4–8	✓	10	✓	9	✓
74	2–5	▮	7–9	▮	6–8	▮	6–7	▮
73	4–7	▮	8		7–8	▮	7–8	▮
72	4–9	▮	6–10	▮	1–4	▮	3	
71	8–10	▮	8–10	▮	7–9	▮	10	▮
70	6–8	▮	7–8	▮	6–8	▮	7–8	▮
69	9–10	▮	8–10	▮	7–9	▮		
68	0		2–4					
67	3–6	▮	8–10					
66	6–8	▮	8–9					

Beaujolais: 76 is the vintage to look for. Mâcon-Villages (white): 76, 75 and 74 are all good now.
Loire: Sweet wines of Anjou and Touraine. Best recent vintages: 76, 75, 73, 71, 70, 69, 64.
Upper Loire: Sancerre and Pouilly Fumé 76, 75, 74 are all good now. Older vintages are in general too old.
Muscadet: 75 is the safest bet at present.

GERMANY

	Rhône		Rhine		Moselle	
76	8–10	✓	10	▬	10	▬
75	0–5	✓	10	▬	10	▬
74	4–7	▮	3–6	▮	2–4	▮
73	5–8	▮	6–7	▮	6–8	▮
72	6–9	▮	2–5	▮	1–4	▮
71	7–9	▮	9–10	▮	10	▮
70	7–9	▮	4–7	▮	4–6	▮
69	9–10	▮	6–8	▮	7–9	▮

N.B. Fully detailed charts will be found on pages 20, 21 (France), 61 (Germany).